Communicating Research

Library and Information Science

Consulting Editor: *Harold Borko*
Graduate School of Library and Information Science
University of California, Los Angeles

The list of books continues at the end of the volume.

Communicating Research

A. J. Meadows
Department of Information and Library Studies
Loughborough University
Loughborough, Leicestershire, United Kingdom

Academic Press
San Diego   London   Boston   New York   Sydney   Tokyo   Toronto

This book is printed on acid-free paper.

Academic Press
a division of Harcourt Brace & Company
525 B Street, Suite 1900, San Diego, California 92101-4495, USA
http://www.apnet.com

Academic Press Limited
24-28 Oval Road, London NW1 7DX, UK
http://www.hbuk.co.uk/ap/

Library of Congress Cataloging-in-Publication Data

Meadows, A. J. (Arthur Jack)
    Communicating research / A.J. Meadows.
        p.   cm. -- (Library and information science)
    Includes index.
    ISBN 0-12-487415-0 (alk. paper)
    1. Research--communication systems.   2. Communication in science.
    3. Communication of technical information.   I. Title.   II. Series:
    Library and information science (New York, N.Y.)
    Q180.55.I45.M43   .1997
    001.4'01'4--dc21   97-23432

PRINTED IN THE UNITED STATES OF AMERICA
97 98 99 00 01 02 QW 9 8 7 6 5 4 3 2 1

Contents

3
Who Does Research and with What Results?

4
Channels for Communicating Research

5
Making Research Public

6

Finding Out about Research

Preface

Communication lies at the heart of research. It is as vital for research as the actual investigation itself, for research cannot properly claim that name until it has been scrutinized and accepted by colleagues. This necessarily requires that it be communicated. Again, the support of research is costly. Such funding is wasted unless the results of the research are presented to their appropriate audiences. Whichever way one looks at it, efficient and effective communication is an essential part of the research process.

I first became interested in the nature of research communication back in the 1960s. Research activity, especially in science, was then expanding rapidly in the Western world. The question inevitably arose—how much longer can this expansion continue? Extrapolation suggested that by the end of the century—where we are now—something would have to give. Growth in funding, and consequently in the number of researchers would have to slow down. The follow-up question, though asked less frequently at the time, was this: Given that funding would be affected, how could the money available be used to produce the maximum amount of high-level research? At that stage, I was working in the Department of Printed Books and Manuscripts at the British Museum (now a part of the British Library) in London. What interested me was a particular aspect of this problem: How could the communication of research be handled most efficiently as funding slowed? The answer again seemed obvious. Computers were already being used for information handling in the 1960s. Their future development would surely allow the rapid manipulation of large quantities of information and make them increasingly effective tools for the communication of research.

After the British Museum, I returned to academic life, working in astronomy, the history of science, and, finally, information and library studies. The first two fields provided an interesting contrast in how researchers in the sciences and those in the humanities handle information. Researchers in these two fields see the world from different angles; their ideas on the nature of acceptable knowledge differ, and their research communities are organized differently. Consequently, their handling of information is dissimilar. Changes affecting the world of research as a whole do not necessarily have identical impacts on research communication in the sciences and on that in the humanities. Such differential change influences, and is influenced by, the activities of intermediaries in the communication chain—publishers, librarians, information scientists, and so on—who try to link authors and readers. They, more than anyone else, need to be aware of new means for improving the efficiency of communication between researchers and their audiences.

Exploring this theme—changes with time acting differentially across research fields—provides my main motivation for writing this book. We are near the end of the 20th century. The expectations of the 1960s are being fulfilled, and research and its communication are under increasing pressure. The essential question that needs answering has now become this: How can the communication activities of researchers best be catered to in a rapidly changing technological environment? The following pages outline some of the main themes of communicating research: what its position is at present and how it has been reached, what factors have been at work, and how these factors can interact with developing information technology to enhance the future of research communication. The main emphasis throughout is on academic research. This bias derives in part from my own background, yet there is some justification for it. In the first place, it is only in the academic environment that all branches of knowledge are pushed forward together, so that a proper comparison is possible. Second, the academic marketplace is both more open and more complex than others in terms of communicating research. It has, correspondingly, been the subject of more intensive study. Several such studies are mentioned throughout the book. It should be remarked, however, that they are used primarily as examples. No attempt has been made to provide a comprehensive survey of what is now a very large and widely scattered literature.

We are currently in a period of transition, which may be interesting, but is rarely entirely pleasant, for those involved. Decisions made now can help or hinder the transition to a more effective handling of research information. Making helpful decisions depends on an understanding of the factors at work. The purpose of this book is to provide some of the background needed for that understanding.

A. J. Meadows

1

Change and Growth

The way a researcher conveys information depends on the medium employed, the nature of the information, and the intended audience. As these change with time, so do the formulation and packaging of the information. For example, the lecture is a traditional way of conveying information: it seems totally uncontroversial. Yet today's lecture is not identical in form to its equivalent of two centuries ago. In terms of medium, lecturers have such newer aids as overhead projectors, microphones, and now, increasingly, computer displays. In terms of information, the theoretical underpinning and the jargon have both changed. In terms of audience, listeners are much more likely to be specialists, so the lecturer will make assumptions about their background. The medium, the information, and the audience interact to produce the package we label a "lecture." Listeners from two centuries ago who arrived to listen to a modern lecture would need time to adjust from the old package to the new. Until that adjustment had been made, they would find it difficult to assimilate information.

Two strands are taken as of prime importance here for discussing these trends—the nature of the medium used for transmitting information and the needs of the research community both as generators and as recipients of information. One obvious question regarding the medium concerns what happens when a new medium appears. Can we assess what has been the impact of printing on the communication of research over the past few centuries? What sort of impact are new electronic media beginning to make? Research information in printed form has been available for many years, but an examination of the physical products—especially scholarly journals and books—shows that their appearance has changed considerably with time. As we shall see, technical changes have often been a less important factor in such changes than the evolving needs of the research community. An understanding of the forces at work when researchers use print for communication may

1

provide some insight into how the research community will react to a shift to an electronic communication medium. This is one of the themes running through the book.

The medium available and the nature of the research community affect not only the way information is presented but also the amount of information in circulation. A small group of researchers living in the same city can clearly use different methods of communication from a community of several thousand researchers distributed throughout the world. Creating a coherent picture of research communication today, including some idea of how it has reached its present position and where it might go in the future, involves an examination of a range of factors such as these. W. H. Auden once referred to history as "the operator, the organizer." We can rephrase this for our purposes as—how has research communication come to be organized so that it assists the operations of the research community?

To answer that question requires some insight into what motivates researchers. For example, why do research? Here is the answer of Sir Francis Bacon, writing around the beginning of the seventeenth century.

> The mind is the man, and knowledge mind. A man is but what he knoweth . . . . The truth of being, and the truth of knowing, is all one . . . . Is truth barren? Shall we not thereby be able to produce worthy effects and to endow the life of man with infinite commodities?[1]

In effect, he is saying that new knowledge is worth gaining for two reasons—for its own sake and for the sake of its applications. These, no doubt, would also be the main reasons offered today. But Bacon goes on to add that the increase of knowledge is inextricably linked with its communication, not simply to contemporaries, but to subsequent generations.

> the images of men's wits and knowledges remain in books, exempted from the wrong of time and capable of perpetual renovation. Neither are they fitly to be called images, because they generate still, and cast their seeds in the minds of others, provoking and causing infinite actions and opinions in succeeding ages.[2]

The concern of this book is with the communication of research. Yet that cannot be entirely separated from the why and the how of doing research. These matters are therefore explored as necessary: in particular, the question of motivation is examined in Chapter 3.

Early Communication

No one can say when research first started and was consequently first communicated. The answer depends not least on your definition of "research." But the earliest activities that made an impact on modern research communication were undoubtedly those of the ancient Greeks. Research can be communicated in various ways, the two most important being speech and writing. The Greeks were involved in both. Thus our "academic" discussion harks back to the Academy, the place just outside Athens where people met in the fifth and fourth centuries B.C. to discuss philosophical questions. Similarly, the original "symposium" was a Greek party at which both debate and drink flowed freely (some things change little).

In terms of the written research tradition, it is the works of the Greeks, headed by Aristotle, which have again contributed most. Their discussions, often precariously preserved in repeatedly copied manuscripts, affected first Arabic culture and then Western Europe. In Europe, exploration and interpretation of the new ideas led to that revival of learning from the fourteenth to the sixteenth century which we label "the Renaissance." Chaucer's Oxford academic, who wanted to have at his bed's head "twenty books clad in black or red, of Aristotle and his philosophy," was far from unique. The introduction of printing into Europe in the fifteenth century made the fulfillment of such wishes much easier. The availability of printed texts increased rapidly. It has been estimated that average book production per year worldwide increased from 420 for the period 1436–1536 to 5750 over the next 100 years (1536–1636).[3] Such a change in a relatively short period had a major impact on the dissemination of information. As one author remarked in 1613:

> One of the diseases of this age is the multiplicity of books; they doth so overcharge the world that it is not able to digest the abundance of idle matter that is every day hatched and brought forth into the world.[4]

Most of these books were not, of course, concerned with research, but the importance of the printed book from the time of its origin for conveying research cannot be doubted. The year 1543, for example, saw the publication of both the founding work of modern astronomy—*De revolutionibus orbium coelestium* (On the revolutions of the celestial bodies) by Copernicus—and the first modern work on human anatomy—*De humani corporis fabrica* (On the structure of human body) by Vesalius. The latter, in particular, represented a step forward in the presentation of research, as it included accurate, detailed illustrations. Works of this sort were often printed under the direct supervision of the author or of a fellow-scholar. Such people were frequently associated with universities, so it happened that some universities set up their own printing and publishing operations. One example is Oxford University Press, which, with some stretch of the imagination, can trace its origins back to the latter part of the fifteenth century.

The ability to multiply copies of a book was a major step toward better and more rapid dissemination of research. It was matched by better transportation of written and printed material, at least throughout Europe. Copies of Copernicus's book, for example, were soon found in major libraries everywhere. Official couriers traveling along regular routes on state business had long existed, and they often carried private correspondence along with the official communications. In the sixteenth century, however, this transmission of nongovernmental mail became increasingly formalized, and postal systems, in the sense we understand them today, began to emerge. Initially, this had only a minor impact on research; though for someone like the Danish astronomer, Tycho Brahe, who tried to establish a network of corresponding astronomers in the latter part of the sixteenth century, good communication facilities were important.

What these facilities especially stimulated was the passage of news. Indeed, postal systems and newspapers can be said to have grown up together. Soon after printing started in Europe, news-sheets were produced, officially or unofficially, to describe events of particular interest. These were mainly local products dealing with a single event, but they soon became intermeshed with existing arrangements for transmitting handwritten news items round Europe. Various news systems connected the leading centers for trade and commerce. A major banking family, such as the Fuggers, regularly supplied customers and friends with newsletters containing information collected via their commercial contacts all over Europe. By the early seventeenth century, demand for this type of information had reached such a level that it was often cheaper and easier to use print for dissemination rather than handwriting. At the same time, the often sporadic distribution of newsletters was made more regular. The publication that resulted from these trends was recognizably the ancestor of the modern newspaper. It also provided a basic model for the development of the research journal.

The transition from manuscript to print did not occur instantaneously. Manuscript newsletters, particularly where a small audience was involved, continued to be produced throughout the seventeenth and into the eighteenth century. Even books continued to circulate in manuscript, though this was now typically because the ideas they discussed were likely to be censored. In fact, from the research viewpoint, it made good sense for ideas to be circulated initially via manuscript letters to a small circle of friends who could discuss and, where appropriate, test them and then reply. If, however, the ideas were to reach a larger group, it was a good deal easier to have the letter printed rather than handwritten. So, in the latter part of the seventeenth century, the first research journals made their appearance.

The Advent of the Research Journal

Seventeenth-century London provides an illuminating illustration of how and why the research journal, in the modern sense, appeared on the scene. The restoration of the monarchy in 1660 brought to an end some 20 years of civil war and parliamentary rule. During that period, small groups, overlapping in membership, had met to discuss philosophical questions, carefully excluding such highly contentious topics as politics and theology. After the Restoration, it was decided to organize meetings in London on a more regular and official basis. This led in 1662 to the formation of the Royal Society—so called because Charles II agreed to give it his patronage. From the beginning, the Royal Society was concerned with communication. Its founders had been influenced by the writings of Francis Bacon, who, in the last of his books, had described the possible activities of a research institute. One requirement, he suggested, was that high priority should be given to the collection and analysis of relevant information. Some members should spend time abroad collecting data by direct discussion and observation, while others should stay at home, reading and abstracting literature from all over the world.

Some Fellows of the Royal Society did travel to obtain information, but other, less time-consuming ways of keeping up with activities elsewhere were relied on more. One was to elect into membership people from abroad, who would then communicate reports on advances in their own country. The first such foreign member was John Winthrop, Governor of Connecticut, a significant researcher in his own right. But the most important means of gathering information was via the correspondence of the Secretary of the new society, Henry Oldenburg. He was an indefatigable writer of letters to correspondents both at home and overseas: a German by birth, he was an accomplished linguist. Oldenburg acted as a clearing-house for information on new ideas and research, much as the Fuggers had earlier collected and disseminated commercial and political news. The scale of this correspondence soon became a major burden: the increasingly obvious answer was to produce a printed publication containing the more important letters and to distribute this.

In Paris, meanwhile, a rather similar situation existed. There Marin Mersenne played a role parallel to Oldenburg's. In 1665, another Parisian involved in the gathering of information, Denis de Sallo, began a periodical devoted to news of what was happening throughout Europe in the "republic of letters." This *Journal des Sçavans* (updated to *Journal des Savants* in the early nineteenth century) has a good claim to be called the first journal in the modern sense. The first issue appeared on 5 January 1665, and Oldenburg read some of its contents to a meeting of the Royal Society held on 11 January—some indication of the speed of communication between important centers at that time. It seems to have crystallized his own ideas for producing a journal, for, in March 1665, the Council of the Royal Society ordered

> that the *Philosophical Transactions*, to be composed by Mr. Oldenburg, be printed the first Monday of every month, if he have sufficient matter for it, and that the tract be licensed by the Council, being first reviewed by some members of the same.[5]

The first issue of *Phil. Trans.* (as it has long been abbreviated) followed immediately on this order.

Though the French and English journals appeared on the scene at the same time, there were clear differences in both their contents and their intentions. In the preface to the first issue of the *Journal des Sçavans,* de Sallo explained that the journal was intended to do a number of different things—to catalog and abstract the more important books published in Europe, to provide obituaries of eminent people, to describe developments in science and technology, to record major legal decisions, and generally to cover all topics of interest to men of letters. The full title of the Royal Society journal—the *Philosophical Transactions: giving some Accompt of the present Undertakings, Studies and Labours of the Ingenious in many considerable parts of the World*—suggests an equally broad coverage. However, the previous limitations on the discussion of such topics as politics and religion remained in place: the Royal Society claimed to be concerned only with "experimental" learning. The *Philosophical Transactions* was thus the forerunner of the modern scientific journal. The *Journal des Sçavans* ultimately found it impossible to maintain the broad spread of topics with which it started and concentrated primarily on nonscientific topics. It can be seen as a precursor of the modern humanities journal.

Scholarly journals appeared in the latter half of the seventeenth century for a variety of reasons. Some were specific (such as the hope that their editors had of making a profit); some general (such as the belief that making new discoveries required communal debate). The clearest thread, however, lay in this need to communicate with a growing clientele interested in new developments in as efficient a way as possible. Though the introduction of the journal was a logical step to take, it held considerable implications for the communication of research. In particular, it meant a formalization of the communication process. To see what this implies, it is necessary to draw a distinction between "informal" and "formal" communication. An informal communication is often ephemeral and is made available to a restricted audience only. Most spoken information is therefore informal, as are most personal letters. In contrast, a formal communication is typically available over long periods of time to an extended audience. Journals and books are published (i.e., made public) and then stored for lengthy periods in libraries, so they are archetypical examples of formal communications. What happened in the seventeenth century was that the existing channels for communicating research—mainly oral, personal correspondence, and books—were supplemented, extended, and to some extent replaced by a new formal channel consisting of journals.

Journal is used throughout this book as shorthand for a collection of research articles by diverse authors. Sets of such articles are collected together at intervals, printed, bound, and distributed under a single title. Other generic terms overlap with this definition. *Transactions,* as used by the Royal Society, evidently refers to a publication associated with the activities of a group. In the nineteenth century, the Royal Society also started to produce a series of *Proceedings,* another word denoting group activity. The development of the journal has also led to changes in the meaning of that word. Originally, a *journal* meant something like a newspaper, but, as we have seen, it came to apply to a periodical publication containing a series of articles in the latter part of the seventeenth century. At about the same time, the word *magazine* also came into use to describe a publication containing a variety of articles. Over the following two centuries, *journal* has come increasingly to mean a serious publication containing original thought, whereas *magazine* now evokes the image of a popular publication of the sort bought on newsstands. However, the old meanings of these words sometimes survive. Some popular publications are still called *journal,* while the *Philosophical Magazine,* founded at the end of the eighteenth century, is currently one of the leading research journals in physics.

The term *periodical* was used previously. This came into common use in the latter part of the eighteenth century, and refers to any publication appearing at specified intervals and containing a variety of articles by different authors. To confuse the matter further, the word *serial* appeared in the nineteenth century as a designation of any publication issued in successive, connected parts. In general, journals (and magazines) are periodicals, but in the humanities especially there are serial publications that have many of the functions of a journal. These fluctuations in word meanings are not peculiar to English alone. In German, for example, early journals were often referred to by the word *Zeitung.* This subsequently came to be associated more with newspapers, and, from the nineteenth century onward, the word *Zeitschrift* came to be preferred in scholarly journal titles.

The Role of Societies

A great deal has been written on the question of why attempts to expand knowledge should have become so much a part of the scene in the Western world during the seventeenth century. Some of the suggested answers have important implications for the communication of the results. For example, there was a rapidly growing belief then that the Ancient world did not have a monopoly in the creation of important new knowledge, as had formerly been supposed. Knowledge, it was argued, in at least some areas of human endeavour was cumulative. New observations and ideas could be added to what was already known to create a higher level of knowledge. It was in this sense that Isaac Newton took over an existing metaphor to proclaim, "If I have seen further it is by standing on the shoulders of giants."

Newton's image implied two things about communication. Firstly, the process of accumulation involved providing information on one's own work to others and, in return, receiving information from them. Secondly, since the accumulation process stretched over time, information must be made available in a durable, readily accessible form. The success of this strategy depended on the existence of groups of people involved in both the formal and informal communication of research. Consequently, the prime vehicle for such communication became the learned society. Societies typically held meetings at regular intervals (so that members could plan their attendance ahead) where informal dissemination of information occurred in a number of guises. Members reported on their own research, demonstrations or exhibitions could be arranged, contacts were established and professional gossip exchanged (always an important way of cementing society membership). Many societies established a publishing program in parallel. In this way, they satisfied the desires of those members who wished to make their work public, allowed nonmembers access to the society's work, and provided a record that could be passed on to succeeding generations.

Societies were soon established to cover all the main areas of scholarship. In France, a similar body to the Royal Society—the Académie royale des Sciences—was established in 1666. By that time, Paris already possessed three academies devoted to subjects other than the sciences: the Académie française (founded 1635), the Académie royale de Peinture et de Sculpture (1648), and the Académie royale des Inscriptions et Belles-Lettres (1663). Initially, creation of new societies was slow, but it speeded up greatly in the eighteenth century. In science alone, some 70 officially blessed academies or societies were set up in that century, along with a considerable number of private ventures.[6] Which of the words *academy* and *society* was used as a description often reflected different organizational approaches. An academy was more likely to receive financial and other support from the state, was more subject to state control, and had fewer dilettante members than societies. In North America, the Netherlands, and the UK, the society approach was commoner: elsewhere in Europe, the academy approach was preferred, at least for national bodies. A contrast can be drawn between the civil servant remuneration of members of the Académie royale des Sciences and the fee-paying demands on Fellows of the Royal Society.

These organizational differences had some consequences for communication. Thus the average attendance at Académie meetings was usually appreciably less than that at Royal Society meetings, where there were considerable numbers of dilettante members. In a similar way, access to publications differed. The Académie produced an annual volume to which only members could contribute. The *Philosophical Transactions* appeared several times each year (the number of issues varied, but was typically five per year) and could include material communicated by nonmembers. Since annual volumes could, and did, slip appreciably in publication date, the more frequent society publication was better placed for providing reasonably up-to-date information. However, these differences must not be overemphasized. In contemporary eyes, academies and societies were all embarked on the same task. In 1766, a member of the Société royale de Montpellier commented:

The usefulness of academies is generally recognized today. One is no longer tempted in our century to call that into question, and one can state with sincerity that the rapid progress that human knowledge has made in our days is due in large part to the indefatigable zeal of the considerable number of learned men, who, assembling in diverse societies and uniting their work and talents, have had as their only goal to enlighten their contemporaries and to transmit useful discoveries to posterity.[7]

The older professions, more especially law and medicine, established officially recognized associations early on, but these were mainly concerned with controlling admission to the profession and supervising standards of professional conduct. During the seventeenth and eighteenth centuries, interest in new knowledge grew (especially in medicine), and the professional societies began to add this concern to their others. In the nineteenth century, new professions appeared and set up their own professional bodies. These typically evinced an interest in research and innovation from the start (and, correspondingly, in questions of communication). In the latter part of that century, new industries developed, based on the advances in knowledge that had now been made. This led to further expansion of societies and of their communication activities, though sometimes creating tension in the process. Developments in chemistry, for example, led to the growth of applied chemistry and chemical engineering alongside "pure" chemistry. At the time, academic chemists were not necessarily interested in the problems of industrial practitioners, and this produced some difficulties in communication. In the UK, applied chemists left the existing chemical society, which was dominated by pure scientists, and set up their own society and publications. In the twentieth century, circumstances have made practical chemists more interested in the activities of pure chemists, and the latter, conversely, more interested in practical applications of their work. In recent years, the two British chemical societies (plus some others) have therefore recombined, with a consequent reordering of their formal and informal communications. As has happened in many other societies, members can now select from a range of publications and meetings that cover the whole pure and applied spectrum.

These ups and downs of history have more than an antiquarian interest. The way in which research communication is organized today often reflects decisions made in the past. For example, many of the older learned societies built up libraries in order to help their members, since, in times past, the acquisition of specialized books and journals was both difficult and expensive. Today, most members have access to adequate collections closer to hand via their institutional libraries. Though the original reason for creating society libraries has therefore largely disappeared, societies find it difficult to dispense with such a rich resource. Users are now as likely to be there for historical purposes as for current research purposes, yet, despite some resistance from members, the libraries often continue to be funded.

Journal Layout

The archetypical example of such fossilized practices is the journal, itself. The way journals present information has evolved gradually over the past three centuries in response both to technological change and to the changing requirements of the research community. Present-day journals contain embedded within them reflections of these pressures.

Take an issue of any journal—say in the sciences—and examine the articles it contains. It quickly becomes apparent that they are organized on the same basic model. First comes a title, followed by the author's name and address. At this point, or elsewhere, there is likely to be a date indicating when the article was received by the journal, together, perhaps with a second date saying when a revised version of the article was submitted. Next comes an abstract, briefly describing the contents of the article. The main body of the article then follows, and this is often structured on a standard pattern (e.g., introduction, methodology, experimental results, conclusion). The article ends with a list of references to other publications mentioned in the text.

To anyone who reads research articles regularly, this description will seem not only familiar, but obvious. How else should an article be put together? But each of these elements has undergone changes with time, which reflect, in part, changes in the research community and the way it communicates. The initial elements—the title and author—are the same for journals as for books: they form the basic items used in distinguishing one book or article from another. Article titles, however, typically contain more detailed information than book titles and so are often longer. In the early days of journals, titles of articles were more similar to those of modern books: they conveyed information appreciably less efficiently than today's titles. (Oddly enough, the converse was true of books: early book titles tended to provide more information than today's.) There remain differences with discipline. Articles in some fields of the humanities tend to have appreciably less information content in their titles than is common in most of the sciences. The author listings, too, have changed, not only in the way the name is recorded, but in the handling of multiauthor articles. A century ago, most articles in the sciences had a single author, whereas today many have two or more. Corresponding conventions have arisen about the order in which author's names should be listed. The proportion of multiauthor articles and the nature of the conventions about name ordering may again vary with discipline, as appears in a later chapter.

The appearance of the date of receipt on an article reflects the desire of the research community to decide on priority claims. Scholars are naturally keen to be given credit for their work. Such credit is typically given to those who explore a particular topic first. Since communication of research results via a published article takes time, authors need some assurance that their claims to originality will be recognized. By including the date on which an article was received, journals cast some light on the question of who first wrote on a particular topic. Similarly, the occurrence of resubmitted articles reflects the importance that the research community attaches to quality control. The quite complex system of editorial assessment and external refereeing that now controls the quality of material published in the major journals has been built up gradually with time. As the research community has grown, so has the need to ensure that only acceptable work is published. Again, there are differences in attitude both to priority claims and to quality control, depending on the discipline. Humanities editors tend to see these things differently from science editors.

Abstracts, too, have changed with time. They first appeared not as part of the article, but as summaries of it reported in other journals. Gradually, abstracts began to appear with the articles, themselves. They could then be used as the basis for summaries in other publications. In the nineteenth century, journals devoted entirely to the reproduction of abstracts began to appear. Again, there are differences between disciplines. Almost all current scientific articles contain abstracts, but they are appreciably rarer in the humanities. More generally, the distinctly unstructured layout of early articles has become more formalized with time. This internal structuring also depends on the field. Thus a section heading of *experimental results* is common in the natural sciences, but is not very applicable to much of the social sciences. Nevertheless, the idea of presenting information in a set sequence is usual across the disciplines, though it may be more strictly applied in the sciences.

The list of references at the end of an article is yet another example of a component that has changed with time. Originally, references to the work of others were made in the main text, usually in a bibliographically unstructured form. Subsequently, references migrated to footnotes and then to the end of the article. In parallel with this development, the way references were cited became increasingly structured: today, quite strict bibliographical standards are usually applied. The exact structure adopted for references can vary with the discipline. Humanities scholars, for example, often annotate their references, whereas scientists rarely record more than the bare bibliographical details.

The various elements of a research article are explored in more detail in subsequent chapters. The point to be made here is that many of the changes in them have been connected with the growing size and complexity of the research community and with the consequent need to improve the efficiency of its communication activities. For example, references act as a connection between new and old work: they represent the mortar holding the new bricks to the old as the building grows. Their increasing standardization represents an attempt to maintain efficient links in an expanding universe of knowledge. The same can be said of changes in titles and abstracts. These have been in the direction of providing information about each article more efficiently, so improving the chances of researchers' retrieving relevant articles quickly, despite the constantly growing number of articles. The improved internal structuring of articles can be seen similarly as aiding rapid retrieval of information from within each article. From this viewpoint, the evolution of journal contents is simply a response to the need for maintaining information flow when the volume of communication is constantly growing.

The Accumulation of Research

To what extent, then, has research information increased in amount over time? Consider first what would happen if the research community always remained the same size. Informal communication would presumably always hover at about the same level, since the number of contacts between individuals would remain the same. The volume of information generated via formal channels by the research community in successive generations might similarly be expected to stay constant. Informal information, by its nature, is soon lost, but the books and journals that provide channels for formal communication remain and would accumulate linearly with time. Each generation would contribute an identical quota of informational bricks to the research edifice, so the volume of research communication would grow at a constant rate.

Such a picture hardly reflects the actual situation, since the size of the research community has certainly not remained the same over time. In the first place, world population has expanded rapidly over the past two centuries. The midseventeenth century can be taken as the starting point for the research community as we know it today. The estimated world population for that time is somewhat over 500 million inhabitants, perhaps twice what it had been in 1 A.D. In other words, it took some 1650 years for the world population to double. Three hundred years later, in the midtwentieth century, the world population was approaching 3000 million. The "doubling" time had dropped to 40–50 years, so that the 1950 population was twice that at the beginning of the century.[8] This rapid growth continues today.

Presuming that the research community expands along with the general population, this means that its activities and, correspondingly, its communications must be growing more rapidly as time passes. Each generation adds an increasing number of bricks to the research edifice, which therefore grows more and more quickly. However, the story does not end here. The level of education has risen considerably faster than population growth over the past century (though obviously at different rates in different countries). For example, recruitment to full-time higher education over the period 1900–1960 doubled every 15 years, on average, in the United States and every 17 years in the UK.[9] Within this overall rise, the number of students taking doctorates has grown particularly quickly over the past half century. Since it is people with doctorates who are expected to provide the next generation of researchers, this growth is important for the communication of research. During the 1960s—a period of rapid expansion in Western higher education—the number of U.S. students taking doctorates doubled between the beginning and end of the decade.[10] At this rate of producing researchers, the research edifice soars from a house to a skyscraper before our eyes. The immediate consequence of such an expansion for a member of the research community is that most researchers are contemporaries. The exact figures depend on the supposed growth rate, but over three-quarters of all researchers throughout recorded history are probably available for a chat today. As was noted some years back, "Today we are privileged to sit side-by-side with the giants on whose shoulders we stand."[11]

The increasing size of the research community has implications for informal communication (which are examined later), but the problems for formal communication tend to loom larger because of the way such information accumulates. Some idea of the growth rate of the research community has been given in the preceding paragraphs. Presuming that other factors, such as productivity, remain constant with time (another point for future consideration), similar growth rates might be expected to apply to the research literature. In fact, pinning down the rate of expansion of the literature is not a straightforward operation. In the first place, the eternal question of what constitutes a "research journal" has to be considered. Are journals containing only review articles acceptable, for example? In any case, how much original research must a journal contain in order to be counted as a research journal? If questions such as these can be answered satisfactorily, the growth rate can be measured in terms of the difference between the number of new titles that appear and the number of old titles that disappear over a given period of time. It is not too difficult to establish which new journals are being published: they are usually advertised by the publishers and recorded in the trade literature. There are always some problems en route, of course. For example, if a single journal splits into two or more separate journals, each of which constitutes a section of the original title, is it one journal still or more? This sort of thing is not uncommon: as far back as the nineteenth century, the *Philosophical Transactions* of the Royal Society split into two parts—*Phil. Trans. A* covering the physical sciences and *Phil. Trans. B* for the biological sciences.

These are minor statistical irritants. A larger problem is gathering reliable data on the death rate of journals. In some instances—for example, when two titles merge into one—publishers may circulate information, but usually the demise of a journal is not widely advertised. For journals that are published irregularly, or at extended intervals, it may be a long time before it becomes clear that another issue is not going to appear. Table 1, which tries to allow for these problems, provides some global figures for the number of journal titles in existence at different times.[12] Table 2 lists similar data for a particular discipline (biomedicine).[13] This latter table illustrates that rapid growth can occur in specific areas of research over long periods, as well as in

Table 1
Estimated Number of Journal Titles Worldwide

Year	Number of titles
1951	10,000
1959	15,000
1970	40,000
1980	62,000
1987	71,000

Table 2
Number of Biomedical Journals Being Published

Decade ending	Number of journals
1799	5
1849	45
1899	426
1949	3,937
1977	19,316

all fields of research added together. These, and other figures, suggest that the number of journals tends to double every 15 years or so.

There is another type of growth that needs to be taken into account. Even if the number of titles remained constant with time, the amount of information contained in journals could still grow, if each title expanded in size. This can happen in a variety of ways—more issues can be produced per year, and/or each issue can contain more pages, and/or more information can be crammed onto each page. Take, as an example, the *Journal of the Geological Society* in the UK, which has adopted all these methods of expansion in recent decades. The number of pages published annually in the journal increased from 200 to 1000 in the 40 years after 1950. At the same time, the number of words per page increased from 900 to 1200.[14] Authors are given little scope to spread themselves in current research journals, so increases in word counts should correspond reasonably well with increases in information content. This means that the information conveyed by this single title each year is now some seven times what it was in 1950.

Table 3 shows the growth in the number of pages published annually for a representative sample of journals in various disciplines during the period of rapid research expansion that characterized the 1960s.[15] It makes clear

Table 3
Average Number of Pages Published by Journals in Different Disciplines

Subject matter	1960	1970
Science and technology	602	1060
Social sciences	352	408
Humanities	382	399

that it was the STM (science, technology, and medicine) journals that particularly grew fat. At the other end of the scale, humanities journals remained much the same size.

Research information is not, of course, conveyed solely by journals. In the humanities and, to some extent, the social sciences, scholarly books are often a more important dissemination channel than journals. (This was formerly the case in the sciences—think of the impact of Darwin's *Origin of Species* published in the midnineteenth century—but most scientific monographs today are mainly concerned with discussing material that has already appeared in journals.) The significance of books for some fields of research suggests an obvious question: has the number of books containing research expanded greatly, over an extended period of time, as journal titles have? As with journals, data gathering is made difficult by the need to define which books are to be included in the count and which excluded. Publishers' statistics do not separate book titles in terms of those that contain research of academic value and those that do not. Indeed, it is often difficult to tell. In history, for example, a biography purchased by the general public can also be a contribution to scholarship. Even when the statistics are available, what should be counted is not always clear. For example, should a revised edition of an existing scholarly book be considered as a new work or not?

One way of circumventing these problems and gaining a general picture of what has happened is to examine how the contents of libraries devoted to supporting research have changed with time. Table 4 records the average number of books held by 10 old-established U.S. university libraries over the period 1831–1938.[16] The data indicate a doubling time of about 15 years throughout the period covered. Compare this with a totally different set of statistics: the number of books on scientific, academic, and professional topics produced by publishers in the UK over the period 1988–1993 (Table 5).[17] These suggest a doubling time of some 10 years. Thus the sort of doubling time found for journals also crops up when examining the growth in numbers of scholarly books.

Table 4
Book Holdings of a Sample of U.S. University Libraries

Year	1831	1849	1876	1900	1925	1938
Average number of books	11,764	28,779	59,380	187,082	744,114	1,182,974

Table 5
Scholarly Books Published Annually in the UK

Category	Number of titles produced	
	1988	1993
Scientific, technical, and medical	10,220	16,931
Academic and professional	17,366	27,264

A comparison of the growth rate of the research community with that of the information it produces suggests that the figures are roughly comparable. If anything, the amount of research information in circulation seems to have grown, in the latter half of the twentieth century, rather more rapidly than the size of the associated research community. The few attempts that have been made to produce direct estimates of the relative rates tend to agree with this. For example, a study of medical information in the United States for the period 1960–1975 found that the number of medical journal titles almost doubled.[18] At the same time, the size of the U.S. medical community grew considerably. Comparing the growth rate of the journals and of the community indicates that the former expanded more quickly but that the difference was relatively modest. The number of medical journal titles per thousand members of the U.S. medical community rose from 15.5 in 1960 to 17.3 in 1975. The overall picture, therefore, is that the number of people involved in research and the number of publications they have produced have both grown with increasing speed from a small base some three centuries ago till they have reached today's massive establishment and literature output.

Rapid Growth and Its Implications

In the preceding discussion, we have measured rate of growth in terms of the "doubling time." It is worth considering what this form of measure implies. There is an old story of a man who was offered a reward by a king. The man took a chessboard and asked for one grain of wheat on the first square, two on the second, four on the third, eight on the fourth, and so on until all 64 squares had been covered. The king agreed, not seeing much difference between this and asking for one grain on the first square, two on the second, three on the third, four on the fourth, etc. Unfortunately for the king, though the latter would have been manageable, the former manifestly was not. The second form of growth has been referred to previously as "linear;" the first form is often called "exponential." Its characteristic, as with the wheat grains, is that the initial development is slow and modest, but numbers then take off and soon become very large. We have already seen this in the growth of journals and books. Until the twentieth century, their numbers were not particularly alarming. Over the past 50 years, this has changed: numbers have soared, and researchers have been increasingly affected by the "information explosion."

With a genuinely exponential growth, the doubling time remains always the same. This is not strictly true for the data on number of researchers or amount of literature: the doubling time for these shows some variation. In part, this depends on problems with data selection and reduction, but some differences are real. For example, the two World Wars in the twentieth century affected the number of research publications appearing for some years. However, the idea of exponential change provides a useful basis for discussing growth and its impact on communication. In particular, it raises the question of how researchers cope with the ever-expanding volume of information. Today's researchers may look back enviously at their predecessors, noting the smaller research world within which they operated. The important thing is that their predecessors did not see it that way. Exponential growth means that the amount of literature expanded at the same rate for earlier generations of researchers as for us. Given a doubling time of 10–15 years, then as now, researchers would see potential formal and informal channels of information at least tripling during their research careers. Consequently, the feeling of being inundated by information has been commonplace for many years. Listen to Faraday complaining in 1826:

> It is certainly impossible for any person who wishes to devote a portion of his time to chemical experiment, to read all the books and papers that are published in connection with his pursuit; their number is immense, and the labour of winnowing out the few experimental and theoretical truths which in many of them are embarrassed by a very large proportion of uninteresting matter, of imagination, and error, is such, that most persons who try the experiment are quickly induced to make a selection in their reading, and thus inadvertently, at times, pass by what is really good.[19]

This complaint sounds odd to modern ears: after all, there is vastly more chemical information to cope with now than in Faraday's time. Consequently, retrieving and assimilating all types of information must presumably be a much more formidable problem today. The answer is that the research community has developed its own defensive mechanism against excessive information input down the years. Chemists no longer try to command the same broad sweep of their subject that Faraday did. They concentrate on much more restricted topics. As research has expanded, so researchers have confined their attention to selected parts of it, in such a way that the information they need to absorb continues to fall within acceptable limits.

Research can be thought of as an expanding balloon. The skin of the balloon is the research front, where new information is being generated. The interior of the balloon represents the volume of information that has already been gathered. If the area on the surface of the balloon that a researcher can encompass remains constant with time, then the proportion of the surface that can be covered necessarily falls. Though the analogy is obviously crude, it points to an important consequence of exponential growth. Researchers must become more specialized in their interests as time passes.

The growth of specialization in research is evident in all forms of communication. Journal titles reflect the trend well, with older titles often implying broader coverage than those of more recently founded journals. *Philosophical Transactions*, when it was established, covered most kinds of investigative activity. Journals appearing since the Second World War do not even attempt to cover an entire field (e.g., physics, psychology) but rather concentrate on specialisms within these larger fields, and this is reflected in their titles. In some cases, this trend toward specialization can be observed in the development of a single journal. The *Philosophical Magazine* was founded in London some 200 years ago with a wide brief, something like that of *Phil. Trans.* By the end of the nineteenth century, it had become recognized as primarily a journal for papers on physics. After the Second World War, further contraction of coverage occurred, and *Phil. Mag.* came to be one of the leading journals in the physics of condensed matter. Subsequently, the journal was split into separately published sections that dealt with different subspecialisms within condensed matter.

A somewhat similar trend can be seen in learned and professional societies. We have seen that learned academies or societies increased in number throughout the eighteenth century. Though some of these bodies covered humanities as well as the social and natural sciences (in the UK, for example, one finds the title "Literary and Philosophical Society" appearing), there was already a tendency for such activities to separate. Topics like medicine and agriculture also saw themselves as distinctive and had their own societies. However, the real diversification of societies occurred in the nineteenth century, as national bodies for geology, chemistry, and so forth appeared in Europe and North America. Though this trend was most obvious in the sciences, parallels can be found in the social sciences and humanities. For example, the nineteenth century saw a considerable increase in the number of societies devoted to particular aspects of literature and language.

Specialization has continued to grow in the twentieth century, with new societies starting as new research areas appear. An obvious example is the proliferation of computer societies since the Second World War and the way that new groups are now forming round specialisms within computer science. In fact, the societies based on broad disciplines have come to realize that their members are typically interested in only part of the field. Sometimes this is reflected by the division of the society's journal into separate sections, as occurred over a century ago with *Phil. Trans.* The division is usually best seen in oral presentations (meetings, seminars, etc.). Apart from jamborees intended for the whole society, meetings are often on a fairly limited topic, intended to appeal to a particular section of the society's membership. The hope is that, by having a range of meetings on different topics, every member will find something of interest in the course of a year's program.

Specialization and Research

Specialization cannot be the sole answer to the expansion of knowledge. Using the balloon analogy again, absorbing the ever-lengthening cone of information beneath a given area of the balloon's surface is a problem that grows with time. What this means is that a new recruit to a specialism needs more time and assistance to reach the research front as time passes. Correspondingly, the education of researchers has become more complex over the years. Undergraduate courses have changed not only in terms of the range of information to be handled but also in the way the information is structured. Subjects have developed an increasingly sophisticated theoretical framework as they have expanded. It is often only after a lengthy exposure to subject knowledge that potential researchers can gain some idea of how to initiate new work. For the actual execution of a research project they require additional training, and this has become increasingly formalized down the years. It now normally requires the intending researcher to study for a higher degree (typically a doctorate) under the guidance of a supervisor, who is presumed to be experienced in the arcana of the research process.

Research supervision is essentially a tutorial activity. A Canadian observer earlier this century remarked on the difficulty of determining how the training actually occurs.

> I gather that what [a supervisor] does is to get a little group of students together and smoke at them. Men who have been systematically smoked at for four years turn into ripe scholars.[20]

Being smoked at is probably less common today, and there are many more female researchers, but the relationship remains one of osmosis. This is particularly true in the many fields of research where the knowledge to be transmitted is not purely verbal or pictorial but includes a craft element. The latter has traditionally been communicated by the supervisor working side-by-side with the student on a specific research topic.

There is a connection here with specialization, for its growth has been paralleled by the growth of group research. Practical work often entails the use of a central store of instrumentation or materials. In the sciences, for example, the laboratory is a major focus of research activity. The idea of research students working together under a supervisor seems to have developed with the establishment of Liebig's chemical laboratory at the University of Giessen in the first half of the nineteenth century. In chemistry, students could be given projects that were interrelated, so allowing the exploration of a whole chemical topic simultaneously. As group research has become increasingly important, so the division of labor has often changed. Now each research student may contribute to a particular type of activity within a single project. The apotheosis of this approach is in high-energy physics, where teams of 50 or more researchers, research students, and technicians may be involved in one experiment. An individual research student is concerned with a very specific activity, such as computer-based handling of the data generated. However, experience varies with the subject: being a small cog in a large wheel occurs in big, expensive research projects. Elsewhere, the model where each research student learns a similar range of skills, though each may be working on parallel projects, remains common.

An interesting example of how specialization can develop is provided by German universities in the nineteenth century. It was then expected that each university would have only one established professorial chair in a given subject. Consequently, the number of academic posts available in that subject could only expand up to the point where all the universities had established chairs. Further expansion depended on the field becoming further differentiated until it could produce a recognizably distinct subfield that deserved its own professorial appointments. Thus physiology originally formed a part of anatomy. However, as research in physiology expanded in the nineteenth century, not all professors of anatomy felt able to teach both topics. A few chairs in physiology were therefore created to supplement the chairs in anatomy. The existence of such positions made it worthwhile for prospective academics to study physiology, and interest in this topic grew. Soon, the background knowledge required for anatomy and physiology became sufficiently different for them to be regarded as separate subjects. In fact, it is possible to discern waves of new specialization as the nineteenth century progressed. Anatomy, itself, only became a distinctive branch of surgery in the first half of the nineteenth century. Chairs in physiology grew in number after the midcentury, but the subject had ceased to expand by 1880. Correspondingly, new specialisms in related topics (such as hygiene and psychiatry) appeared and began to command their own chairs. These spurts of growth in terms of posts can be related to growth in terms of research and its communication. Thus a study of important advances in physiology published by German scientists in the nineteenth century suggests that there were 168 during the period 1835–1854, 321 during 1855–1874, and 232 during the 20 years from 1875.[21] This corresponds quite well with the rate of expansion of the subject in German universities as measured by the number of academic positions. As this example may suggest, the quasi-exponential growth of published research discussed earlier really applies to research publication as a whole. Though individual specialisms may expand in the same way (as biochemistry in Table 2), they often have their ups and downs: this phenomenon is looked at in a later chapter.

A growing number of researchers implies not only a greater degree of specialization but also more finance to support them. Some of this increased funding has come from public sources, and some from private. In the academic world, it has been forthcoming because of the ever-growing demand for a well-qualified workforce. This, in turn, has been an inevitable consequence of the expansion of industrialization in the nineteenth and twentieth centuries. In the case of an occupation such as engineering, the link is direct and obvious. The original core subject of civil engineering splintered during the nineteenth century as new specialisms—mechanical, chemical, electrical—developed and required their own courses. Government, industry, and commerce have increasingly demanded specialist graduates from the nineteenth century onward. But industrialization also affected specialization indirectly. It required a better educated workforce at all levels, which meant better teaching in schools for the whole population. This led to a demand for larger schools and more teachers. Within such schools, it became more efficient for each teacher to concentrate on a limited range of topics. This, in turn, made feasible the creation of more specialized courses in higher education for them to attend. The trend toward specialist university courses, and the corresponding appointment of specialist staff to teach them, therefore affected not only applicable subjects, such as science and technology, but also the humanities. History teaching in universities, for example, has become increasingly divided by period, geographical area, or approach (economic, social, etc.). This specialization in teaching has paralleled the increasingly specialized nature of historical research.

The Professionalization of Research

The increasing complexity and specialization of research has tied in with a further development—the professionalization of research. There are many ways of defining a "profession." All agree that it should form one's main paid occupation, that it involves a high level of specialist knowledge, and that it should entail maintenance of appropriate standards of competence both individually and across the professional group. General acceptance that research satisfies these requirements only came in the decades around 1800. This does not mean that recognizably professional researchers had not existed before 1800. Medicine is a typical example of a profession, and some of its practitioners were famous researchers long before that time. Similarly, surveying was a well-regarded profession in North America from the early days of European settlement, and some of its members contributed to early American research. However, in virtually all these cases, the research was regarded as ancillary to their work, rather than as an essential component of it. Even in the academic world, though a number of professors or fellows of colleges contributed to research, the main justification for their posts was teaching.

The belief that university posts should require ability in both teaching and research grew gradually throughout the nineteenth century. Again, Germany led the way. The different German states competed to obtain the most eminent staff for their universities. Such eminence was assessed most readily in terms of what they had published. Professors acquired research students to help develop their research programmes. These students needed some certificate of their research ability, and so grew up the process of awarding the Ph.D. The research reputation of German universities and the availability of doctorates attracted both German students and others from abroad (not least, from the United States and the UK). In the latter half of the nineteenth century, the possession of a German Ph.D. was a widely accepted sign of a professional researcher. Though Germany especially attracted would-be researchers in science-based fields, its importance for research training extended into other fields (theology and philosophy, for example).

The success of Germany in developing training for the potential professional researcher was gradually copied elsewhere. In the United States, it led to the formation of graduate schools from the 1870s onward. It is interesting that a continuous growth in the numbers of research personnel in Germany and the United States starts at about the same time that the academic world in the two countries established organized postgraduate training (in the first and second halves of the nineteenth century, respectively). In France and the UK, where the introduction of systematic research training was delayed until the twentieth century, so, too, was a continuous growth in numbers of research personnel. In the twentieth century, the more diversified nature of university organization in the United States, as compared with Germany, allowed graduate schools to develop into a flexible system for research training of all sorts. In terms of such training, the position of the United States in this century has been in some ways equivalent to that of Germany in the last century as a focus for professional researchers. Hardly surprisingly, leading countries and pioneering institutions in the provision of research training, whether in Germany, the United States, or elsewhere, have also typically taken the lead in the production and dissemination of research results.

Though the academic world absorbed many of the aspiring researchers, the development of industrialization produced a growing need for researchers elsewhere. Early industrialization—in coal and steel, for example—did not require many employees with a strong background in the fundamentals of the subject and a research orientation. Industries that became important later in the nineteenth century, particularly the chemical and electrical industries, did require some such employees. Starting again with Germany, professional research scientists working in industrial fields began to increase in number.

A third group of researchers are those directly supported by funding from some level of government. From the nineteenth century (and sometimes before), work on a range of topics—from standards to agricultural innovation—has been widely seen as requiring state support for their continuance and (often) impartiality. Government work embraces a wider span of subjects than the industrial scene. Social scientists have some opportunities for research-related activities in the industrial and commercial worlds, but they are not as varied as those available in the government sphere. Neither industry nor government is a major employer of humanities graduates interested in research, though there are some jobs in fields such as history and archaeology. A league table of the opportunities for research outside academia might therefore run as follows: science-related subjects, social sciences, and humanities. In contrast, the contributions of amateurs to research in these fields today runs in the opposite direction.

Amateurs and Others

The word *amateur* originally meant that, unlike a professional, the person concerned was not paid for participating in the activity. However, the definition of *professional* suggested earlier in this chapter involves more than a paid position. It stresses specialist knowledge and maintenance of standards as well. The problem for amateur researchers in the twentieth century has been keeping up with the requirement for specialist knowledge. This is not simply a matter of the amount of information to be absorbed. The increasingly complex theoretical framework of much research, often accompanied by a requirement for expensive research facilities, entails lengthy training in well-equipped institutions. This typically prevents amateurs from acquiring the same research background as professionals. This, in turn, has led professionals to doubt whether amateurs are able to maintain the standards expected of "acceptable" research.

The width of the amateur–professional divide varies considerably with discipline. At one end of the scale, there are few amateur brain surgeons: at the other, there are many amateur local historians. Although factors favoring professional-only participation occur more commonly in the sciences than in the humanities, the distinction is not clear-cut. Sciences can be divided roughly into two kinds—the experimental and the observational. The former category includes wide swathes of physics, chemistry, and the biomedical sciences, which today require expensive equipment and complicated techniques centered on a laboratory. The latter category includes some areas of such subjects as astronomy, meteorology, geology, and biology, which rely on direct observation of the phenomena nature supplies. Though professional work in these latter fields may be costly (as in the purchase and running of astronomical or meteorological equipment), some observations can be made at relatively little cost. Moreover, observational activities in these fields often need only a fairly low level of theoretical backing. For example, counts of animal or plant populations, though they may contribute to theoretical studies, do not usually entail too much by way of a theoretical framework for their execution.

This last statement applies even more widely to subjects outside the sciences, from archaeology through to historical and literary studies. There are, however, important differences between amateur research in the sciences and in the humanities. Amateur and professional scientists tend to concentrate on different types of topics in their research, whereas amateur and professional research in the humanities overlaps appreciably more in terms of research interest. Humanities subjects also have the virtue that their research techniques are often more readily self-taught than scientific techniques. The differences between the subjects that attract amateurs and those that do not are reflected in the membership of amateur societies. Topics such as archaeology, natural history, or literature attract the largest numbers of adherents. Indeed, amateurs in these fields may be more numerous than professionals.

Differing amateur and professional attitudes to research are naturally reflected in their communication activities. In the early nineteenth century, amateurs and professionals happily cohabited in the same societies. By the end of the century, societies catering specifically for amateurs, and so paralleling professional activities, were appearing. These had their own meetings and publications. The research presented increasingly differed—often because of disagreement on what constitutes "acceptable" research. In geology, for example, studies of local geological structure represented research acceptable to everyone in the nineteenth century. In the twentieth century, such studies are still acceptable to amateurs, but professional geologists expect local data always to relate and contribute to broader themes. Similarly in archaeology, professional standards in the presentation of information were being identified by the end of the nineteenth century and were being related to the value of the research, itself. A paper read to an archaeology society in 1899 was criticized in the following terms:

> [He] ventured to question the utility of such communications as the foregoing, in which no plans of the excavations or even of the district were produced to the meeting . . . . He strongly deprecated [excavation] by any but competent explorers. Incompetence destroyed evidence.[22]

This difference in approach has been emphasized by the spread among professional journals of refereeing, which acts to impose the research norms of the community on the material accepted for publication. Though some amateur journals have also introduced refereeing, what the referees are asked to look for often differs. Amateurs and professionals continue to interact readily and retain a considerable overlap of interest, but the differences in their approach can affect intercommunication significantly.

Beyond the amateur–professional divide lies the division between those who carry out research in any form and those members of the general public who are interested in hearing about the results of research. The dividing lines between the various groups are porous. Some amateurs become professionals; some members of the general public become amateurs. Indeed, a single individual may be a professional in one subject, an amateur in another, and an interested member of the general public for several others. At the local level, amateurs often interact more than professionals do with the public in their locality. However, direct contact is much less important as a source of information than the mass media. In terms of local media (newspapers, radio, etc.), amateurs often contribute as much as professionals, but professionals typically dominate media presentations at the national level. Public interest tends to mirror that of amateurs in preferring, for example, topics that can be absorbed without requiring too much in the way of theoretical knowledge. The type of research emphasized shows some variation with the information channel employed: television, hardly surprisingly, favors visually attractive topics. Television is easily the most popular channel for public consumption of research, but this has to be qualified for particular groups within the public. For example, politicians often use newspapers relatively more as information sources on research because they can glance at them easily as they travel around. As this indicates, there is not actually a single audience for media-communicated research, rather there are several overlapping audiences.

In the nineteenth century, researchers often presented their results directly to the public. Indeed, there was often competition for their services. T. H. Huxley wrote to the editor of one popular magazine—the *Fortnightly Review*—in the following terms:

> Many thanks for your abundantly sufficient cheque—rather too much, I think, for an article that had already been gutted by the newspaper.
>
> I am always very glad to have anything of mine in the *Fortnightly*, as it is sure to be in good company; but I am becoming as spoiled as a maiden with many wooers. However, as far as the *Fortnightly* which is my old love, and the *Contemporary* which is my new, are concerned, I hope to remain as constant as a persistent bigamist can be said to be.[23]

Even so, the rapidly growing professionalization of research was leading the research community as a whole to regard with increasing suspicion anyone who spent too much time writing for the general public. One such professional commented sourly on Huxley's friend, Tyndall:

> Dr. Tyndall has, in fact, martyred his scientific authority by deservedly winning distinction in the popular field. One learns too late that he cannot "make the best of both worlds."[24]

Though there remained significant differences between disciplines in this respect, the divide between the professional and the public became generally more marked in the first half of the twentieth century. At the same time, the growth of the mass media inevitably led to demands for more information on research activities that would interest the general public. After the Second World War, specialist reporters of research became increasingly common. In essence, they formed a kind of information filter between the researcher and the public, and provided a way of maintaining public access to research information despite the increasing difficulties caused by specialization and professionalization.

Information Growth and the Researcher

Today's members of the general public are not the only ones who have experienced difficulty in maintaining access to research information. It was clear still earlier—by the latter part of the nineteenth century—that researchers needed more assistance to help them pin down the material they required from all the literature available. Part of the problem was the lack of bibliographical standardization in reporting research (and the corresponding omission of relevant data). This point is highlighted by the following complaint from a chemist in the 1890s:

> I am referred by an author to a paper by Schmidt, in the *Berichte* of the German Chemical Society, vol. xx. Not possessing this journal, I hope to be able to find an abstract of the paper in question in the *Journal* of the Chemical Society, to which I subscribe; but as I have no notion in what year vol. xx of this *Berichte* was published I have to search through numerous indexes in order to find the abstract.[25]

His comments also indicate the most important method that was being developed to tackle the problem of access—the use of abstracts and indexes. It was commonplace in the nineteenth century for journals to report the contents of recent issues of other journals, especially ones from abroad, that overlapped in interest. For a while, this helped overcome the difficulties caused by inefficient access to the publications themselves, but the increasing number of journals and pressure on space began to make any kind of systematic and comprehensive coverage in this way impossible. The answer was evidently to publish separate journals, or separate sections of existing journals, that contained only abstracts. Because the problem was not simply one of identifying relevant material but also of obtaining access to it, early abstracts were often intended to act as substitutes for articles as much as guides to them. When the Chemical Society in the UK introduced its system of abstracts, the intention was that:

> The reader will thus not only have a good general notion of the extent of the researches made by any particular author, but also be able to repeat any of the experiments, or prepare any of the substances from the directions given.[26]

In an industrially important subject such as chemistry, abstracts were produced in more than one country, with a corresponding overlap in effort. In the 1890s, U.S. chemists became sufficiently dissatisfied with European coverage of their work that they established a *Review of American Chemical Research*. As its title indicates, it, too, was not intended to have a universal coverage of chemistry. However, in 1907, the American Chemical Society decided to supersede it with *Chemical Abstracts*, a publication with a wider remit. Under its familiar abbreviation of *Chem. Abs.*, it has become the bible of chemists everywhere and has squeezed out most potential competitors.

The success of *Chemical Abstracts* is simply one reflection of the growth of U.S. involvement in abstract journals, paralleling the increasing impact of U.S. research worldwide. In the latter part of the nineteenth century, national production of abstract journals was in the order—Germany, France, UK, United States. Early in the present century, the United States moved ahead of the UK and then overtook France after the First World War. The decline of Germany after the Second World War left the United States in a dominant position in the production of abstracts. Major abstract series were produced elsewhere—for example, the *Referativnii Zhurnal* in the then USSR—but the significant English-language abstract journals to survive were those that had long since reached a modus vivendi with North American readers. For example, the main source in physics—*Physics Abstracts*—which is still published in the UK, established links with the relevant U.S. societies as long ago as 1903.

Abstract journals provide condensed versions of the articles appearing in research journals. Just as the latter represent part of the primary literature (along with books, etc.), so abstract journals form part of the secondary literature (along with indexes, etc.). Abstract journals were created in the nineteenth century in order to ease the task of retrieving information from the primary literature. It is hardly surprising therefore that, as the number of primary journals has grown rapidly over the past century, so has the number of abstract journals. In fact, if the former's growth can be approximated by an exponential curve, so, too, can the latter's. Consequently, a new problem has arisen in recent years—how best to track down information in abstract journals.

If it is even difficult to keep up with guides to the primary literature, how can the problem of information overload be resolved? A major obstacle to coping is the acceleration of information growth. Clearly this cannot go on forever. It was already being remarked in the 1960s that something would have to give by the middle of the twenty-first century. Otherwise, by then, not only would every adult and child in the world be engaged in handling research, but so would every dog and cat. How is this affecting communication at the end of the twentieth century?

An initial period of exponential growth is common in nature. What happens usually is that, as soon as growth becomes really rapid, an opposite trend comes into play, so the growth dies off almost as a mirror image of the initial increase. The growth curve therefore looks rather like an elongated letter S. Such "logistic" growth (as it is often termed) is typical, for example, of the way in which many plants increase in height. If a similar sort of trend is going to hold for research information, there should be some sign of this flattening off occurring now, since we are not many doubling periods away from the crunch point of the mid-twenty-first century. We have looked at journals previously as one way of measuring growth in the communication of research. What do they suggest about current growth trends? An examination of new science periodicals introduced annually over the period 1945–1988 indicates that numbers of new titles peaked in the early 1970s and have been dropping since.[27] The fall in number of new journals does not appear to have been balanced by further increases in the size of existing journals. Hence, it seems a fair guess that the rate of increase in the amount of information contained in research journals is now declining.

This looks like a cautious way of saying that, as judged by journal publication, we are entering the upper branch of the postulated S-shaped curve of information growth. There is good reason to be cautious, for the real point at issue is not how many research journals exist, nor, for that matter, how many monographs and research reports are being published. The fundamental question is how much research information is being put into circulation annually. A comprehensive answer to this requires an examination of all channels of communication. In recent decades, researchers have become increasingly involved in handling information in electronic form, to the extent that electronic storage and communication of research information is now commonplace. It is commonly supposed that current developments foreshadow a large-scale transfer of research communication from print media to electronic media. If so, this will be a major revolution, for the research community has relied on print from its infancy. How has this situation come about?

The New Electronic World

Although early computers were thought of primarily as "number-crunchers," it was obvious that they could also be used for alphabetic sorting. The first electronic computers were introduced in the 1940s. By the 1960s, electronic computers were already being employed to handle bibliographic information. As we have seen, the growth of research had by then reached a stage where individual researchers were finding it difficult to keep up with all the relevant primary literature. Even tracking it via the secondary literature was becoming hard work in some subjects. Electronic computers could offer two advantages here. They could store large quantities of information, and they could also sort through it rapidly. The question was how best to use these assets in order to find items in the literature that were relevant to the researcher's needs. The standard method came to be via "keyword" searching. (A keyword is any word, or phrase, that helps pinpoint the contents of the item concerned; i.e., it excludes words such as *the, of,* etc.).

Since the 1960s, computers have become an increasingly acceptable conduit for secondary publication. Electronic abstracts have been essentially modeled on printed abstracts, and, in many cases, both printed and electronic forms have been made available for researchers to use. In the earlier electronic versions, titles of abstracts were searched for keywords specified by the researcher (usually working in conjunction with a trained information officer, who actually handled the computer input and output). Matches of keywords with titles were recorded, and the corresponding abstracts provided, if the researcher so wished. The speed with which a search could—in principle, if not always in practice—be done was only one of its advantages. At least as important was the coverage of the search. A computer could examine a much wider spread of the secondary literature than could easily be managed by a human being, including sources that might not be available to the researcher in printed form.

Electronic computers were, of course, expensive items of equipment, at least until microcomputers became common in the 1980s. Much of the early activity with information on computers was subsidized by funding from military sources. The abstracts handled, therefore, mainly related to the scientific and technical literature. Some social science material was provided in this way, but the availability on computers of large amounts of secondary literature in the social sciences and humanities awaited the 1970s and 1980s, when computers became both cheaper and easier to use, so that the need for a specialized intermediary to help with the actual retrieval process became less pressing. Almost inevitably, the number of electronic databases began to increase exponentially. Now the advice of information experts is still needed, but more to identify the appropriate databases to access, rather than to help with actual retrieval.

Thus computers entered research communication once removed from the research front—handling secondary, rather than primary, information. From the viewpoint of research communication, however, the electronic medium becomes really interesting only when it can handle every type of information that interests researchers. The transition from supplying secondary information to supplying primary information via computers has taken a little time to accomplish for three basic reasons: the capabilities of the computers, themselves; differences in the nature of primary and secondary publications; and differences in the way researchers handle these two types of publication.

Sorting through large quantities of text can be time consuming, even for a computer. As computers have become more powerful, so the amount of text they can handle rapidly has increased. In the beginning, keyword searches were carried out on titles; then they expanded to cover the contents of the abstracts as well. Now searching of full-text documents—books, as well as journal articles—is commonplace. In other words, the transition from handling secondary information on research to handling primary information has depended on the technical development of the computer. But primary information differs in content from secondary information, and this, too, has affected the transition. One obvious difference is the presence of extensive graphical material in the primary literature. An old saying has it that one picture is worth a thousand words. So far as computers are concerned, most pictures equate to far more than a thousand words in terms of the computer power required to handle them. Even modern computers can be hard pushed to operate rapidly when flipping backward and forward between high-resolution color images. The ever-growing power of computers is undoubtedly overcoming such technical problems, but differences in content are linked to differences in usage, which can complicate attempts to resolve the situation. For example, there are not many different ways in which the title of a journal article can be read. An entire article or book may, on the contrary, be read in several different ways, with different starting points and a variety of jumps between sections. Hence, what is needed for reading an electronic journal or book is not simply a powerful computer, but also one that can react flexibly, according to the needs of the user. These requirements can prove very testing in terms of demands on the software.

The discussion so far covers only half the story. To use a computer for communication necessarily implies communication channels—what of these? In the early days, communication with computers had to be immediate: the people inputting or outputting data typically came into the physical presence of the computer when carrying out their work. Remote access gradually became commoner, with devotees providing and receiving data over a cable (usually a leased telephone line). Further developments hastened the growth of remote access. Different computers were linked together to form a network, so that users could call on the resources of more than a single computer. Interactivity between users and computers increased, and it became possible for a number of users to access the same computer simultaneously. The increasing interdependence of computers and networks led to the coining of a new label—*information technology*, sometimes abbreviated to IT—to describe the two together. By the 1980s, the development of information technology had reached the stage that it could begin to compete with print-on-paper as a universal means for disseminating research information. Within the last few years, therefore, it has become reasonable to examine the potential for transferring research information from a print medium to an electronic medium. The questions this raises are looked at in more detail in later chapters. Here, we look briefly at such a transfer in general terms, using our previous discussion of the development of printed research communication as a basis.

Consider, first, the type of argument that can be made for the advantages of computer-based information. The development of anatomical research from Vesalius onward relied, in part, on the ability to disseminate detailed, exactly reproduced drawings. This is something that print can offer, but handwritten documents cannot. Is computer-based communication similarly able to offer advantages that printed material cannot? One affirmative answer, also in the biomedical field, is supplied by current work on the human genome. The analysis of human DNA is producing a vast amount of information, all of which must be rapidly available to researchers, who must also be able to add new information to the corpus. It would be impossible to satisfy these requirements using only print, so the work has been computer-based from the start. Here is an instance where electronic information handling allows the research community to carry out a major new type of investigation. Of course, printed matter continues to have some advantages over computer-based material. For example, many people still find it easier to read long stretches of text from the printed page, than from the computer screen. But the balance of advantages and disadvantages is changing rapidly, not least because—as with the human genome—computers are affecting the type of research that can be undertaken.

The development of the printed research journal has hinged on resolving a series of problems—the need to provide the information in a standard form, to support quality control mechanisms and establish priorities, to disseminate a large number of copies internationally, and so on. An electronic journal can follow similar approaches to the printed journal in trying to solve many of these problems, but it also has the potential for being more flexible. For example, the standard layout of a printed journal can readily be reproduced on-screen (allowing for the differing shapes and capacities of a printed page and a screen), but the computer provides additional possibilities. One relates to the references attached to an article. A reference in a printed article to another article or book entails a separate literature search, if the reference is to be followed up further. In an electronic journal, it can be arranged so that other material referred to in the course of an article can be brought up immediately on the screen at the press of a button. Again, it is straightforward to referee electronic articles in a similar way to printed articles. (Access to an electronic document can be restricted to named individuals initially; then it can be thrown open to a wider readership.) But, information technology can offer greater flexibility, if it is desired. For example, the effort involved in interacting with referees usually restricts the number used. The easier communication provided by computer networks makes it feasible to involve more referees, should the editors consider it helpful.

International dissemination of research journals can obviously be effected much more speedily for information in electronic form. It can also be done more cheaply, given that research networks are usually subsidized. The main problem concerns the proportion of the potential audience that can access an electronic network and so receive the journal. This depends not only on the country concerned, with poorer countries, in the main, having greater problems of access to electronic journals. It also varies from one subject to another, with scientists still tending to have better access to networks than researchers in the humanities. However, networking is developing so rapidly that it is no longer easy to assess who will be the "have-nots" for electronic research information in the next century.

At a more fundamental level, there is the question of how the exponential growth of research information will be affected by the rise of information technology. Computers can obviously handle incomparably more information than printed sources; since their power and storage capabilities are still growing very rapidly, there is no immediate obstacle to further growth. (There are problems relating to the organization of electronic information, and these are discussed in a later chapter.) There remain the limitations due to human resources. If the growth in the number of researchers tails off, as it appears to be doing, the amount of computer-based research information in circulation will presumably do the same. After all, a finite number of human beings can only absorb and produce research information up to a certain limit. From this viewpoint, the question is whether the productivity of the individual researcher can be enhanced. If so, then some further growth is possible.

A distinction must be drawn here between "data" and "information." The raw data obtained from direct measurements or observations can presumably continue to increase in amount into the indefinite future, so long as researchers continue to expand their use of automated instrumentation. Research information derived from the analysis and discussion of these data may nevertheless be limited in its growth because of the need for human interaction. The crucial question is whether data analysis and deductions from it can be automated. This is certainly happening in some research fields. For example, in high-energy nuclear physics not only are the experiments automated, but so, too, is the analysis. The researchers are left with the activity of discussing the small number of events that the equipment shows to them. (For the moment, they also have the communication task of conveying the results of their experiments to the outside world.) What has happened, in this case, is that the productivity of the researchers has been enhanced by the introduction of automation. Computers can similarly act to enhance the amount of information transferred. For example, their speed and storage capacity mean that raw data can be published as part of a research report along with the data analysis (something that can rarely be done in print). The overall result, if this were done consistently, would be to increase still further the amount of research information in circulation, prolonging the exponential growth phase.

The vast capacity of computer systems creates a problem when comparing dissemination via electronic and printed means. A classification of activities that has been worked out for the latter cannot necessarily be transferred to the former. In the foregoing example, it was noted that the electronic medium can readily intermix the raw data and the refined information, unlike a printed journal or book. (Indeed, it may be possible in the future to include appropriate software for making deductions from the data and information, so adding a knowledge function to these two.) In traditional research work, the data were likely to be in one source (e.g., a laboratory notebook), information in another (e.g., books or journals), and knowledge in a third (the human researcher). Hence, use of electronic media can begin to blur traditional distinctions drawn between data, information, and knowledge. More particularly, basic assumptions about categories of information will need to change. For example, the distinction between formal and informal information channels sits uneasily with the use of computers and networks. The difference between a handwritten letter and a published journal is very clear; the distinction between an electronic mail message and an electronic journal article is not. Both can be sent to any size of audience from one individual upward; both are disseminated via the same channels and can be accessed by readers via the same computer screens. This blurring of function does not only apply to researchers' disseminating information to a research audience. The growth of information technology is increasingly making it possible for computers to act as channels for the mass media, more especially television. In principle, and already sometimes in practice, researchers can provide information to a mass public via the same information technology they use for contacting fellow-researchers.

This blurring of traditional divisions is a key factor in the transfer of information from traditional to electronic channels. It inevitably affects not only the way information is handled but also the institutions involved in information handling. For example, if the traditional distinction between formal and informal information is disappearing, how will this affect the publishers of printed books and journals, who have only hitherto been concerned with the former? Will the impact be different for learned societies, who, alongside their formal publishing activities, have always been active in using informal channels (organizing meetings, etc.)? Questions of this sort are followed up in subsequent chapters.

2

Research Traditions

A great deal has been written about the differences between the major divisions of learning—science, social science, and humanities—not least because these divisions are seen to reflect basic beliefs about the nature of knowledge. How such differentiation affects communication has been less studied; yet drawing distinctions between subjects necessarily implies some form of imagined barrier between them. A striking example of this, in concrete form, is provided by research libraries, where the science, social science, and humanities books and journals may be on different floors. To the extent that the divisions reflect different ways of doing research, the methods of communicating the results are also likely to differ. In this chapter, we look first at the nature of the differences between subjects. We then look at some examples of how these are reflected in the process of communication.

The Development of Disciplinary Divisions

How clear-cut and stable are the divisions between subjects? There has certainly been some change with time. In the seventeenth century, studies of the world around us were all considered to constitute some kind of philosophical investigation. Much of what we now call the physical sciences came under the heading of natural philosophy, whereas some of the modern social sciences, along with history, were regarded as moral philosophy. Natural philosophy, it was believed, provided especially significant knowledge of the world around us because it relied on the logical, quantitative approach to be found in mathematics. When Isaac Newton wrote a book on the nature of the universe, he entitled it *Principia Mathematica Philosophiae Naturalis* (or, in English translation, *Mathematical Principles of Natural Philosophy*), so establishing its claims to containing fundamental knowledge. In these terms, biology was not a part of natural philosophy, since it did not yield to mathematical treatment. The name given to many biological studies in the early days—natural history—indicates that their links were seen to lie with other nonmathematical subjects. It was in this vein that Ernest Rutherford, one of the great physicists of the twentieth century, claimed there were only two sorts of research—physics and stamp collecting.

This classification of disciplines was already changing in the seventeenth century. Baconian ideas of ways of studying the world affirmed that empirical investigations based on observation and experiment could provide knowledge, which, if less certain than mathematical proofs, was still acceptable as an objective account. Henceforth, scientific knowledge could be derived either analytically or empirically, so long as there was agreement on the basic data involved. This definition of *scientific* extended widely. Until the nineteenth century, it could include such subjects as history and economics, as well as physics and biology. Then things began to change:

> In the United States shortly after the middle of the nineteenth century, the meaning of the word "science" began significantly to change. Before, any well-organized body of knowledge or speculation had been called a science. Science connoted orderliness and system, in ethics no less than in geology.[1]

Now, in English-speaking countries, geology became a science, but not ethics. In these countries, *science* by the early twentieth century, meant the natural sciences (physics, chemistry, biology, etc.). In other countries, this narrower meaning has still only partly established itself. The older approach, which lumps some social science and humanities subjects together with the natural sciences as *empirical sciences,* is still maintained elsewhere. Indeed, in communist countries, it was almost axiomatic, since Marxist analysis of such subjects as economics, history, and politics was considered to be on a par with his account of the natural sciences. It is worth quoting one attempt to provide a definition of science that would be acceptable in all countries in order to see how broadly it extends, as compared with the standard English-language meaning (that is employed in this book). The quotation is essentially about knowledge, but it has implications for a number of the divisions we often make: for example, those between amateur and professional researchers and between pure and applied research.

> science is a body of coherent, systematic knowledge of any subject, formal or empirical, natural or cultural, arrived at by any method whatever, provided it (1) is based on hard, honest and serious study and research and

reaches insights not available to laymen or superficial observers and (2) is designed for either intellectual or general-pragmatic purposes, but not for immediate practical application in a concrete case or situation.[2]

These national differences in interpreting the word *science* have had some influence on international communication. At one level, the lack of a common meaning has often led to contrary interpretations of what a book or journal should contain. At another, it has led to organizational differences that affect communication. The Royal Society constitutes an interesting case study. By the end of the nineteenth century, a majority of its members had come to believe that the Society's original broad spread of interests should be restricted to the natural sciences only. In 1901, there was a meeting of a newly formed International Congress of Academies, which the Royal Society was invited to attend as the representative body for the UK. It was decided to divide the Congress into two sections—scientific and literary. This was a simple exercise for most of the national academies involved, but not for the Royal Society, which by now had no literary members. As an immediate result, a British Academy was founded to act as parallel literary body to the Royal Society. (Originally, it was designated as being for the promotion of historical, philosophical, and philological studies, but its brief subsequently widened to cover most of the social sciences and humanities.) In terms of communication, this divided responsibility has proved a less efficient method of organization than the unified body found in many other countries. One example is the handling of borderline subjects, such as archaeology or the history of science, where there have been times of doubt as to which body should take the initiative.

If the word *science* creates difficulties, so, too, does the label *humanities*. Originally, humanities referred to classical studies. Thus a degree in *Litterae Humaniores* at Oxford University entailed a study of Greek and Latin literature and philosophy. This is still the sense in which the word is used in many languages. In English, it has gradually come to have the wider sense of literary, historical, and philosophical studies in any language. Its widespread use is quite recent: it can be dated to the latter half of the twentieth century. An older word that is also in use with a somewhat similar coverage is the *arts*, as in those universities that award Bachelor of Arts degrees. Unfortunately, this word, too, has its ambiguities. Until the twentieth century, it was mostly employed when talking of the practical arts, which ranged from the fine arts, such as painting, through various crafts, to activities related to engineering, often including en route music and the theatre. In principle, research on all these topics is distinct from creative work in them and can be separated off for inclusion under the "humanities research" banner. In practice, the distinction has often been blurred, with an uncertain boundary between research and creative work.

This points to one of the fundamental problems of discussing research communication in the humanities—namely, determining what exactly constitutes humanities research. For example, the constitution of the Modern Language Association states that it aims to promote study, criticism, and the advancement of research in the modern languages and their literatures. Now many scholars would dispute the use of words here: they would claim that criticism, properly practiced, is a form of research. In the humanities, more than in other subjects, part of the communication of research involves a continuing discussion of what actually constitutes research. As one eminent historian has observed concerning his own subject:

> Since historians are naturally given to sharpness of tongue, the debate is likely to look savage to the outsider.[3]

The description *social science* has had a somewhat less variegated career than *science*, or *humanities*. It has not, however, managed to avoid conflict altogether. The main dispute relates again to the restricted use of the word *science* in English. Is the study of society a science in the narrow sense of that word? The former Social Science Research Council in the UK had its name forcibly changed to the Economic and Social Research Council when the politician in ultimate charge decreed that the subjects that concerned it were not real sciences. A more important query is how the social sciences should position themselves intellectually relative to science and the humanities. This uncertainty became particularly acute in the United States when the U.S. Congress set up agencies to sponsor research in science, the humanities, and the arts but failed to provide one for the social sciences. Social scientists were then faced with the urgent question of which funding agency to approach. (Their choice often hinged on the fact that the sciences had much more funding available than the humanities.)

Researchers see the boundary line between the social sciences and the humanities as being particularly blurred, though, for a subject such as psychology, the boundary line between the social and the natural sciences can be just as uncertain. A symposium of the American Council of Learned Societies, arranged to discuss the relationship between the social sciences and the humanities, gives some indication of the vast range of opinion that exists on this topic.

The sociologist George Caspar Homans held that "between the social sciences and many of the so-called humanities no intellectual line can be drawn: all are social sciences (or, if you like, all are humanities)." To those who emphasized the humanities' basic concern with human values, Homans replied with a rhetorical question: "In what sense is the study of Romance philology a study of human values rather than a study of the way men have behaved?" With regard to the place of history, the classicist Paul L. MacKendrick suggested that Gibbons' *Decline and Fall of the Roman Empire* was "a humanistic work, because it was written with a profound sense of individuation," but the *Cambridge Ancient History*, "because it was written by a team, is not: it is social science." The historian Hugh R. Trevor-Roper found the distinguishing criterion of "humane subjects" in the fact that they have "no direct scientific use; they owe their title to existence to the interest and comprehension of the laity; they exist primarily not then for training of professionals but for the education of laymen." Carl J. Friedrich, the political scientist, held that "the focus of the humanities is upon critical examination and evaluation of the *products* of man in cultural affairs . . . whereas the focus of the social sciences is upon the *way* men live together, including their creative activities."[4]

Or, as another contributor to the symposium suggested:

> Those who think and get somewhere are mathematicians. Those who think and don't get anywhere are philosophers. Those who don't think and get somewhere are the natural scientists. Those who don't think and don't get anywhere are the humanists.[5]

Subject Development

To a significant extent, the present location of a subject in the spectrum from the sciences to the humanities depends on where within that spectrum it first emerged. As we have seen in the first chapter, one typical way for a subject to originate is via specialization within a broader topic. Physics and chemistry emerged in this way from natural philosophy and have always been seen as having significant similarities in the way they operate: so they continue to be grouped together. In a similar way, economics emerged from moral philosophy and then helped give birth to sociology. Both economics and sociology remain classified as important components of the social sciences.

In these cases, the broad subjects that have split off are distinguished not only by their differing areas of interest, but also by the differing approaches researchers take when studying them. Within such subjects, many specialisms exist: they are often more concerned with narrowing the area of study than with different methodologies. Local history and the history of science, for example, take over much of the intellectual baggage of history but apply it to a restricted topic. Though development of subjects by "twigging" is common, the opposite process involving the union of two branches of research to form a new specialism is also important. The combination of part of biology with part of chemistry to produce biochemistry is an excellent example of the way in which a major new research field can be produced by fusion. This sort of process is particularly important for the progress of research because it alleviates a basic limitation of specialization. Each subject, such as biology and chemistry, can be thought of as a mining activity that digs deeply within a specified field of interest. The individual shafts are sunk, but they typically leave regions in between that remain unexplored. The combination of two specialisms helps ensure that such intermediate territory is exploited. For biochemistry, and for a number of other combined specialisms, the union is reflected in a compound name. In other combinations of topics, the parent subjects may still appear as separate words, as, for example, in economic and social history.

Francis Crick, a physicist who won a Nobel prize for his work on the biochemical problem posed by DNA, suggested that new specialisms to explore could readily be devised by the simple process of yoking together two distinct areas of research. He proposed as an example—tongue in cheek—molecular theology. As the mining analogy may suggest, the actual process of cross-fertilization between specialisms is somewhat subtler. The two specialisms being mined usually need to be in some sense adjacent, if the ground in between them is to be explored. Genuinely, interdisciplinary topics can arise, but only when a new unifying concept brings together a wide range of knowledge. For example, cybernetics brought together a range of scientific, social scientific, and engineering ideas. Even subjects that are regarded as very stable now may have originated by a process of aggregation of adjacent specialisms. For example, it was not until the nineteenth century that the various branches of physics were recognized as forming a unified whole. Similarly, geology has managed over the past century to bring together elements, such as mineralogy, which were originally regarded as distinct.

Both entire subjects and the specialisms that compose them can thus arise via more than one process. The expansion of research means that new specialisms arise from old ones all the time. This does not mean that the rate of evolution is the same in all fields. The speed with which changes occur depends on such factors as the intellectual priority given to the subject and the number of researchers in the field who can be supported. However, it seems obvious that the more comprehensive the research field, the longer it takes to produce a major change in it. For example, one study of physics divides it into a hierarchy of four categories.[6] This starts with the entire discipline (physics) and progresses down through subdisciplines (e.g., condensed matter) and fields (e.g., the transport properties of condensed matter) to the ultimate subfields (e.g., electrical conductivity in metals). The corresponding periods for major change are suggested to be 100 years, 50 years, 20 years, and 10 years. Large-scale change is not the same as total disappearance, so when we talk about whole disciplines, we can assume they have a reasonable long-term stability—as, indeed, is suggested by past history.

To some extent, the appearance of specialisms on the intellectual scene can be identified from the dates at which university chairs in the subject have been founded, since these often reflect the period when particular topics began to come to the fore. When the first Professor of English Literature at Cambridge University started to give lectures, he listed all the previous Chairs founded at Cambridge, in order to emphasize how long it had taken before English Literature was regarded as a proper subject for study at the University.

> It began in 1502 with the Lady Margaret's Chair of Divinity, founded by the mother of Henry VII. Five Regius Professorships follow: of Divinity, Civil Law, Physic, Hebrew, Greek all of 1540 . . . . Close on a hundred years elapse before the foundation of the next Chair—it is of Arabic; and no more than a hundred before we arrive at Mathematics . . . . Then follow Moral Philosophy (1683), Music (1684), Chemistry (1702), Astronomy (1704), Anatomy (1707), Modern History and more Arabic, with Botany (1724), Geology (1727), closely followed by Mr. Hulse's Christian Advocate, more Astronomy (1749), more Divinity (1777), Experimental Philosophy (1783): then in the nineteenth century more Law, more Medicine, Mineralogy, Archaeology, Political Economy, Pure Mathematics, Comparative Anatomy, Sanskrit and yet again more Law, before we arrive in 1869 at a Chair of Latin. Faint yet pursuing, we have yet to pass Chairs of Fine Art (belated), Experimental Physics, Applied Mechanics, Anglo-Saxon, Animal Morphology, Surgery, Physiology, Pathology, Ecclesiastical History, Chinese, more Divinity, Mental Philosophy, Ancient History, Agriculture, Biology, Agricultural Botany, more Biology, Astrophysics, and German, before arriving in 1910 at a Chair of English Literature which by this time I have not breath to defend.[7]

An examination of this list suggests a number of points regarding specialization. The first recognized professions—law, medicine, and the church—were also those that were first catered for by the provision of chairs, reflecting the link between professional and subject development. The dates of the individual chairs not only indicate the increase in specialization, but also suggest the different times at which individual subjects became recognized as coherent wholes. For example, "chemistry" appears in 1702, but the mention of "physics" is delayed until the latter part of the nineteenth century. Many of the topics mentioned can be identified as readily today as when the chairs were founded. Most fall either in the sciences or the humanities. The social sciences are not only poorly represented, their titles—political economy, mental philosophy—also have an odd sound to modern ears. Correspondingly, the split between science and humanities subjects is usually fairly clear. It is the borderlines between these disciplines and the social sciences that tend to be most hazy. The interesting subjects, from the classification viewpoint, are those that hover vaguely around one of the science–social science–humanities borderlines.

Psychology is a good example of a subject whose development reflects an uncertain affiliation. Academic interest in psychology as a discipline developed first in Germany during the nineteenth century. Some psychological research was being done at that time in the English-speaking world, generally under the banner of "mental philosophy." But the appearance of psychological research as a distinctive activity in the United States is usually attributed to William James, who began teaching the subject at Harvard in 1875. James's background was in physiology, but he by no means believed that the only approach to psychology was via work in the laboratory. Nevertheless, psychology was generally regarded in the United States as being an experimental subject. In the early years of the twentieth century, for example, behaviorism made a major impact on U.S. psychological research, and, according to the behaviorists, psychology was a purely objective experimental branch of natural science. Their view was purveyed via both journals and meetings. Thus one of the leading behaviorists, John Watson, was an influential editor of the *Psychological Review*, and subsequently president of the American Psychological Association.

As time passed, this view of psychology as a natural science underwent modification. Clinical psychology represents an extreme example. Originally, the Freudian approach was seen as essentially scientific, but, for a number of years now, it and related approaches have been seen in a different light. The change is reflected in this comment from the 1950s:

> There is a prevailing sense of the scientific untenability of clinical psychology among many psychologists. Frequently, clinical psychology is envisaged

as an art; or if the critic is inclined to be more critical, it may be conceived of as an attempt to obtain knowledge mystically and effect changes magically.[8]

The fact that different areas of psychology were being investigated in different ways raised a basic query. The natural sciences have developed views of what they are about and how research should be tackled, which are widely accepted by researchers in these subjects. Is psychology capable of developing a similar unified approach, or must it remain a group of distinct specialisms—some more akin to the natural sciences and some less? Are there generally applicable laws in psychology as there are in (say) physics? This is a question that affects all the social sciences. As the following quotation implies—perhaps it depends on which specialism you are considering.

> Nevitt Sanford, then of Stanford University, said in 1963, "The great difficulty for general psychology is that the 'general' laws so much admired and so eagerly sought are never very general. On the contrary, they are usually quite specific."
>
> This could mean that psychology was simply not advanced enough to permit anyone to conceive an over-arching theory. But it could mean something quite different: that psychology is not a science in the same sense as physics, chemistry, or biology; that it is a cluster of scientific fields that, though related, are too disparate to fit into the framework of a single theory . . . in fact the field of psychology has burst apart and become autonomous areas of specialization. The American Psychological Association now recognizes fifty-eight fields of psychology, and forty-two of the APA's forty-five "divisions" (membership subgroups) represent such fields or, one might say, fission products of psychology.[9]

The groupings in the APA are distinguished not only by differences in practical approach, but also by theoretical stance. As the number of divisions may suggest, particular groupings can be quite specific in the research methodology that they regard as suitable. For example, one division was set up to concentrate on research using the behaviorist methodology advocated by Burrhus Skinner. Despite the specificity of the topic, it is covered by four research journals. Such specialization via methodology, rather than subject matter, occurs quite frequently in the social sciences. Two European sociology journals circulating after the Second World War had very similar remits. Their independent existence derived from the fact that the training of pre-war and postwar researchers took rather different paths. The theoretical stances of the two groups were incompatible, so their communications went to separate destinations.

The Conceptual Basis in Science

As this last example implies, differences within and between subjects are often as much a question of approach as of content. Many psychologists would, no doubt, define their subject as the study of the mental characteristics or attitudes of a person or group of people. Where they differ is in how to study such characteristics or attitudes. This question of the conceptual framework to be used in carrying out research is a major factor in determining differences in communication pattern between subjects. Much of the debate about such frameworks to date has revolved round the idea of a "scientific method." This therefore makes a good starting point for discussing the relationship between conceptual framework and communication.

Many working scientists would regard talk of "conceptual framework" and certainly of a "scientific method" as unnecessarily high-flown. They have learned to study the world around them by a variety of ad hoc methods. The assumptions they make in carrying out such studies seem mostly too obvious to require mention. Nevertheless, their assumptions ultimately affect the way they communicate. Scientists believe there is a real world out there that has its own characteristics independent of the hopes and desires of human beings. They automatically suppose that they can dissociate themselves sufficiently from this world to be able to examine it with a degree of impersonality. They believe that obtaining reliable information about the world entails a rational, quantitative approach, accumulating data via observation and experiment and interpreting them via an appropriate theoretical framework. Progress in scientific investigations depends on an intermixed application of practical and theoretical work, each component checking and aiding the other. This approach leads to the discovery of regularities, which can ultimately be subsumed in "laws of nature." For example, the study of regularities in how the planets move led to the law of gravitation.

The identification of such laws permits predictions to be made—for example, where a particular planet will be at a particular time. Should the predictions fail, it is a question of back to the drawing board: scientists must be prepared to modify their ideas when the evidence suggests strongly enough that they are wrong. Such growth by modification ensures that the picture we have of the world continually increases its scope. In other words, science progresses as time passes not only by accumulating more data, but by providing more general and more sophisticated insights into the nature of our world. All these assumptions led to the belief among scientists that, though science may not be the only way of exploring the world, it does so in a unique way. Indeed, many scientists suppose that the development of modern science was, itself, a unique event—something that happened in Western Europe during the sixteenth and seventeenth centuries—though some historians are less sure.

These beliefs influence the way science is communicated. One example is the belief that there is just one real world waiting to be explored, which implies that specific discoveries about it can only be made once. Since several scientists may be working along similar lines at the same time, this means that the first to give public notification of a discovery preempts the work of the others. Consequently, the communication system must be able to establish clearly who has priority for each new step forward. Or, to take another example, the emphasis on impartial observation and quantitative analysis links in with the way in which research results are typically presented—an impersonal style often interlaced with mathematics. This form of presenting science is indigestible to nonscientists and so has led to the rise of science popularizers. Even a belief in the uniqueness of science has implications for the diffusion and acceptance of research information internationally. It suggests that all countries should adopt the forms of communication developed in the leading science countries.

These various beliefs about science necessarily imply that scientific research is bound up with social interaction. The need to accumulate data, to develop theory and experiment in parallel, and to modify ideas, all involve scientists in communication. This is not to say that science needs to be considered only in sociological terms: the research styles of individuals, which involves their psychology, are also important. But communication is, by definition, a communal activity. Consequently, it is the social aspects of science that most concern us here. In other words, what do scientists believe about the way they should act as a member of a research community?

This is basically a question about rules of conduct, or—as they are often called—social norms. Various attempts have been made to define sets of norms for the scientific community. The most influential, by Robert Merton, proposes the existence of four basic norms—universalism, communality, disinterestedness, and organized skepticism.[10] "Universalism" means that the scientific community assesses new work on the basis of preestablished, impersonal criteria, independent of such personal factors as sex, race, nationality, religion, and so on. New results depend ultimately on interaction between scientists and must, in turn, be made available to the scientific community. "Communality" reflects the requirement that scientific knowledge should be made common property. "Disinterestedness" instructs scientists that their prime concern should be the advancement of knowledge. They should not be emotionally involved in the acceptance or rejection of particular ideas. Finally, the scientific community should continually be subjecting the knowledge they accept to critical scrutiny—that is, to "organized skepticism"—looking for possible errors, whether of omission or commission.

A variety of comments can be made about these rules of conduct. One is that they are not necessarily true. For example, the likelihood of a radically new idea being accepted is often considerably enhanced if its progenitor is highly committed to it. Many scientists would regard this as normal practice and so implicitly question the norm of "disinterestedness." Again, there may be additional norms discernible in the scientific community that are not included in Merton's four. It has been suggested more than once, for example, that scientists also believe strongly in a norm of "originality." This entails a scientist only putting forward research results that contain some genuine novelty. At another level, it is clear that all the suggested norms are broken, sometimes frequently, by scientific researchers in their actual practice. In a sense, there is nothing surprising in this: the ten commandments laid down in the Bible are broken even more frequently. The difference is that the ten commandments represent an ex cathedra statement, whereas scientific norms are meant to be generalizations based on the actual outlook of the community. One of two conclusions seems to follow. The first is that there must be a continuing tension between what scientists think they should be doing as members of a community and their own personal predilections. Alternatively, we can reject the idea that the scientific community actually adheres to such a set of social norms.

This latter action seems too extreme. Merton's norms at least reflect what scientists would regard as a perfect research world. However, there is an important proviso: these norms apply to academic science. They need major surgery to fit the aims of many scientists working in industry. Even within academic science, different specialisms may take rather differing attitudes, and the members of each specialism are, in any case, likely to hold a range of views. For example, there have been a number of debates between and within specialisms on the problems of accepting research funding from military sources. One point at issue here relates to the norm of communality—the belief that scientific knowledge should be made freely available to the whole community—which is often impossible to fulfill on defense projects. It should be added that, though acceptance of Merton's norms can also be found in the past history of science, attitudes can change with time. For example, senior scientists in the nineteenth century debated whether acceptance of any government funding at all might limit the freedom of their research activities. This more general worry is rarely heard today.

The existence and acceptance of norms can affect the process of communication. Take the concept of universalism first. An example of this at work can be found in the scrutiny of articles submitted for publication in scientific journals. Editors are usually anxious to ensure that articles are accepted on their merit and not just because their author is well known. As becomes evident in a subsequent chapter, editors expend considerable effort in trying to handle submitted material even handedly. The norm of communality is also well illustrated by journals. Authors, however important their work, cannot, when they publish it, lay down conditions for its further use and development. The fact that authors do not expect to be paid for having their research work published in journals (indeed, they sometimes have to contribute to the cost) is, in turn, one illustration of disinterestedness. The refereeing of research articles is, equally, an excellent example of organized skepticism at work. (The same critical function can be found in informal communication, as speakers at seminars or conferences are cross-examined.) If originality is accepted as an additional norm, then this, too, appears in the article review process, where it is a basic requirement for acceptance. It also acts as a crucial objective in the training of new researchers, since a basic condition for the award of a Ph.D. is that the candidate must have produced new knowledge. Any, or all, of these Mertonian norms might be disputed in terms of representativeness and level of communal acceptability. Nevertheless, the scientific communication system, and more especially the reviewing process, clearly presupposes some such agreed rules of conduct in order for it to work. The existence of this agreement is perhaps best illustrated when it is ignored. An obvious example is the harsh treatment by the scientific community of individual researchers who are clearly breaking the "rules," either by plagiarizing the work of others or by forging data.

The foregoing discussion leads to the conclusion that two conceptual factors have a significant influence on the process of communicating science—the basic assumptions that scientists make about the work they do and the beliefs they hold concerning the research community and the way it should operate. The obvious question to ask next is—to what extent does science differ in these respects from other fields of academic research? We shall approach this question via a slight detour, by asking first of all how and why research leads scientists to change their views of what the world is like, and the way it should be investigated.

Science and Other Disciplines

The most obvious changes in science are, naturally, the big ones: from believing that the earth is a few thousand years old to believing it is several billion years old; from believing that the earth is at the center of the solar system to believing that the sun is; from believing in Newton's picture of the universe to believing Einstein's picture; and so on. Thomas Kuhn has argued that scientific research can be divided into periods of relatively calm development, which he has labeled "normal science," interspersed with periods of major upheaval, labeled "revolutions," such as the three mentioned in the previous sentence.[11] During a period of normal science, the field concerned is governed by a generally accepted "paradigm." The paradigm, essentially a conceptual framework involving both theory and practice, provides researchers with guidance on what problems deserve investigation and how they should be tackled. As research proceeds, anomalies begin to accumulate, which the paradigm finds it increasingly difficult to accommodate in a convincing way. Eventually, the whole structure is overthrown by a conceptual revolution. Thus, in the early nineteenth century, one generally accepted paradigm in biology was that all species were uniquely created. However, in an increasing number of instances this supposition led to problems of interpretation. In the midnineteenth century, this led to a revolution in biology that introduced a different paradigm—Darwinian evolution. The new paradigm put forward its own specification of which research tasks were important and how they should be investigated.

Kuhn's analysis treats the top end of the market, where the big changes can be found. What about the other end: the smaller scale changes that occur as part of the activities he has labeled "normal science"? One common model of scientific research supposes the scientists typically apply a hypothetico-deductive approach.[12] This can broadly be regarded as a "bootstrap" approach. The scientist hazards some guesses—labeled "hypotheses"—about some aspect of the natural world. These hypotheses are then subjected to practical tests, the results of which are compared with the original guesses. Disagreement may lead to a modification of the hypotheses, followed by further tests, and so on until the scientist is happy with the match. A well-tested hypothesis may become embedded in the scientists' world picture, but there is never an absolute guarantee that some new finding will not supplement it. Karl Popper has argued, in fact, that the important factor in the development of science is this potential that research has for showing ideas are false. Whereas a whole program of investigation will not ensure that any particular hypothesis is true beyond any shadow of doubt, a single experiment may suffice to show that it is wrong.

A picture, or more accurately a series of vignettes, of science built up from conjectures such as Kuhn's and Popper's provides a helpful framework for discussing research and communication in science. But no single picture provides a definitive description of how the system of science works. For example, at the top level, scientific revolutions are seldom as clear-cut as Kuhn originally postulated (his views changed somewhat with time). When, in early twentieth-century physics, the classical model of the world was "replaced" by the quantum model, this did not mean that all research on the classical model immediately ceased. On the contrary, it still continues today, and researchers acknowledge both classical and quantum models to be useful, depending on the context. Similarly, not all research can be classified as consciously hypothetico-deductive à la Popper. Prior to its series of lunar landings, NASA set up a program for mapping the front face of the moon. This mapping process no doubt involved a number of implicit hypotheses, but they were mostly regarded as too obvious to require explicit mention, let alone discussion. Even Popper's falsifiablity criterion is only part of the story. There are a range of instances where new evidence seems to contradict an accepted hypothesis, yet scientists continue blithely to make use of the hypothesis in their work. For example, in the years following Einstein's announcement of his relativity theory, some experiments seemed to contradict the predictions that followed from it. They were not considered sufficiently significant to cause scientists to drop their belief in the new theory.

All this seems to be saying is that scientific research is a messy activity, so it is hardly surprising if scientific research can only be partly described by simple models. The interesting point, however, is the queries these models raise about the nature of scientific knowledge and, consequently, about how it should be communicated. Kuhn's picture of a paradigm change sees the state of knowledge in the research field concerned as undergoing a complete transformation before and after the revolution. Many of the data remain usable, but the information derived from them is different. As a result, earlier communications cease to be consulted:

> When it repudiates a past paradigm, a scientific community simultaneously renounces, as a fit subject for professional scrutiny, most of the books and articles in which that paradigm had been embodied.[13]

More generally, this model sees scientific information as only accumulating to a limited extent, with beliefs and consequent information use being transformed at each paradigm change. As Kuhn remarks:

> We are all deeply accustomed to seeing science as the one enterprise that draws constantly nearer to some goal set by nature in advance.
>
> But need there by any such goal? Can we not account for both science's existence and its success in terms of evolution from the community's state of knowledge at any given time? Does it really help to imagine that there is some one full, objective, true account of nature and that the proper measure of scientific achievement is the extent to which it brings us closer to that ultimate goal.[14]

What is being attacked here are some of the basic assumptions that scientists make about their work. In particular, Kuhn is challenging their belief that they can obtain reliable information by rational investigation of an external world from which they can stand apart. More generally, the challenge to scientists in recent decades has come from three directions. The first extends Kuhn's approach and basically asks whether scientific knowledge is really any different from other kinds of knowledge. The second asserts that scientific investigation is so tied up with other social activities that research cannot be seen as constituting a separate entity distinct from them. These two points can be combined:

> it is vital not to be diverted by the myth that says that there is a gap between science and politics and that the two are, or should be, separate. Our argument . . . is that science is politics by other means and, accordingly, that the study of science takes us straight into politics . . . . The idea that there is a special scientific method, a realm where truth prospers in the absence of power, is a myth.[15]

The third strand relates to the language that scientists use. The problem is that scientific words are necessarily laden with theory, however straightforward they may seem to be. For example, *force* seems a simple enough word, but its scientific meaning is much narrower than its use in everyday life and is best defined via a mathematical equation. The process of understanding words involves an interaction between the provider of information (whether a human being, a printed text, or words on a screen) and the person receiving the information. From this viewpoint, the transfer of information is not only a difficult activity, it also involves a considerable degree of subjectivity in effecting the transfer process.

> Thought ... is not, then, to be sought only in theoretical formulations such as those of philosophy or science; it can and must be analyzed in every manner of speaking, doing, or behaving in which the individual appears and acts ... as subject conscious of himself and others.[16]

For the present purpose of looking at differences between disciplines, the first two strands are the most important. At one level, what is being asserted is no more than that we should investigate science and its communication in terms of the hypothesis that scientific knowledge is no different from any other knowledge generated by research.

> If there is no royal road to scientific truth, but instead a way only to be found by applying complex, technical standards of evaluation, then bias and irrationality are not the only reasons why one might get lost .... Patterns of meaning and standards of evaluation can no longer be taken for granted in studying scientific controversy, whether intra or extra-institutional; full examination of actors' points of view becomes necessary. As we are interested only in how actors evaluate the claims of scientists it is as well, in such an investigation, temporarily to suspend our own faith in their truth.[17]

Obviously, however, it is only a small step from this to the assertion that there really is no perceptible difference between scientific and other kinds of knowledge. This is a step that has been taken by some sociologists and philosophers of science. Their assertion makes a good starting point for the query—how is knowledge in nonscience fields perceived? Presumably if we see what beliefs about science are being denied, it will give us some insight into what beliefs are being held about other types of knowledge generation. The following description suggests just where the most significant difference between science, on the one hand, and the humanities and social sciences, on the other, is deemed to lie.

> these [humanist] tendencies ... attempt to get the "actor" back into the picture: the actor not as an abstract unit of analysis or a positivistic robot, but as a human being who has emotions, conflicts, inconsistencies, and who does not live in a social vacuum but rather mediates between the wider socio-political and cultural context and the kind of science which results from it.[18]

Research in the humanities and social sciences is often characterized as not involving—indeed, not permitting—a clear-cut separation between the world around us and the person describing it. One of the consequences of this assumption is that investigations in these fields do not necessarily involve anything like the hypothetico-deductive approach that has been suggested for science. The studies are often not quantitative and, even if they are, do not lead to anything like laws of nature. "Progress" in these fields may well be difficult to define. The Kuhnian idea of a paradigm change in science, where the old conceptual framework (and much of the accompanying information content) is discarded and an entirely new one accepted, fits the picture quite well for a number of major changes that have occurred in the humanities and social sciences, but with a fundamental difference. The old and new paradigms may well continue to coexist in these disciplines rather than one replacing the other. Such coexistence can depend on personal factors—age, nationality, and so on.

As this last point suggests, social norms derived from the scientific community are not necessarily applicable to research communities in the humanities and social sciences. Many in these disciplines would reject the idea of universalism for at least some types of research, claiming that a whole range of personal factors can affect the approach, and therefore the acceptability, of the results. Similarly, disinterestedness, with its criticism of emotional involvement in the results of one's work, would not be seen as a worthwhile ideal by many researchers in the humanities and social sciences. In sum, both the basic assumptions made regarding research and the rules of conduct tacitly approved by the research community may differ between science and other disciplines. This can lead to differences in the nature of communication in these fields, as will be illustrated. Before doing so, we need to remember, as was remarked earlier in this chapter, that all borderlines between subjects and disciplines are to some extent blurred. We now look briefly at how this affects the question of the nature of knowledge in a discipline.

Knowledge Divisions

Numerous attempts have been made down the years to classify knowledge into basic categories. The parameters used have varied greatly. For example, Shiyali Ranganathan in India, who has been widely quoted on knowledge classification, outlined a scheme based on a traditional Vedic view of the nature of knowledge. The resulting categorization revealed differences in emphasis from most Western schemes. What is noticeable about all these classifications, whichever parameters have been chosen, is that they rarely lead to clear-cut divisions between different academic disciplines. Even if we turn to schemes specifically devised for looking at knowledge and the educational curriculum, the mismatch with subject fields still occurs. Thus, one scheme distinguishes six categories of knowledge.[19] The first category, "symbolics," includes all subjects involved in some form of symbolic communication. The next, "empirics," concerns factual information (i.e., derived from direct observation), and so on. In terms of the conventional subject boundaries, this knowledge classification brings together topics usually placed in separate disciplines. Symbolics brings together language, normally associated with the humanities, and mathematics, which is usually placed with the sciences. Similarly, though empirics obviously forms a basic part of the natural sciences, it is also important in the social sciences and, indeed, is an element in a range of humanities subjects. Even the third category of knowledge on this list—aesthetics—spreads across disciplinary divides. Its main focus may be in the humanities, but many theoreticians in the sciences would claim that their work involves in a very fundamental way a feeling for the aesthetic. As this example illustrates, the reason there are blurred boundaries between different subjects and disciplines is because the match between types of knowledge acquisition, on the one hand, and subjects defined by information content, on the other, is far from perfect. Different subjects have varying mixes of knowledge type, which leads to a greater or lesser amount of overlap between them in the way they operate and how they handle information.

This point can be taken further. Even within a particular subject, different branches may have differing approaches. In studies of the Bible, it used to be the practice to distinguish between "lower criticism" and "higher criticism." The former kind of research concerned itself with such activities as defining the meanings of words, trying to establish a definitive text, and so on. The latter kind was concerned primarily with establishing a theoretical framework in terms of which the biblical text might be interpreted. This sort of division is common in the humanities. It leads not only to different research methodologies, but also to differing understandings of what constitutes acceptable research. Here is a reflection on this difference in the field of New Testament studies:

> In the study of New Testament externals—what used to be called the "lower criticism"—we may at least hope for certain results which in their scientific validity will be comparable to the achievements of the physical scientists. In more central matters [i.e. "higher criticism"] we may hope to find that certain theories have so successfully resisted criticism that they may at least for the time being be accepted as useful working tools.[20]

This might be paraphrased as saying that certain parts of New Testament studies have well-defined methodologies and the results accumulate in rather the way they do for a science. Other parts, generally those that are more explicitly oriented toward theory, are less certain, in the sense that agreement both on methodologies and conclusions is only tentative.

In a similar way, a discussion of the research interests of an English faculty in the 1980s found that there were at least five different research strands at work.[21] These were defined as: traditional scholarship (historical, biographical, linguistic); textual studies; study of literature in social and cultural contexts; alignment of literature with other modes of communication (mainly television and films); international approach (structuralist, poststructural, etc.). This listing moves from a more objective stance at the start to a more subjective approach at the end. It also proceeds from older established studies at the beginning to newer style studies at the end. What has happened is that the nature of scholarship in literary studies (and not only in English) has changed. Formerly, researchers took the text as given: it was the scholar's job to set it in context. Now many researchers see the interaction of the reader with the text as of prime interest. This has entailed a shift in what is regarded as acceptable research: for example, the role of literary criticism has become increasingly a matter for debate.

> You won't find it easy to name an important critic who was a critic, and nothing else; that is, until quite recently. The world is now full of literary critics, some held to be important, who do nothing else but write literary criticism, and they all work in universities.[22]

This growth in criticism as a form of research has been paralleled by an increasing emphasis on conceptual, as compared with factual, knowledge. The shift has led to rapidly fluctuating debates on the acceptability of different theoretical approaches. Few conceptual stances that were popular a few decades ago are still highly regarded today. At the same time, the emphasis on the conceptual means that the discussion of theory now receives great attention. This move from the specific and empirical to the general and theoretical can be found in other fields besides English literature:

> For a generation now [up to the 1990s], the humanities have actually penalized narrow specialization and reserved their highest rewards for work that propounds sweeping cultural theories and broad interdisciplinary generalizations, work that promises to revise the paradigm for thinking about its subject.[23]

The battle over the role and significance of theory is not limited to the humanities. It is waged just as fiercely in the social sciences, where it is heightened by a strong tradition of empirical research. The question at issue is not the need for theory, but whether all-embracing theories are really viable in the social sciences. For example, Merton has emphasized the need for employing middle-range theories in sociology. (A middle-range theory is one that helps unify empirical studies in a particular area, without attempting to provide an all-inclusive picture.) He observes that:

> sociology will advance insofar as its major (but not exclusive) concern is with developing theories of the middle range, and it will be retarded if its primary attention is focussed on developing total sociological systems.[24]

Merton compares in some detail the role of theory in sociology with its role in the natural sciences. This tendency to position other research fields relative to the research processes in science has long been characteristic of the social sciences and the humanities. History provides a good example of the way that views on this have changed with time. Most nineteenth-century historians saw their subject as firmly attached to the scientific camp. The influence of German scholarship, then very strong, emphasized this link.

> The German historicism of the nineteenth century . . . took its first inspiration from two sources: the textural criticism of the philologist, and the mechanics of physical science . . . . Towards the end of the last century, the dominant sciences of physics and philology were replaced by biology, anthropology and sociology, with the result that history became both subtler and less certain, more relativist . . . . These three influences have remained strong ever since.[25]

The question of what conceptual model is chosen for research in a particular field has behind it another question. How can the development of a research specialism influence what model is acceptable? For example, the physical and biological sciences followed appreciably different approaches to research earlier in the twentieth century. The former were particularly concerned with processes at the atomic or molecular levels and depended strongly on theory. Neither of these statements applied to biology. Developments in recent decades have brought the physical and biological sciences increasingly close together. The conceptual model that biologists have of their subject has changed to bring it more in line with that of the physical scientists.

It was often supposed in the nineteenth century that different disciplines were at different stages of development. As time passed, so their characteristics would tend to converge. Auguste Comte, for example, drew up a sequence of fields of knowledge that might be summarized as follows: physical sciences—biological sciences—sociology. In his view, this not only moved from more basic knowledge to less basic knowledge, but was also a developmental sequence. Sociology should become more akin to the biological sciences with time, and both should ultimately move toward the rigor of the physical sciences. In the twentieth century, and more especially in the past few decades, researchers in the social sciences and the humanities have moved strongly away from this view. Increasingly, they have come to see knowledge acquisition in relativist terms. Indeed, some consider this to be the appropriate way of viewing all knowledge. They assert that scientists are wrong to believe that they can achieve objective knowledge. Scientists deny this, asserting, in turn, that only scientific knowledge is capable of systematic development. One biologist has phrased this belief in Comtean terms:

> In a sense, all science aspires to be like physics, and physics aspires to be like mathematics. But too great an aspiration can lead to frustration. In spite of recent successes, biology has a long way to go when measured against physics or chemistry. But sociology? Biologists can still be full of hope and are going through exciting times, but what hope is there for sociology acquiring a physics-like lustre?[26]

The fact that universities are organized into departments and faculties, both subject based, is an obvious acknowledgment of differences between subjects. Rather than talk in general terms about differences between disciplines, it is possible to ask academic researchers which other departments they feel close to and why. Their assessments can be analyzed to indicate the factors that influence their judgment. Researchers usually seem to judge other departments in terms of a few basic antitheses.[27] One important parameter relates to where the subject is seen as lying along the pure–applied axis. But the most significant factor in terms of knowledge is the extent to which a subject is seen as "hard" or "soft." (Here "hard" means quantitative and rigorous, whereas "soft" means the converse.) Academics, it seems, typically divide subjects into the hard (natural sciences and technology), the soft (humanities), and those in between (social sciences), so reproducing the traditional distinctions we have been discussing.

The overall impression given by this continuing debate is that there are genuine differences between disciplines in terms of the kind of knowledge researchers seek and how they handle it. This is not the same as saying that knowledge in science subjects is of one sort and in humanities of another. Even using a simple dichotomy, such as "hard–soft," research is not usually all one or the other. In subject terms, a single field of study typically mixes these components. For example, the work of literary researchers ranges from (very soft) literary theory to (quite hard) linguistics. Equally, a specific research project can be a mixture. In physics, research activities range from thinking up new ideas (often quite soft) to deriving results (hard). Perhaps one should think of hard research as being like water and soft research like alcohol. They can be mixed in various proportions—with noticeably differing effects on those who imbibe the resultant concoctions.

Examining Subject Differences

If these distinctions between subjects and disciplines are as meaningful as it seems, it is reasonable to suppose that they should also be reflected in communication patterns. In the early 1970s, Derek Price suggested that such differences could be discerned in the way scholarly articles cite each other.[28] Almost all articles contain references to related publications—in order to justify claims, to criticize earlier work, and so on. These references can be viewed as a networking mechanism that integrates the research literature together. The way in which they do it should provide some insight into the process of relating new to old information; Price proposed that there are subject differences in operation here. To explain what the differences are requires a detour to discuss the results of "citation studies."

The word *citation* is widely used to describe the activity of referring from one article to another. It is customary, in this context, to distinguish between the citing article (the one that contains the reference) and the cited article (the one mentioned in the reference). As noted in the previous chapter, the amount of research literature has grown approximately exponentially with time. If all this literature is of equal interest to researchers, the time distribution of references to it would be expected to follow a similar pattern, with many more references to recent publications than to older ones. This proves, indeed, to be the case, but, in some research fields, the proportion of recent literature cited is even higher than an exponential growth rate would predict. Price referred to this overcitation of recent publications as the "immediacy effect." He suggested that it could be measured very simply by determining the overall proportion of references in a given field that related to literature published in the previous 5 years. He determined this proportion—which he referred to as "Price's index"—for a range of research journals. The science journals had an index of 60–70%: the social science journals were 10–20% lower, and the humanities journals scored appreciably lower still.

The data were interpreted as meaning that the immediacy effect indicates the existence of a "research front." The characteristics of this research front relate, in turn, to the nature of the information being handled. Thus one of the characteristics we have noted of scientific information is its cumulative nature. Accumulation, in this sense, does not mean that the information just piles up. It means that the information is systematically codified and absorbed. As a result of this process, scientists usually need to be aware only of recent work when carrying out their own studies. In contrast, information in the social sciences is often less readily codified, so older literature continues to be mentioned. The humanities form a special case, since older literature for them often represents the raw data of their investigations. As we have noted, certain "science-like" characteristics, including the way information accumulates, appear not only in the sciences: they can also be discerned in some types of research in both the social sciences and the humanities. There is, consequently, some scatter in Price's index at the level of particular specialisms.

The existence of a research front implies there is a tight citation linkage between recent publications because the research community is trying to understand and assimilate the results that they contain. As time passes and this occurs, the older publications are relegated to the general archive of accepted research and so need to be referred to less often. Price, himself, estimated that an article in the research front might be cited by other articles somewhat less than twice a year, whereas an archival article might only be cited once every 2 years. He tried to illustrate these arguments concerning the research front by carrying out a detailed study of publications on N-rays.

These rays were "discovered" early in the twentieth century: the name *N-rays* was modeled on the already known *X-rays*. The new rays aroused lively interest for a short period of time. It then became apparent that their detection was spurious, and the topic was consigned to oblivion. As a result, a couple of hundred articles on N-rays were published that form a small, isolated block in the scientific literature. Price believed his analysis of these publications clearly showed how a "research front" worked. Subsequent study has cast doubt on this.[29] One reason, interestingly, resides in the different way researchers then communicated as compared with now. Nevertheless, the concept of a "research front" remains a useful way of thinking about the immediacy effect.

As would be expected, statistical fluctuations of a few percent occur each year in the Price index for a given subject. Systematic changes can also occur, more especially when a subject experiences a major breakthrough or a period of controversy. For example, when one specialism in psychology underwent a major change, it was found that the Price index increased considerably. Once the change had been absorbed by the community, the index dropped again.[30] There seem to be two factors at work here. One is the higher level of interaction between researchers during a period of major debate. The other is the lack of earlier literature to cite when there have been significant changes in the accepted research model. This latter becomes particularly evident when a new research topic appears suddenly. For example, pulsars were detected quite unexpectedly by astronomers. There was little relevant material already in existence, so the early pulsar literature contained a great deal of cross-reference between the articles being produced. Consequently, the field at this stage had a very high Price index, which subsequently decreased as work on pulsars expanded in scope. There may also be long-term trends. For example, a comparison of the references attached to articles in British physiology and geology journals at the end of the nineteenth century and in the 1960s suggests that the Price index increased for both subjects over this period. The difference in index between the two subjects remained throughout this period, reflecting the basic difference in their natures. An observational science, such as geology, always needs to refer back to older material than does an experimental science, such as physiology. The trend implies, however, that the level of integration of the research front has become tighter for both with the passage of time.

The immediacy effect is not the only way of examining how tightly integrated subjects are. Another approach is to investigate directly the degree of linkage between articles dealing with the same topic. The most-used method again employs the references attached to the end of each article. We have been talking of citations as reflecting how research in a topic relates to previous work. If this is true, two articles written on precisely the same topic should presumably look back to the same body of prior research. Hence, they should cite much the same literature. Such overlap can, indeed, be found. Some years ago, the journal *Nature* received two simultaneous, but independent, submissions (one from the United States and one from the UK) on an identical topic—the identification of certain airborne organisms. The editor of *Nature* commented:

> The incident may also interest connoisseurs of scientific literature, particularly those who like cynically to maintain that 90 per cent of any list of references is aimed at displaying the erudition of the author rather than the antecedents of his paper. Seven of the eight references by both [authors] are identical.[31]

The existence of an overlap suggests a different way of examining the divisions between specialisms. If such divisions are real, the citations provided by publications within a particular specialism should presumably overlap more between themselves than they do with the citations from articles devoted to other specialisms. Can such overlap be examined in a statistically viable way?

The Institute for Scientific Information in Philadelphia has been compiling computer-based citation indexes since the 1960s. (A "citation index" is a codified list of cited articles alongside the articles that have cited them.) Though the original focus of interest was science, medicine, and technology, coverage subsequently expanded to include the social sciences and humanities. Several thousand journals—the list is up-dated regularly—are scanned each year to provide this database. All these citation data are stored in digital form: the coverage now is not only broad, but also extends back over a considerable time period. Clearly, this material offers the opportunity to carry out a detailed study of overlapping citations.

Despite the *Nature* example, the degree of overlap between the citations in different journal articles is typically found to be small, not least because they are rarely dealing with absolutely identical topics. Consequently, the linkage between two articles has come to be described in a rather more general way. It is usually defined in terms of how many times a given pair of articles are cited together in the lists of references attached to other articles. The argument is that the more often researchers link the two articles together in their writings, the more likely it is that they relate to the same topic. A study of such co-citations should therefore indicate whether citations can be used to establish the existence of groupings of journal articles, with each cluster relating to a specific topic.

When the exercise is actually carried out, it does, indeed, lead to a distinguishable clustering effect, rather than to a uniform sea of co-citations. The clustering is typically hierarchical. Some co-citations link articles on a specific research topic together, but others link them to wider groupings and so on to an entire discipline. For example, articles dealing with a particular type of spectroscopy may link together strongly. At another level, this group may link to other articles dealing with the study of plasmas. At yet another level, plasma studies may link to groupings across a wide swathe of physics research. It is possible to draw co-citation maps of science, showing the clusters that appear for linkages of different strengths. The maps for science as a whole typically show, in this case, a physics cluster that has links with other disciplinary groupings, more especially with mathematics and chemistry, but nevertheless remains distinct.

Such mapping of fields of knowledge has been subject to appreciable criticism. One problem, in particular, is that the results can depend quite critically on what instructions about sorting the data are given to the computer. Despite this, there can be no doubt that some groupings, which maintain a fair stability from one year to the next, can be discerned. Many of these can be related to the mental models that researchers have of their world. For example, academics tend to see a connection between all subjects that deal with life and, therefore, often link the biological and social sciences together in their minds. Such a connection also appears on co-citation maps, but these provide more information on the nature of the link. They show that it occurs via such topics as classification or methods of data analysis and interpretation. The maps can go further in pointing to the influence that one subject area can have on another—for example, biomedical research on chemistry—so drawing attention to interdisciplinary activities, which thread their ways through the conventional divisions.

Investigations of similarities can employ almost any distinguishing feature of journal articles—author's name, title of article, institutional affiliation, etc.—when looking for clusters. Content analysis is especially interesting, since the text of an article contains much more information than its references. The argument here is that articles dealing with the same topic will have a number of keywords in common. Thus if two chemical articles refer to the same chemical compounds and the same types of instrumentation, it seems reasonable to suppose that they cover an overlapping area of interest. Similar sorts of methodology to those employed for co-citation analysis can be applied to co-word analysis. Study of words offers some advantages over study of citations. It can, for example, be applied to any kind of document—books and reports, as well as journal articles. The words can also be chosen to look for similarities of different kinds between articles: not only whether the object of the investigation is the same, but whether they are applying similar conceptual approaches or similar methods of analysis. For example, a study of biotechnology by co-word analysis found that different approaches to research could be discerned as between universities, government research establishments, and industry.[32]

Although co-word studies can thus be used for different ends from co-citation studies, both demonstrate the ability to separate research topics into a series of clusters. To what extent do these clusters coincide with the boundaries drawn by experts in the field? More specifically, how well do the mental maps perceived by experts coincide with bibliometric maps? This actually proves quite difficult to determine. Not only are experts often dismissive of groupings obtained by bibliometric means (grading clusters as either obvious or wrong), but they tend to feel that the one- or two-dimensional plots used to present bibliometric results do not fit well with their own mental maps of research. Another problem is that the responses given by experts can vary according to their particular interests and background. Hence, to get a communal map entails averaging over a number of respondents. In a rather similar way, different bibliometric analyses can produce rather different maps of a given topic. The overall result is that a somewhat blurred set of expert views has to be superimposed on a somewhat blurred set of bibliometric maps. When this is done, it appears that the mental maps and the bibliometric maps do resemble each other in terms of their main features, but not (hardly surprisingly) in their details.[33]

Subject and Communication Differences

It appears that major divisions of knowledge—such as those traditionally drawn between the sciences, social sciences, and humanities—correspond to something real, though blurred. They lead to differences in what is regarded as acceptable research activity in each field and, similarly, in what is regarded as acceptable research information and its communication. This suggests that subject differences should be apparent for many different aspects of research information or communication. We look next at some examples of this (the factors at work are discussed at greater length in subsequent chapters). As a beginning, Table 6 compares some of the characteristics of the journal articles published in a number of different subjects.[34]

We have noted previously that a highly quantitative approach is one of the markers of the boundary usually drawn between the natural and the social sciences. The first column of Table 6 indicates a trend in the expected

Table 6
Characteristics of Journal Articles by Subject

Subject	Contain quantitative analysis (%)	Include tables (%)	Include graphics (%)	Acknowledge external funding (%)
Biochemistry	98.1	73.5	91.0	74.2
Psychology	75.1	70.7	41.5	43.4
Economics	72.1	46.8	39.6	34.3
Sociology	52.6	65.0	22.6	27.0

direction (with psychology, as usual, lying on the borderline), though the difference between economics and sociology is as large as that between biochemistry and economics. The next two columns show how different subject approaches affect the way information is presented in an article. Tables can be employed to display either quantitative or qualitative information: so their use shows no particular trend. Biochemists need both graphs, to convey numerical data, and pictures (of specimens, etc.). The difference between biochemistry and the other subjects in terms of graphics is correspondingly marked.

The final column acts as a reminder that the production of research costs money. Scientific research normally requires more financial backing than research in the social sciences, which, in turn, often requires more funding than humanities research. These differences in funding requirements can affect the communication of research. A simple example relates to page charges. A few major U.S. scientific journals have employed a system of asking authors to pay a certain amount toward the cost of publishing their articles. It is expected that this payment (usually charged in terms of so many dollars per printed page) will come out of the funding scientists receive to forward their research. A similar scheme could hardly be imposed in the social sciences and humanities, since not only are grants smaller, but fewer researchers have access to them. A more significant example concerns the extent to which publication can occur. It is not uncommon for the provider of research funding to impose restrictions on how and when research results are made publicly available. This is commonplace in some areas of science (e.g., research supported by the pharmaceutical industry or by defense grants), but occurs less frequently in the social sciences, and is rare in the humanities.

Table 7 draws attention to another aspect of the divide between the sciences, social sciences, and humanities—the level of cooperative activity

Table 7
Number of Authors per Article

Subject	One author (%)	Two authors (%)	Three authors (%)	Four or more (%)
Biochemistry	19	46	22	13
Psychology	45	36	15	4
Economics	83	16	1	–
Sociology	75	21	3	1

within a subject.[35] In terms of communication, one reflection of the level of cooperation is the proportion of articles that have more than one author. Cooperation can occur in various ways. It can become necessary, for example, if the research requires a diversity of skills. Again, it may be because a supervisor is working on a particular project along with a group of research students. Whichever mechanism is at work, the need for cooperation and the means for achieving it are usually greater in science than in the social sciences and greater in the social sciences than in the humanities. In fact, since teamwork tends to require more funding than working on one's own, it is not surprising to see some correlation between the data in Table 7 and the final column of Table 6.

One of the important factors in disseminating research is obviously the extent to which the results are actually made public. The general rule is that publication is easiest in the sciences, harder in the social sciences, and harder still in the humanities.[36] The actual rejection rates vary appreciably with the journals selected for examination, but the sequence of difficulty remains fairly stable. Various forces are at work here, but one, certainly, is the level of agreement on what constitutes acceptable research. As we have seen, this is not a purely disciplinary split: there are topics in the social sciences and humanities where agreement on how research should be tackled is reasonably good. For topics that fall into this category (e.g., linguistics), journal rejection rates are closer to the science end of the spectrum. Another factor relates to standards—what experts in the subject expect of an acceptable article. In science, for example, articles not only have a standard layout, but also a generally similar approach. Editors and referees typically see their job as examining submitted articles to see if they can find anything wrong with them. In the humanities, articles may differ in layout and may reveal a range of views as to what represents appropriate research. Editors and referees are less interested in looking for things that are wrong, than for significant, creative steps forward. When stated in these terms, it becomes less surprising that rejection rates are much higher in most humanities subjects than in most science.

Yet another factor is the availability of resources. Journal publication consumes money. (It also requires time, but, given sufficient funding, the necessary expertise can be bought in.) Research communities that command large amounts of funding find it considerably easier to support a range of journals than do those with little funding. This means that scientists have more journal outlets for their work than do their colleagues in the humanities. From this viewpoint, the rejection rates in different subjects have their basis in economic considerations: articles are selected for publication from the total input on the basis of what publishing space can be provided in the subject.

This brings us to the question of publishing research via outlets other than journals. In all subjects, journal articles are one of the commonest types of research publication, but that does not mean they are always rated as the most important type of publication. Some light on this can be obtained by studying the references attached to publications. Table 8 compares the spread of citation distribution found in the sciences with that in the social sciences.[37] Clearly, journals form the most important information source in the sciences, but are supplanted by books in the social sciences. Studies of the humanities indicate a similar sequence to the social sciences (though "other sources of information" are more likely to include critical editions, etc., rather than reports).

These findings can be interpreted in terms of the differing pressures at work. In terms of content, the nature of research in the social sciences and humanities is such that its presentation often entails lengthier discussion than in the sciences, as data from a range of project work are brought together. This is often difficult, or impossible, to achieve via a series of journal articles. At the same time, speed of journal publication in these fields is often slow: book production will not necessarily take much longer. Economically, books may prove viable when a series of journal articles would not. All these factors can change with time, as well as with subject. One of the key science publications of the nineteenth century—Darwin's *Origin of Species*—was published in book form because Darwin wished to develop his ideas at length. It was economically viable to do so because Darwin's narrative, unlike most science writing today, was couched in language that did not deter a wide readership.

Table 8
Distribution of Citations to Different Types of Publication in Science and the Social Sciences

Type of publication	Science (%)	Social sciences (%)
Journals	82	29
Books	12	46
Other (especially reports)	6	25

Communication to a Wider Public

This question of breadth of readership is another that reveals character-istic differences between subjects. Table 9 lists some results of a Dutch survey that examined how many publications aimed at a general audience, rather than fellow-researchers, came out of various university departments.[38] (The results listed refer to the maximum found for a given type of department.) These differences can be related to the question: what characteristics of a research topic make it more, or less, suitable for communication to the gen-eral public?

A first answer can be found by considering what type of research receives preferential mention in the mass media. Media reporters and produc-ers are particularly concerned with topics that can be considered "newswor-thy." Such topics have a number of characteristics. Firstly, to be regarded as important, an event should have happened recently, or, even better, be about to happen. Secondly, it should be in some way relevant to ordinary human life. Finally, it should have an element of entertainment. It is not expected that all newsworthy events will contain all three elements in equal amounts. In reporting research, the last element tends to be toned down; although any researcher who claims to have defined a sense of humor, or shown that astrol-ogy is true, will almost certainly be reported.

As these examples may suggest, the priorities of the mass media in reporting research differ considerably from those of the research communi-ty. This affects the extent to which different subjects are reported in the media. Table 10 compares the space devoted to different branches of science in a "quality" daily newspaper during the course of a year.[39] These propor-tions bear little resemblance to the relative amounts of research that are

Table 9

Maximum Proportion of Publications Aimed at a General
Readership Produced by Dutch University Departments

Subject	Maximum proportion of "popularizing" publications (%)
Linguistics	8.5
Experimental psychology	10.4
Social history	35.0
Dutch literature	43.0

Table 10
Relative Space Devoted to Different Scientific Topics
in a Daily Newspaper

Topic	Space devoted to topic (%)
Biomedicine	48
Technology	30
Astronomy/space	17
Earth sciences	3
Chemistry	1
Physics	1

being published. Chemistry, for example, is one of the major producers of research articles in the sciences, yet it rarely rates a mention in the newspaper. One study of the contents of popular science magazines has compared subject coverage with researcher population (measured by the number of doctoral graduates being produced in each subject). Chemistry again performed well below expectations, whereas astronomy (including space science) scored higher than the size of the astronomical research population would suggest.[40]

These differences are not difficult to understand in terms of the media priorities previously outlined. Much chemical research cannot be related easily to immediate human concerns. Understanding its significance requires an extensive theoretical and practical grounding. Hence, major developments can be difficult both to identify and to interpret. Compare this with research in botany or zoology. Though the research may be just as complex, members of the public find it easier to relate to the objects of study and to be interested in the research outcome. From a media viewpoint, in fact, sciences fall into the two groups mentioned previously—the experimental or the observational. Laboratories are not part of everyday life for most people. Sciences, such as physics or chemistry, that rely mainly on laboratory experiments therefore lie at one remove from most human experience. By comparison, such sciences as astronomy, geology, and the "natural history" part of botany and zoology are concerned with observing things that form a part of the human environment. Consequently, these latter sciences tend to be overrepresented in the media in terms of their research output. The observational sciences are also often more photogenic than the experimental sciences, which is a bonus for science reporting on television. So astronomy and space science, the progenitors of many exciting graphic images in the last few decades, are even more overrepresented on television than they are in newspapers. The major exception is biomedical research, that may be laboratory-based but is widely reported (as Table 10 indicates). Here the negative factors are offset by its great relevance to human life.

The same mass media priorities also apply, of course, to research in the social sciences and humanities. It might be expected that these disciplines would benefit from them comparatively more than the sciences. Archaeology, for example, concerns itself with matters that relate both to human life and to the environment in which we live. Little background is necessary in order to understand the significance of new discoveries. Archaeological excavations and the objects found are often pictorially satisfying. So archaeology is reported by the media more often than would be expected from the amount of archaeological research produced. But there are some counterinfluences at work. The nature of research in these disciplines means that "breakthroughs" are less easily definable than in the sciences. In addition, the increasing research emphasis on abstract theory has distanced some parts of these disciplines from the general public.

The public presentation of research in the humanities poses an intriguing conundrum. Across a broad swathe of humanities subjects, media interest is mainly in the object of study, rather than in the research, itself. For example, a television program may be devoted to a painting. Discussion of the painting is often based on a variety of research investigations; but it is the painting and its painter that dominate the program. It may not be at all evident to the viewer how much research lies behind the discussion. Similarly, the production of a play may rely heavily on many years of research, but this will usually not be obvious to the audience. Even where the mix of research and production has been especially intimate—for example, in exploring and restoring the scores, musical techniques, and instruments used in early music—the research element can be easily ignored. The problem is increased for some humanities subjects, where the borderline between investigating an object and creating an object can become confused. An obvious example is provided by university staff in departments of English literature who write novels, which may be turned into television programs. These novels and television programs may, in turn, become the objects of scholarly study.

Media reporting priorities do not change greatly with time, but coverage of particular topics may. One reason is because the nature of the research changes, making it more, or less, appealing to the general public. Thus earlier in the twentieth century, there was relatively more reporting of chemical research because it was seen as being more immediately relevant to human life. There have been fluctuations, too, in the wider appeal of social science and humanities subjects. Literary criticism provides an example:

> until the advent of American and English New Criticism the job of a critic was an appreciation of work as much for the general reader as for other critics. Functionalist criticism makes an extremely sharp break between the community of critics and the general public.[41]

Another obvious reason for fluctuating coverage is because of major changes in the comparative amounts of research being done. For example, media reporting of space research grew from virtually zero in the early 1950s to reach a peak around 1970 with the first manned landing on the moon. After that, it tailed off as the American space program was cut back. Table 11 compares the coverage of astronomy and space science in two British daily newspapers at two epochs 15 years apart.[42] Clearly, medicine took over from astronomy and space science during this period as a focus for media attention.

A more direct route by which research can reach a wider audience is for the researchers to present it themselves. The two main ways of doing this are either by contributing articles to popular magazines or by writing books at the appropriate level, though some researchers also appear on radio or television. There are disciplinary differences here, too. In a subject such as history, many books that present the results of scholarly investigations are written in such a way that their contents are accessible to nonspecialists. In this case, the scholarly text and its popularization are the same thing. In other areas of the humanities—literary criticism, for example—the theory and jargon of many scholarly books may now be too much for a nonspecialist reader. At the same time, there may not be much of a market for popularized versions of literary theory. The average reader is therefore left with the few scholarly

Table 11

A Comparison of the Number of Articles Devoted to Astronomy/Space and Medicine at Two Epochs

Newspaper	Topic	1974–1975	1989–1990
The Times	Medicine	86	183
	Astronomy/space	69	68
Guardian	Medicine	22	125
	Astronomy/space	26	34

titles in this field that are sufficiently straightforward to be readable. Science is different again. Scientific research normally appears in journals, so any book intended for a wider audience has to be specially written. This may be done by the researchers themselves, but many science popularizations are written by nonresearchers—for example, by people with scientific qualifications who report advances in the mass media. These disciplinary differences in the way the researcher and the general public are linked can be related back to the distinctions drawn earlier in this chapter—for example, between "hard" and "soft" research—and to the discussion of specialization and professionalization in the first chapter. Changes in these latter mean that subject differences in the way research is presented to the general public have grown with time. In the nineteenth century, all types of research were more likely to be presented to a wider public in similar ways than they are today.

Information Technology and Subject Differences

The examples of subject differences cited in this chapter have mostly stemmed from print-based communication. We have noted briefly that criteria for public presentation may differ as between newspapers and television. Might subject differences themselves change somewhat according to the medium employed? For example, we have seen that books are more important for research in the humanities than in the sciences. Two of the factors involved in this are finance and speed of communication. Both of these relate, in part, to the medium. Books and journals are financed in different ways—that is to say, they represent different ways of packaging print-on-paper—and which is chosen depends, in part, on the sources of finance available for production and consumption. The time taken over production and distribution is likewise related in part to the handling limitations imposed by the print medium. How would a change in medium affect factors of this sort?

The rapid growth of computer networking is beginning to throw some light on the answer to this question. We can begin by considering how the move to computer-based communication may affect research communities differentially. Reading printed matter requires the application of a number of skills (a point to be taken up in a later chapter). For many years past, education at all levels has been designed to help develop these skills. They are subsequently kept in practice by the requirements of everyday life (e.g., reading newspapers). In contrast, widespread access to computers has only become possible relatively recently, and information handling by computer is still an arcane topic for an appreciable number of researchers. The differences in computer literacy across the research community are therefore much greater than any differences in literacy relating to printed matter. Differences in computer usage can be found for groups, as well as for individuals. For example, the keenest users of electronic networks are young males. Female users of electronic bulletin boards and similar communal discussion groups may be deterred by this, especially if they are not experts in computer usage and networking activities. Again, the level of access to information technology is often determined by the ability to provide the necessary funding for equipment, etc. This has meant that humanities subjects have usually been disadvantaged vis-à-vis science subjects. Though these financial differences are being gradually alleviated, there remains a difference in the level of computer expertise available to researchers in different subjects. Assistance and advice is still usually more readily available for researchers in the sciences than for those in the humanities.

Historically, use of computers by researchers has depended on what the computer can offer them. Different disciplines have turned to computers at different times and for differing purposes. In the beginning, computers were designed as number-crunchers. They were therefore used mainly by researchers in the hard sciences, though social scientists concerned with analyzing large sets of statistical data also made use of them. More recently, efficient text-crunching has become commonplace, which has extended regular use of computers throughout all disciplines. There are still differences between researchers in terms of access to computers, but they are less predictable than formerly. It is generally agreed that regular use of a computer for information purposes requires that access to it should be immediate—either in the office or laboratory. A large-scale survey of UK researchers in the early 1990s found, as would be expected, that most physicists and mathematicians have such immediate access.[43] More surprisingly, they were matched by the social scientists who, in this respect, were well ahead of the biologists, chemists, and engineers. This reflects the high importance many social scientists now attach to computer access. Even within specific subjects, use of information technology can differ according to what it can offer the researcher. For example, in the world of chemical research, organic chemists tend to make most use of computer-based information systems, followed by inorganic chemists, with physical chemists coming at the bottom. This order correlates quite well with the number and range of information systems available in the different branches of chemistry.[44]

By the early 1990s, both scientists and social scientists were using information technology for a range of applications, including on-line communication. Researchers in the humanities were more restricted in their interests,
with a much greater emphasis on using computers in isolation for their
word-processing capabilities. However, on-line access to texts has been available for some time, and the range of other humanities information resources
on-line in increasing. Consequently, the use of networks for communication
in the humanities is rapidly coming to resemble that in other fields.
Differences of perception are likely to linger. For example, a survey carried
out for the American Council of Learned Societies found that sociologists
were considerably more likely than their colleagues in the humanities to see
computers as aiding the quality and creativity of their research.[45] The basic
property of computers—that they can store and handle large quantities of
data (numerical, textual, graphical)—is particularly helpful in empirical
research. It is less obviously helpful to qualitative theoretical analysis, such as
is common in the social sciences and humanities. But discussions of such theory can be aided by the communication properties of the new medium—
more especially by the creation of electronic lists and journals. In fact, some
two-thirds of all the electronic journals made available on-line in the first half
of the 1990s were devoted to social science and humanities topics. Many
(e.g., *Postmodern Culture*) had an especial interest in conceptual issues.

Most of the electronic journals devoted to research in the first half of
the 1990s were "free" (i.e., no fee was charged for accessing them, though
readers might need to expend money in order to get on the network). They
were put together by groups of enthusiasts, usually in the academic world in
North America. The emphasis on social sciences and humanities in these
journals may seem surprising, since rapid publication is less important in
these fields (though practitioners obviously do not object to it). A major reason is the limited space available in the printed journals in these subjects and
their high rejection rate for articles. To the extent that these are related to
lack of finance, electronic networks, which are usually free to academics at
the point of use, offer a practicable way of circumventing the limitations.
Moreover, the prime concern of much research communication in the social
sciences and humanities tends to be with text. Handling this via information
technology is fairly trouble-free today. In contrast, science articles often contain graphics and, perhaps, mathematical equations, as well as text. Until
recently, the handling and transmission of such material has been considerably more complex than for text, which has meant that electronic journals
have been harder to create in the sciences.

A more general academic query relates to the quality control of information communicated electronically. How does the social norm of "organized skepticism" apply to the new medium? Because electronic communication is fast and not usually limited by space considerations, on-line discussions of research can be both more informal and more prolix than printed discussions. This has led to a feeling, especially among scientists, that electronic publications may be less carefully controlled as regards the quality of the research they report than printed publications. It is undoubtedly true that idiosyncratic material may circulate electronically. It has been suggested, for example, that some distinctly odd ideas about AIDS were first mentioned in electronic discussions, from whence they contaminated the mainstream research literature. Rigorous refereeing is, of course, as feasible for an electronic journal as for a printed one. The increased ability to use different methods of refereeing and to be flexible in their application may, however, prove particularly helpful in the reviewing of discursive articles such as are often encountered in social science and humanities research.

Where the sciences undoubtedly gain from a change to electronic communication is in the speed of dissemination and response. The debate over cold fusion at the end of the 1980s provides an interesting case study. The idea that energy from nuclear fusion could be tapped by what were essentially chemical means was first announced in March 1989. If true, this result was of great significance, so a large number of researchers immediately moved into the field. Within a month, some 40 articles on cold fusion had been sent to refereed (printed) journals. It rapidly became apparent that research was proceeding at too great a pace to use the traditional outlet of printed publications. An electronic newsletter on cold fusion was started. This, together with individual electronic-mail messaging, came to be the main method of exchanging information during the few months that the topic was at the center of debate. In fact, by the time the refereed articles were actually appearing in printed journals, most of the research community had already decided that the topic was not worth pursuing further.

There is an implicit question raised here about the "research front" discussed earlier in this chapter. It seems that the duration in time of research front activities may diminish with the introduction of electronic communication, whereas what is meant by a research front publication may also change to encompass something less formal than has been customary with printed sources. At the same time, the fact that the scientific community obtained much of its early information about cold fusion from mass media sources provides an unusual illustration of the value of multimedia presentation. One attempt to reproduce the apparatus of the original researchers—Pons and Fleischmann—was described in the following way:

> We used photographs from the *LA Times* of Pons holding the cell, and you could see pretty well how it was made. We used Pon's finger for a scale. [A post-doctoral student] figured his hand was about equal-size, so he scaled it to his own finger.[46]

This is an illuminating example of the flexible use of the media mix that now exists to transmit research information to its various audiences. Researchers must increasingly cope with information that is transmitted and handled in a variety of ways. Their reward lies in the better information they acquire. Subject-based differences in researchers' use of media certainly exist. They reflect varying matches between the current capabilities of the medium and the continuing needs of the researcher. (This point is explored further in subsequent chapters.) Overall, the nature of electronic handling tends to favor a more informal, flexible style of communication than has been customary with print-based handling. This suggests that it may prove particularly congenial to researchers in "soft" specialisms.

3

Who Does Research and with What Results?

The Reason Why

Why decide to do research? For some, the opportunity to develop their own abilities and to explore topics that fascinate them is sufficient. For others (and, especially those who wish to continue in research), the question is whether their lengthy training will also lead to an acceptable career. Though it is nice to obtain insight and some element of prestige from being a researcher, it is also pleasant if it leads to a satisfactory job. As one nineteenth-century scholar reassured his students:

> the study of Greek literature . . . . Not only elevates above the vulgar herd, but leads not infrequently to positions of considerable emolument.[1]

A researcher today is usually a person whose training involved the acquisition of a Ph.D. So, instead of asking a complicated question about why people do research, it is possible to ask a simpler one. Why do people enter graduate school? One extensive study of U.S. doctoral students came up with the most important reasons as being those listed in Table 12.[2] Though the respondents may have exaggerated the purity of their motives a little, intellectual curiosity was clearly dominant. The other main reasons might be summarized as—making a name for oneself; forging a satisfactory career; benefiting others.

The extent to which these different motivations are emphasized depends on the subject field. For example, studies over many years have indicated a considerable motivational difference between the average scientist and engineer.[3] The former are more often self-motivated and concerned with

Table 12
Reasons for Entering Graduate School

Reason	Percentage claiming
To continue intellectual growth	96.9
To make significant contributions to knowledge in field	83.1
Because of intrinsic interest in field	81.6
To prepare for an academic career	81.6
To increase earning power	74.9
To serve mankind better	74.1

having freedom to pursue their own interests. The latter are less bothered by external control of their work, but more influenced by questions of status.

The range of jobs available to researchers in a particular field obviously influences the span of their motivations. Those in science and technology can look towards industry and government service for careers, as well as to the academic world. So can some in the social sciences (e.g., economists). This is not true of most fields in the humanities. As one guide for postgraduates in the humanities remarks: "the principal reason, in practice, to undertake literary research for a higher degree is an ambition to become a university teacher."[4] Hence, the reasons motivating entrants to doctoral research in the humanities are likely to be more restricted in range than those for entrants in science and technology.

Even within a single field of research, there can be considerable differences in motivation. One study of chemistry students found that they were in generally good agreement as to the relative benefits of working in universities or industry (Table 13).[5] Which they preferred as a career depended mainly on three factors, two of them related to motivation. These two were work conditions and scientific identity. The former is obvious, the latter less so. We have noted the proposition that members of the scientific community tend tacitly to agree on a set of norms, which should, in principle, guide the community in the way it acts and communicates. Acceptance of this proposition is strongest in the academic scientific community. Scientists working for other types of employers are much less likely to operate within the same norms. The chemistry students reflected the full gamut of opinion—from acceptance of all the standard norms to doubts about them all. Depending on which sort of "scientific identity" the students possessed, they were more or less likely to prefer academic or industrial research careers. In other words, those who identified with the standard norms were more

Table 13
Perceived Advantages of Different Research Environments

Category	Offered by universities (% agreeing)	Offered by industry (% agreeing)
Freedom to publish	94	19
Freedom to choose projects	78	10
Holidays	63	38
Social and welfare facilities	60	54
Equipment availability	57	82
Salaries	24	75

likely to seek careers in the academic world and vice versa. The nonmotivational factor in career choice was the level of degree that the student expected to obtain. The majority of those who hoped to achieve top-grade degrees also wanted to pursue academic careers. This can be related back to Table 12. Making a significant new contribution to a research field is usually seen as requiring a considerable intellectual ability.

The reasons for being involved in research evidently link with the reasons for communicating research. So it is important to note that an essential part of the basic motivation—curiosity and the wish to develop one's own understanding—does not of itself imply publication. In fact, some of the most famous researchers in times past have been notoriously uninterested in publication. Thus the British scientist, Cavendish, left at his death a great mass of research in manuscript form, of which it has been said, "the most careful scrutiny of his unpublished work has all gone to show that a great deal of it is of the highest value, and has left permanent marks on the subjects which he studied."[6] Cavendish was a very wealthy man, whereas the German mathematician, Gauss, came from a poor background. Yet Gauss had an attitude toward publishing that was similar to Cavendish's.

> Gauss said that he undertook his scientific works only in response to the deepest promptings of his nature, and it was a wholly secondary consideration to him whether they were ever published for the instruction of others .... Not till long after his death was it known how much of nineteenth-century mathematics Gauss had foreseen and anticipated before the year 1800. Had he divulged what he knew it is quite possible that mathematics would now be half a century or more ahead of where it is. Abel and Jacobi could have begun where Gauss left off, instead of expending much of their finest effort rediscovering things Gauss knew before they were born, and the creators of non-Euclidean geometry could have turned their genius to other things.[7]

The last two sentences here indicate well enough why "communalism" is one of the norms of the scientific community, but they do not explain why individuals should feel compelled to disseminate their work. For enlightenment, we turn again to Table 12. The desire to make a significant contribution to knowledge immediately raises the question—who judges whether it is significant? The answer is, of course, the relevant research community, and that requires, in turn, the discussion of each individual's work by the community. A continuing theme for researchers—indeed, for all creative people—is the need for reassurance at intervals that what they are doing is worthwhile. This is what communal appraisal of work can give. Shortly after T. H. Huxley was elected to the Royal Society, he found himself in the running for one of its medals. He wrote to his future wife:

> Except for its practical value as a means of getting a position I care little enough for the medal. What I do care for is the justification which the being marked in this position gives to the course I have taken. Obstinate and self-willed as I am . . . there are times when grave doubts overshadow my mind, and then such testimony as this restores my self-confidence.[8]

Elsewhere in the same letter he rhapsodized on the way in which the sense of community reinforced his intellectual curiosity.

> I have at last tasted what it is to mingle with my fellows—to take my place in that society for which nature has fitted me . . . the real pleasure, the true sphere, lies in the feeling of self-development—in the sense of power and of growing *oneness* with the great spirit of abstract truth.[9]

Huxley's letter relates the motivation of the individual researcher to the activities of the research community. The motivation of researchers can, correspondingly, be discussed in terms both of the individual (psychological factors) and of the research community (sociological factors). It makes sense to tackle the former first.

Psychological Factors

Some requirements are prescriptive for any researcher. An obvious one relates to intelligence. It is true that particular aspects of research, such as the accumulation of data, do not require outstanding intellectual ability. Thus measurement of air temperature, counting the number of words in a text, and so on are straightforward, routine activities. But researchers are expected to do more than this: they must make original, creative contributions. To do that requires an above-average intelligence. It has been estimated that the average IQ for high-school graduates in the United States is 110. For college graduates, the corresponding average score was 120, and, for Ph.D.s, 130.[10] Given the normal distribution of IQ in the population, this simple measure suggests that only a limited proportion can hope to achieve a research qualification. In fact, there are significant differences between the average IQ scores for Ph.D.s in different subjects: one study put physics highest and education lowest.[11] The differences presumably relate to the role of mathematical and literary assessment in the IQ test itself, as well as to the differing abilities of the candidates.

In a number of cases, particularly in the sciences, it has been found that researchers, subsequently eminent, became interested in the general field of their lifework at an early age. Such precocious involvement is especially well-documented in mathematics. Gauss is again an example. He corrected a payroll calculation by his father at the age of three. Evidence of various kinds has been adduced for the influence of family background in encouraging or discouraging an inclination toward research. For example, there have been lengthy debates on whether first-born or only children are more likely to have a research orientation, and whether such an orientation is affected by the religious affiliations of their parents.[12] Though such questions may seem far removed from a discussion of research communication, they actually provide pointers to potentially significant queries. In the first place, they raise the question whether individual characteristics can affect the research career chosen.

An interesting insight into this is provided by a study of teenage schoolboys in the UK.[13] This tried to divide them into two groups—convergers and divergers. (Other work has invoked more categories but come to generally similar results.) The basic characteristics attributed to each group are set out in Table 14. Many of the boys exhibited a mix of characteristics, so they could not be uniquely allocated to one group or the other. Nevertheless, the data indicated a correlation between these groupings and the subject areas that the boys found most congenial. Convergers tended to be attracted to the physical sciences or the classics, whereas divergers were more likely to prefer the biological sciences or the humanities. The difference may be more emphasized in the UK than elsewhere because subject specialization starts early in British education, but the overall trends seem to be paralleled in other countries.

A further study looked at the images such schoolboys had of people who studied science or humanities at university. Table 15 compares the sort

Table 14
Differences between Convergers and Divergers

Topic	Converger	Diverger
Intelligence tests	Good at conventional IQ tests	Good at open-ended questions
Courses	Prefer settled syllabus	Prefer flexible syllabus
Attitudes	Conventional	Unconventional
Interests	Mechanical, technical	People
Emotions	Inhibited	Uninhibited

of responses obtained. Perhaps the most fascinating thing about this list is that it reflects good agreement between the respondents, regardless of their own subject preferences. Overall, scientists are seen as more oriented to things than to people, and as more single-minded and introverted than their peers in the humanities.

A variety of studies have shown that most outstanding researchers exhibit a mix of divergent and convergent characteristics, but with the emphasis clearly on the divergent, regardless of field. For example, a study of female mathematicians remarks: "The emphasis is upon genuine unconventionality, high intellectual ability, vividness or even flamboyance of character, moodiness and preoccupation, courage, and self-centeredness."[14] The picture of an average scientist, derived from Tables 14 and 15, looks rather different from this. It may be that creative scientists, therefore, experience particular difficulty in passing through the standard educational system. Certainly, they may become impatient of the long period of learning expected of them before they can produce original results (compare this with the greater creative freedom in the humanities). Many leading scientists have not had out-

Table 15
Images of Science and Humanities Graduates

Supposed characteristics of science graduates	Supposed characteristics of humanities graduates
More hard-working	Less hard-working
More valuable to society	Less valuable to society
Unsociable	Sociable
Cold	Warm
More dependable	Less dependable
Less imaginative	More imaginative

standing records of undergraduate achievement. An illustration of this is the story of how Schwinger, later a leading theoretical physicist, gained entry to Columbia University.

> Well, it turned out that he was a sophomore at City College, and he was doing very badly—flunking his courses, not in physics, but doing very badly. I talked to him for a while and was deeply impressed. He had already written a paper on quantum electrodynamics. So I asked him if he wanted to transfer, and he said yes. He gave me a transcript and I looked at it. He was failing—English, and just about everything else.[15]

The character traits attributed to scientists might be expected to make informal communication less pleasurable for them than for researchers in the social sciences and humanities. Thus Cavendish was famous for his distaste for discussion, while Schwinger preferred to work at night, coming to work just as his colleagues were going home. In fact, scientists are found to be as involved in informal communication as social scientists and often more than researchers in the humanities. One reason is certainly the pressure toward teamwork in the sciences. Another is the greater urgency attached to communicating research information in science because of the need to complete projects rapidly. (By way of contrast much humanities research is still done by individuals, and a single research project may extend over many years.) Not least, however, researchers in any field show a spread of characteristics. One study, based on psychological tests, suggested eight categories of scientist, each distinguished by a different style of working and by different ways of interacting with colleagues.[16] Yet, though Table 14 must be hedged around with many qualifications, it does suggest a generic difference between entrants to the different fields of research. The convergers prefer topics where it should be possible to find a definite answer, which ties in with the idea of cumulative knowledge discussed in the previous chapter. The divergers are happy working on topics for which no definitive answer may be possible. Though this is not a straight science–humanities division, it suggests that the average entrant to each of these fields may have somewhat differing psychological characteristics.

Productivity

In terms of communication, the two most important characteristics of a researcher are the quantity of information he, or she, communicates and its quality. How can these be investigated? One measure of quantity for acade-

Table 16
Differences in Total Number of Articles Published by Field (%)

Number of articles	Humanities	Social sciences	Sciences	Technology	Medicine
0–4	37	37	20	41	9
0–10	24	21	23	30	13
More than 10	39	42	57	29	77

mic researchers is the number of journal articles that they publish. Table 16 compares the number of articles published by a group of academics working in different subjects.[17] It indicates that, for this sample, scientists, and especially medical researchers, publish more than researchers in other fields.

This supposes that productivity is best measured in terms of articles published. However, many researchers in the humanities prefer to publish their results in book form rather than in journals. This presumably evens out the publication imbalance—but by how much? In crude terms, how many articles equal one book? Similarly, engineers are often oriented toward the development of products and patents. How can these be compared with articles in journals? The simple answer is that they cannot, though various attempts have been made to do so (e.g., rule-of-thumb estimates equate one book to anything from two to six articles). Table 17 reflects what happens when this kind of adjustment is made (in this case, from a study of Norwegian academics).[18] What it underlines is that productivity comparisons between science and medicine, on the one hand, and social science and humanities, on the other, depend greatly on the weightings that are adopted for the different categories of publication.

Even this attempt at refinement does not solve all the problems. For example, it is necessary to be clear that the books being counted actually contain research (i.e., that they are research monographs rather than text-

Table 17
Average Number of Publications with Their Article-Equivalents per Researcher over a 3-Year Period

	Humanities	Social sciences	Sciences	Medicine
Number of publications	3.5	4.6	5.1	8.2
Number of article-equivalents	4.7	5.9	3.9	5.2

Table 18
Average Number of Articles Published over a 5-Year Period

	Field					
Type of article	Humanities	Social sciences	Physical sciences	Life sciences	Technology	Medicine
Research	11.5	13.2	8.6	8.6	5.5	11.0
Professional	9.6	10.3	3.8	6.0	5.1	7.9

books). Production of textbooks in a field such as engineering can actually correlate negatively with research as measured by number of published articles.[19] Even the articles themselves need scrutiny. Not all contain research: some are aimed at discussing current developments or matters of professional interest. For example, a study of Croatian researchers came up with the results in Table 18.[20] In this case, researchers in the humanities and social sciences proved to be the most productive, but more of their effort went into articles that did not contain original research.

The foregoing discussions deal with averages over large groups of researchers. They, therefore, fail to reveal how skewed the production of research publications actually is. At the upper end of the scale, remarkable rates of production are achieved. Many years ago, Lotka examined this question of individual productivity by looking at the publication of journal articles in chemistry.[21] He counted the articles published by different authors over a period of a decade, and found that the number of authors publishing fell off approximately as the inverse square of the number of papers published. In other words, for every 100 authors who produced a single article during the decade, 25 produced two articles, 11 produced three articles, and so on. This type of distribution is now called "Lotka's law."

There is another way of looking at this skewed productivity. In each field of research, a small number of high producers will publish a significant fraction of all the articles in the field. One suggestion is that the number of high producers will vary as the square root of the total number of authors.[22] In other words, if a field contains a hundred authors, 10 of them are likely to be producing half (say) of all the articles. A similar rule-of-thumb can be applied to the staff within individual academic departments.[23]

This general picture of productivity requires modification in detail. At the top end of the productivity scale, the researchers with the highest number of publications to their credit actually fall below the line predicted by

Lotka's law. In other words, they publish relatively less than would be expected. This is not too surprising when the implications for them in terms of publication rate are considered. Suppose the normal maximum number of publications a researcher can produce is a thousand (the nineteenth-century British mathematician, Cayley, published 995). Given a working life of 50 years, this corresponds to a publication rate of one item every two or three weeks: no easy task, even if the researcher remains alive and well for all that time.

Perhaps more importantly, the way in which the number of publications declines with number of researchers depends on how the measurements are made. In obtaining his results, Lotka relied mainly on sampling *Chemical Abstracts*, counting the number of publications per author over a fixed period of time. This cross-sectional approach includes all researchers, whether they move in and out of the field or stay there. For example, it includes Ph.D. students who may publish one or two articles on their doctoral research before they move on to a different career. If counting is restricted to researchers who remain active in the same field throughout the period of measurement, a rather different result is obtained. There are, again, a few high producers and a larger number of low producers, but the curve is flattened: the number of low producers relative to high producers is considerably reduced. Both methods of measurement are equally valid, of course: which is chosen depends on the application in mind. If it is a question of information production, Lotka's original method is appropriate. The second approach—cohort analysis—may prove more useful when comparing research productivity in different institutions.

A form of Lotka's law, though not necessarily fitting exactly an inverse-square relationship, can be found across most creative activities. It applies, for example, to the relative amounts of music produced by different composers. In one investigation, it was found to hold for the number of works by different English-language authors that were translated into Danish during the nineteenth century.[24] This is an interesting example because it illustrates the importance of defining appropriately the units to be measured. In this case, dealing with books, the falloff comes closest to Lotka's law if only the original titles are counted. When reprints or new editions are included, the fall-off becomes appreciably less steep (because there are fewer authors with only one "publication" to their credit).

It is not only publications at the individual level that produce a skewed distribution pattern. The numbers of publications from different research institutions typically fall off in a similar way. For example, a study of research and development publications on telecommunications from West German universities found that six universities produced 53% of the annual output, whereas the other 34 universities produced the remaining 47%.[25] Even at the highest level—the analysis of productivity by country—the same skewed distribution can be found. Thus a study of the scientific publication activities of 32 countries showed that six (approximately the square root of 32) could be credited with some 50% of the total.[26]

Differential productivity between institutions or countries is clearly not the same as individual productivity differences. In the latter case, the unit of comparison—the individual researcher—can be made the same, whereas the number of staff in a research institution, or the number of research institutions per country, can vary widely. Most studies show that, at the institutional level, there exists a cluster of factors that correlate with high productivity.[27] These include the size of the university (in terms both of staff and students), its wealth, and the level of provision of support services (such as the library). Of these, the fundamental factor appears to be finance. A wealthy university can afford to provide good research conditions for its academic staff. This attracts high-quality researchers, which enhances the prestige of the university, and so attracts better students. As a result of these developments, more finance comes into the university, and so the process continues. Although these factors can be analyzed reasonably easily within a single country, comparisons between countries require more caution. What passes as a wealthy university in one country may be rated as less than wealthy in another. There are parallels in this between factors relating to high institutional productivity and high individual productivity. More productive researchers tend to have access to more research funding and to more research assistants and students than others—factors that also appear for more productive institutions. There is a direct connection, of course, in the sense that more productive researchers tend to work in more productive institutions.

Quality

This examination of differential productivity leads to the next question. To what extent does high productivity correspond to a high quality of research publication? Does productivity result from churning out large quantities of trivia, or does it reflect the self-motivation of a high-quality researcher? One way of estimating quality is by assessing the level of interest of others in the research. The simplest method of measuring this is via the number of citations to the research in later literature. Such use of citations obviously needs careful attention, since interest in a piece of research can be evoked for a number of reasons. For example, it might be thought that citing a research article because its contents are deemed to be incorrect hardly indicates it is highly significant. An example is the original paper on "cold fusion" in 1989, which was subsequently cited several hundred times, mostly by people who believed it to be wrong. However, the case is arguable. Such citation depends on the importance of the topic: questionable articles dealing with less important topics are likely to be ignored rather than cited. Some articles containing erroneous results have actually proved fruitful in stimulating further research: the original work on gravitational waves is an example. In any case, since a researcher who continually produced incorrect results would soon find it hard to publish in reputable journals, this type of citation represents a small fraction of the whole. So it seems worthwhile considering citation counts as a measure of quality a little further.

There have been a variety of attempts to explore why one researcher cites the work of another. For example, one listing puts forward 15 possible reasons, such as—paying homage to pioneers; giving credit for related work; identifying methodology, equipment, etc.; providing background reading.[28] The majority of the reasons suggested in the list can be counted as positive, they are recommending the work cited rather than condemning it. Unfortunately, such categorization does not identify what proportion of journal references appear under each heading nor whether each should be considered as of equal significance. Will two people writing on the same piece of research come up with the same citations and attach the same importance to each? As was noted in Chapter 2, sometimes they do, but, more often, different articles written at the same time on the same topic only show a limited degree of overlap in the choice of citations. The fit is usually far from perfect for reasons attached both to the research and the researcher. For example, it depends on the specificity of the subject: the more specific the topic, or the approach followed, the greater the likelihood of overlap. Equally, it can depend on the researcher's background: researchers from different countries typically select somewhat differing sets of citations.

To tackle the question of the intrinsic significance of different citations requires some easy way of classifying them. The simplest approach divides citations into three groups—essential, supplementary (both seen as positive), and negative.[29] One study of business administration literature, which obtained feedback from the original authors, found that less than a third of the citations were actually considered to be essential.[30] Presumably, if citations reflect importance, the authors of those graded as essential should gain the most kudos. However, even supplementary references are not chosen at random. Where possible, researchers naturally prefer to cite work of their own. Such self-citation accounts for some 10% of all citations, and is, no doubt, better ignored as an impartial assessment of research excellence. Otherwise, authors are likely to cite work that has been drawn to their attention, or is readily available. This limits what is likely to be chosen. For example, research mentioned in reviews, or appearing in major journals found in all libraries, is more likely to be cited. Both of these sources are likely to contain the higher quality research. Hence, supplementary references (other than self-citations) still tend to pick out the more important research.

First, a word of caution: most research on citations has relied on the work of Eugene Garfield and the Institute for Scientific Information (ISI). This has created a range of citation indexes that can be used for investigations. The references attached to articles from a wide range of scholarly journals are brought together and sorted under various headings. It is therefore possible to look up a specific name and to count how many references have accumulated over a given period to the various publications authored by that person. But, as Garfield has frequently pointed out, the process is subject to uncertainties. In the first place, a surprising proportion of the references in journals contain some kind of error. Then again, authors do not always record their names in the same way: it can depend on publishing policy. Let me cite my own case as an example. Some journals prefer initials, so my articles appear in them under the byline A. J. Meadows. Others prefer the commonly used forename to be given: for me, this means the byline Jack Meadows. The latter is abbreviated to J. Meadows for handling in the citation database. Consequently, should anyone be foolish enough to cite my research, some citations will appear under A. J. Meadows and some under J. Meadows. Anyone counting citations could be pardoned for not knowing that these two are the same person. The opposite error occurs when two authors with the same surname and initials are conflated by the database. The world contains a considerable number of people called J. Smith (and its even more numerous parallels in Asian countries), who may appear as a single major producer of information. For all these sorts of reasons, simple counts of citations can have their problems.

The argument so far suggests that citations may be able to provide a measure of quality, but there are various pitfalls to be avoided en route. The obvious way of testing this conclusion is by looking at other measures of research quality and seeing whether they correlate with citation rate. For example, we can look at how researchers are rewarded, since it seems reasonable to suppose that rewards are mostly given to those who produce the highest quality research. Some types of reward—such as promotion and higher salaries—are common to almost all types of endeavor. Other forms of recognition are more commonly confined to the academic world. Starting at the top, the most evident recognition of research merit is the award of a Nobel Prize. A study of physicists who won the Nobel Prize during the period 1955–1965 found that they received 10 times as many citations per year as the average.[31] Nor was this a spin-off effect from receiving the prize, since recipients were being cited as highly beforehand as afterward. The results placed them in the top 1% of all scientists in terms of level of citation. At a more general level, various studies have looked at links between salaries (or position), external recognition and citations. These suggest there is a significant correlation between such variables, to the extent that attempts have been made to calculate the monetary value for a researcher of each publication.[32] Perhaps the most convincing point in linking recognition to citations relates to prediction. Identification of high citation rates has proved to be a moderately successful way of forecasting which researchers will receive recognition in the future.

We now have two things we can quantify—productivity and quality of research. This takes us back to the original question. Are productive authors also highly cited authors? Four combinations are possible—high productivity/high citation rate; high productivity/low citation rate; low productivity/high citation rate; low productivity/low citation rate. The first corresponds to a researcher who publishes a lot of high-quality work. The second indicates a researcher who is producing a large amount of relatively low-quality work. The third suggests a researcher who is a perfectionist, producing a limited quantity of high-quality work. Finally, the fourth group is likely to contain relatively marginal members of the research community. When these various options are put to the test, by comparing the productivity of researchers with the citations that their publications attract, each of the four groupings contains some members. But categories 1 and 4 are appreciably better populated than categories 2 and 3. In other words, most studies find a significant correlation between productivity and citation rate.[33]

Most of the studies of quantity versus quality have concentrated on the sciences. The available data on the humanities and social sciences strongly suggest that they show similar, though perhaps less strong, links between productivity and the level of recognition accorded to researchers.[34] The main difference is that the number of published articles is not always the best criterion: publication in book form is often of equal or greater importance. Some measure other than articles is also often necessary in nonacademic environments. In some areas of industry, researchers are encouraged to apply for patents rather than to publish articles. Here, there appears to be a link between the number of patents registered and the perceived quality of the researcher's work.[35]

The conclusion from all this seems clear. There is a good, though by no means perfect, correlation between the amount researchers publish and the quality of their work (measured in terms of its recognition by the research community). Psychological studies of researchers underline this link. Outstanding researchers are distinguished by their high level of motivation: they are driven by a desire to be both productive and creative. An early study of the backgrounds of people generally regarded as geniuses noted that:

> high but not the highest intelligence, combined with the greatest degree of persistence, will achieve greater eminence than the highest degree of intelligence with somewhat less persistence.[36]

This motivation manifests itself in all types of communication, not only in the publication of articles and books. As compared with the average researcher, not only are such people more motivated to involve themselves in formal communication, they are also more concerned with informal communication. "Highest producers . . . express more of an interest in research, communicate more frequently with scholars at other institutions, and subscribe to more academic journals."[37] But the driving force must be internal. External factors, such as salary and work conditions, may help, but are no substitute. Researchers in industry may be more influenced by such factors, a reflection of the fact that the ultimate aim for many of them is a managerial position rather than more research. However, it remains the high producer who dominates research communication in most environments. Such people must therefore be an important focus for studies into the communication of research.

Leading Researchers

One aspect of high motivation in research is often a desire to be in touch with others who are equally highly motivated. This manifests itself from the start, when potential high-flyers seek research training. An examination of Nobel Prize winners shows that an appreciable fraction were trained by people who had themselves been awarded a Nobel Prize. More generally, present-day eminent researchers are frequently found to have been trained by eminent researchers of the previous generation. Being themselves highly motivated, these latter researchers have tended to congregate in a core of élite institutions, where they attract the best research students nationally and often internationally. So the system perpetuates itself. Which institutions produce the largest amounts of high-quality research can change with time, but the pecking order usually alters fairly slowly. For specific subjects, it can change more rapidly, especially when the creation of a new specialism (for example, mass-media studies) is involved. In fields such as the humanities— where research remains low cost, and the identification of important new work less straightforward—the institutional spread of eminent researchers is rather greater than in the sciences.

As an example of the kind of differences that can be found between institutions, Table 19 compares data from two groups of British universities— the élite institutions of Oxford and Cambridge, on the one hand, and a group of minor universities, on the other—in terms of their highest producers. These figures date from about 1970.[38] The major expansion of the British university system two decades later has expanded the gap between the top and the bottom. The research differences between universities in the United States have always been large.

What do highly motivated researchers pass on to their students that those less highly motivated do not? In general, it is not factual knowledge, though that may be easier to acquire in the well-supported research environment of a major university. It may be practical "know-how"—the craft knowledge that is usually thought to be learned by apprenticeship. But eminent researchers are not necessarily good communicators. A biologist at a major Australian research institute is reported as believing

> that this kind of doing-thinking which arises out of work at the laboratory bench is to some extent incommunicable. Scientists are very bad at communicating to other scientists what they are about. He had attended a con-

Table 19
Proportion of Staff (in %) at Different Universities Who Have Published More Than 10 Articles

	Humanities	Social sciences	Science	Technology
Oxford and Cambridge	50	70	80	46
Minor universities	40	23	46	9

ference at Versailles which brought together sixty top scientists from various fields . . . The idea was that each scientist would explain to his colleagues what he was doing . . . However, not only were they incapable of communicating, they were also quite uninterested in listening to others.[39]

In fact, the most important type of knowledge passed on is more intangible, yet has an impact on all forms of communication. It is having a feeling for research style—more especially, for the appropriate selection of topics to investigate—and for how the research community works. Much of this is not transmitted explicitly. For example, an understanding of the norms of the research community (and when and how they may be transgressed) is usually learned by example rather than by discussion. Illumination concerning the research community comes to research students obliquely and by inference. The same is often true of research style, which embraces such matters as the approaches, methods, and types of evidence that are regarded as acceptable by one's research peers in a particular field of research. Perhaps the most important characteristic that outstanding researchers can pass on to their students is the ability to foresee which research topics will be most worthwhile pursuing in the immediate future. The people most likely to receive widespread recognition are naturally those who pioneer successfully a new research trend.

There is, of course, an element of self-fulfillment in all this. High-flyers in research are the people most widely known to their peers. Hence, high-flyers help their juniors indirectly by making them more visible more quickly to the research community and directly via their significant role in the allocation of recognition (and jobs) to new researchers. At the same time, association with eminent researchers can have disadvantages. For example, when a young researcher publishes an article or book jointly with a famous researcher, it is often the latter who receives more of the credit. But, for highly motivated young researchers, the overall effect is clearly positive. They work in an institutional climate that expects publication of high-quality research from its members. Such publication is readily recognized by the research community. This recognition represents feedback, encouraging young researchers to publish more; indeed, building up the expectation that they will publish more. Correspondingly, low producers receive little feedback and little encouragement to publish more often. Various studies have shown that high producers start that way and attract citations to their work from the beginning. Conversely, low producers rarely become high producers later in their career and seldom attract significant numbers of citations.

One point, however, must be noted. Leading researchers are rarely accorded that status because all their publications are considered to be of major importance. Some publications are seen by the research community as much more important than the remainder. If citations are a measure of the relative impact of different publications, then, even for a high producer, they typically follow a skewed distribution. Consider, as an example the publication record of R. A. Daly, a leading U.S. geologist during the first half of the twentieth century.[40] Daly produced 136 publications, 50 of which were never cited. The remainder had received 859 citations by 1968 (14 years after the appearance of the last of them). In this case, recognition was slow to come in Daly's early years. By the time he had completed his first 45 publications, he had only received 23 citations (some of them self-citations). He then published two influential monographs, based on his research, and these soon came to be widely cited. Unlike physics or chemistry, monograph publication continued to be important in geology during the twentieth century as a way of conveying original research. By the time he had produced 65 publications—about halfway through his total production—he had acquired 77 citations. From there it built up by an order of magnitude as he completed his list of publications. Overall, the top 10% of his publications received 52% of all his citations; at the other end, 50% of his publications received 9% of the total citations.

The distribution of people who cited Daly's work was also skewed, but not so much as the citations themselves. Self-citations accounted for 10% of the total—the standard rate. The top 10% of other citers produced 45% of the total citations, whereas the bottom 50% produced 20% of the citations. The frequent citers proved, hardly surprisingly, to be productive geologists whose interests overlapped with Daly's. The people who cited Daly only once were a mixture of low producers in the same fields or higher producers in adjacent fields. These latter were mostly people with a relatively limited knowledge of the topics on which Daly worked. They are the ones who may have been encouraged to cite Daly's publications because of his high level of visibility in the world of geological research. Even this could only be true of citations made in his later years, so not many citations of Daly's publications can be attributed primarily to his status.

What these particular results are telling us—and it has been confirmed by other studies—is that, though high producers are highly cited, a limited number of their publications receive most of the citations. This does not imply that the other publications should not have appeared: there are several reasons why "minor" articles may be useful. Many research projects produce interesting, but somewhat peripheral, information as part of their progress.

For example, in the course of writing a biography of a politician, a historian may come across new material concerning (say) education during the period. It may not be relevant to the planned book, but still be worth publishing as a separate article. Again, a long-term project in chemistry may involve a series of experiments. These will probably be written up and published as the series progresses, though the clinching article may only come at the end. Another factor is invited publications, where the researcher is asked to contribute an article or book chapter. Such contributions may be useful as summaries, or "think-pieces," but, like the previous categories, they will not necessarily be highly cited.

A more interesting factor in looking at the output of leading researchers is their choice of topics to be investigated. As remarked previously, an outstanding researcher typically latches on to an important topic early and leads in its investigation. The difficult balance lies in moving into the field at just the right time. Enter it too late, and the pioneering work has already been done. Enter it too early, and the research community may not be interested. In addition, even eminent researchers are not necessarily the best judges of their own work. They have won acclaim by boldly going where others have not. This is a high-risk strategy. The research literature is littered with new initiatives that failed to take off and are rarely cited.

A distinctive feature of key publications is not only that they are highly cited, but that they are cited over a longer period of time than other publications. Indeed, work can be cited long after an author's death. In a rapidly changing field, such as astrophysics, there may be some increase in the citations to well-known researchers immediately after their deaths, but the rate of citation then falls off fairly rapidly.[41] In other fields, especially the humanities, citation can continue for much longer. Owing to the expansion of the research literature and the corresponding growth in numbers of citations being made, a classic work may actually be increasingly cited long after its first appearance. Thus citations to Darwin's *Origin of Species*, which first appeared in 1859, rose significantly in number during the latter half of the twentieth century. This long-term attention is partly due to what has been called "ritual" citation—a reminder to readers of where the research topic originated—but certainly not all. Important concepts and results are sooner or later absorbed into the general consciousness, when they no longer require referencing. No biologists would consider it necessary to refer to Darwin today purely because they were discussing natural selection. Similarly, no scientist when using Newton's laws, would consider it necessary to cite the *Principia*. The remnant of the citation is contained here in the use of the phrase Newton's laws. Unfortunately for the recipient, the research community often fails to bestow eponymous recognition of this sort until after death.

Old research continues to be cited for a variety of reasons. Results that have been round for some time may be given a new application—a not unusual happening with mathematical techniques. Again, the research community may catch up with a piece of research that was carried out ahead of its time. The obvious example is Gregor Mendel's work on genetics, which appeared in the 1860s, but was only developed in the early twentieth century, long after his death. Here there was a delay of some 40 years between the appearance of a publication and a significant number of citations to it. A less-pronounced example of such a delay is a paper on jumping genes published by the U.S. geneticist, Barbara McClintock, in 1951. It received a reasonable number of citations in subsequent years, but only achieved its full impact in the 1970s, at which point citations to it began to rise rapidly as its real importance was realized. In fact, an examination of citations to a large enough number of publications reveals a range of ways in which citations to a particular work can change with time.[42] Nevertheless, it remains true that most significant research begins to be recognized soon after its publication.

Age

Our discussion of productivity has so far concentrated on the total number of publications produced throughout a research career. It leaves open the question—how does productivity vary during a researcher's lifetime? There must obviously be an initial gestation period while the future researcher grows up and receives training. At the other end of a lifetime, there will presumably be a decline in productivity as researchers enter old age. What happens in between?

The data are not so hard to gather, but their interpretation can be difficult. For example, it is necessary to allow for a researcher's age at death; otherwise, the number of researchers who die relatively young will boost the apparent level of productivity of younger researchers as compared with older ones. Once allowance is made for factors such as these, the typical pattern seems to be that researchers begin to publish in their twenties. This is a crucial period in their development, when their growth rate in terms of publications produced is maximum. Productivity then increases more slowly to the late thirties or early forties. This is followed by a decline during the remainder of the publishing career.[43] Where the peak occurs depends on the subject. For researchers in the physical sciences it tends to occur earlier in the thirties; for those in the biological sciences, later in the thirties; for humanities researchers, some years later still. These differences are related to the nature of the subject. Where the knowledge is highly codified and understanding of a restricted area can be gained quickly, it is easier to become a productive researcher earlier.

Because of these differences, when the productivities of different groups are averaged together, what appears often looks more like a plateau than a peak. This is illustrated in Table 20 from data averaged over members of the National Academy of Sciences.[44] The table also shows that a subject such as psychology, which embraces a range of different research styles, has a similarly flattened profile. Different groups of researchers may have greatly differing levels of productivity, but their publishing profile as a function of age remains much the same. Not all studies agree in detail. Some, for example, suggest that the productivity patterns of researchers may have two peaks, with a dip in the forties or fifties. The differences between these various results may well depend, at least in part, on the selection of data and the mode of analysis. Longitudinal and cross-sectional studies, for example, are likely to come up with rather different answers. It is probably best to accept the overall picture previously described and not to expect too much agreement on details.

What factors are likely to be affecting the productivity of researchers as a function of their age? Unfortunately, there are so many contenders that it would be difficult to list them all. For example, successful researchers are usually promoted. Once in a senior position they are given increased responsibilities and administrative duties, which can certainly have an adverse effect on productivity. At the same time, their promotion may give them access to more research assistance and funding, which enhances their publication rate. In any case, the impact of extra duties is not always obvious. Thus university

Table 20
Average Productivity of Researchers during Their Lifetime

Group	Decade of life				
	20–30	30–40	40–50	50–60	60–70
National Academy of Sciences	15.0	48.4	47.1	47.3	37.6
Psychologists	1.5	7.4	11.4	11.7	11.7

staff are supposed to be involved in teaching and administration, as well as research. It would be expected that the less time they have for research, the fewer publications they produce. Up to a point, this is true. However, it seems that researchers who do a small amount of teaching and administration can be more productive than those who concentrate solely on research. It depends whether they find an occasional change in activity mentally stimulating. Besides such influences on individual researchers, there are also influences on cohorts. For example, researchers who are less successful in their early years may drop out of research altogether. This boosts the apparent productivity of the cohort as it ages. As with other aspects of productivity, the key factor is undoubtedly motivation. The best predictor of how much researchers will publish during their next decade is how much they published during the past decade. Similarly, the drop-off in publications that can occur after retirement represents more often a loss of motivation than a loss of capacity to do research.

There may be something of a self-fulfilling prophecy here. Evidence, though often anecdotal, suggests that the most creative researchers are precocious and produce important research early on. For example, the key publications that established quantum mechanics in the 1920s were mainly produced by young researchers in their twenties. The belief therefore seems to have established itself in the sciences, less so elsewhere, that older researchers are less likely to produce important results. One study of eminent scholars found that most mathematicians and physicists in their forties thought that they had already made their most significant contributions. In contrast, a considerable proportion of researchers in the social sciences and humanities thought they might have more significant contributions still to make.[45] In fact, major contributions, even in the physical sciences, can be made by older researchers. For example, the British physicist, Sir Nevill Mott was awarded a Nobel Prize, in part, for work which he started in his fifties. The widespread belief that, for research, young equals good is hardly designed to help motivate older scientists in their pursuit of research and its publication.

One factor in a researcher's career that can affect not only productivity, but communication, is mobility. This takes two forms—physical mobility from one place to another or intellectual mobility from one field of research to another. It seems that the former leads to a productivity increase mainly for younger researchers, who are still developing their research career.[46] The impact of intellectual mobility is less age dependent.[47] It appears to have a generally positive effect on the research of scientists. They may show a decline in productivity while the transition to the new field is taking place, but this is normally more than balanced by their subsequent productivity increase. Intellectual mobility seems to be less productive in the social sciences. One reason is the rapidity of change in different disciplines. In some sciences, a new development may have run its course in 10 years, so any productive researcher must of necessity migrate to another topic. Topics in the social sciences and humanities usually take longer to exhaust, so mobility between research topics is less important.

The Research Community

All these studies of productive researchers suggest, when aggregated, that each subject area contains a relatively small group of people who dominate their chosen fields. They are highly visible not only to people in their own specialism, but to others outside. This picture chimes with the way most researchers, themselves, view their peers. The Russian physicist, Lev Landau, is reported to have classified his fellow-physicists on a logarithmic scale:

> This means that a physicist, say, of the second class has accomplished (precisely *accomplished*, we are dealing only with accomplishments) a tenth as much as a first class physicist. On this scale, Einstein was of class one half, and Bohr, Schrödinger, Heisenberg, Dirac and a few others first class. Landau placed himself in a two and a half [class] (i.e., only one hundredth of an Einstein!).[48]

Researchers pick up this sort of vision along with their training. It is often part of a heroic, and grossly oversimplified, image of how their subject developed. Historians of the various disciplines sometimes seem aggrieved that researchers are not as interested as they should be in acquiring a more rigorous view of their heroes and heroines. This misses the point. Researchers' images, like the norms of research, are intended as a reflection of, and a guide to, the way things ought to be rather than as they actually are. The use of earlier generations of researchers as exemplars of conduct is not, however, totally unproblematic. "Good" research conduct three hundred years ago may not be entirely applicable to the modern world. Thus the traditional picture of great researchers is of people who succeed on the basis of their own talents and efforts. As Wordsworth described Newton: "a mind for ever voyaging through strange seas of thought alone." In a world where cooperation is increasingly important, this traditional description of a researcher may be a less useful guide for young researchers than it has been in the past.

The tendency of researchers to see their famous peers as mountain peaks, towering above the foothills that represent the average researcher, is reflected in the communication system. For example, an analysis of physics articles published in the 1920s found that those now considered to be classics were immediately cited very highly.[49] However, this high citation rate lasted only for a short period of time. By way of contrast, articles that were cited equally highly, but over a longer period of time, are not now regarded as classics. The reason probably relates to the speed with which these major advances were incorporated into further research. Really epoch-making work was absorbed so quickly that it soon became unnecessary to refer to the original article. The implication is that the distinctive research peaks we now discern in quantum mechanics were equally identified by contemporaries. In communication terms, if not in purely historical terms, there are some similarities between the researchers" pictures of their subjects and the way things actually operate.

Yet it may be that this is again, in part, a self-fulfilling prophecy. Outstanding researchers naturally attract more attention than their colleagues. This acts to emphasize their significance and so attracts still more attention to them. Such snowballing of attention has been labeled the "Matthew effect,"[50] from a passage in St. Matthew's gospel: "For unto everyone that hath shall be given, and he shall have abundance: but from him that hath not shall be taken away even that which he hath." The quotation underlines the fact that in attracting attention to themselves and their work, leading researchers can, often unwittingly, attract attention away from their less-known colleagues. It raises the question—is the difference between outstanding researchers and others on the logarithmic scale suggested by Landau, or is it actually smaller, and simply being amplified by the Matthew effect? The extreme assertion that the difference is unimportant was formulated by the Spanish philosopher, Ortega y Gasset:

> it is necessary to insist upon this extraordinary but undeniable fact: experimental science has progressed thanks in great part to the work of men astoundingly mediocre, and even less than mediocre.[51]

Ortega is actually echoing here the viewpoint of Francis Bacon in the early seventeenth century. Bacon believed it was true of branches of knowledge that depend on the accumulation of information—especially therefore, but not solely, what are now labeled the "natural sciences." It is certainly for the sciences that the Ortega hypothesis, as it is called, has been most widely examined. Clearly, the citation data do not seem to support it. A detailed study of research articles in physics led to the following conclusion:

> The data allow us to question the view stated by Ortega . . . that large numbers of average scientists contribute substantially to the advance of sci-

ence *through their research*. It seems, rather, that a relatively small number of physicists produce work which becomes the base for future discoveries in physics. We have found that even papers of relatively minor significance used to a disproportionate degree the work of the eminent scientists."[52]

The italics (which appear in the original) are important. Citations, and even publications, only reflect part of the range of interactions that take place between researchers or of the assistance they give each other. For example, designers of equipment may not be prominent in terms of publications or citations, but work using their instrumentation may be vital for others who achieve a high level of citation. It may be that cooperative research is making these hidden supporters more apparent. Thus a high-energy physicist, however bursting with genius, would make little headway by experimenting alone today. Reports of high-energy experiments have therefore increasingly stressed the research team rather than the individual. It is true that the people in charge still receive much of the kudos, but at least the literature is beginning to reflect a little better their dependence on others.

The picture described so far comes particularly, though not solely, from studies of male researchers in Western countries. Must the conclusions be modified when looking at other groups? Studies of female researchers, mainly those involved in science in Western countries, have been made in increasing numbers in the last two decades.[53] They show that the proportion of women involved in research has been growing. In the United States, the proportion of scientists and engineers who were female rose from 6% to 13% from the mid-1970s to the mid-1980s. There has always been an imbalance between male and female recruitment to different disciplines, with the proportion of females increasing along the line from the physical sciences, through the biological and social sciences, to the humanities. For example, in the early 1970s, women in the United States obtained 2% of all doctorates in engineering, 7% in the physical sciences, 17% in the biological sciences, and 22% in the social sciences. Though numbers of doctorates increased for all these fields in subsequent years, it rose most rapidly for the social sciences. This growth in female participation allied to differences between disciplines is nothing new. Table 21 gives some comparative data for the first half of the twentieth century.[54]

The continuing change in numbers makes it difficult to assess communication differences because, for example, the proportion of women researchers in each age cohort can differ significantly. One conclusion seems clear: male and female researchers of the same age differ appreciably in productivity. On average, women produce 50–60% of the publications of their

Table 21
Female Researchers Holding Posts in the U.S. Academic World

Field	Number (1921)	Number (1938)
Physical sciences	60	227
Biomedical sciences	228	870

male counterparts, and this holds true across different subjects, institutions, and even countries. The consequences are equally clear. Women are cited less than men, more or less in line with the productivity difference. Taking publications by women alone, there is a skewed distribution of authorship, mirroring the usual Lotka law. However, differences in productivity between men and women are particularly marked at the more productive end. In view of the strong link between being a high producer and visibility as a researcher, it is hardly surprising if women researchers often appear less visible in their research field than their male colleagues.

Various reasons for the difference in productivity have been put forward, some of which relate to points raised earlier in this chapter. For example, young women researchers, if they are married, often experience limitations on their geographical mobility. Since such mobility, up to the early thirties, can be helpful in improving productivity, this may have an adverse effect, especially in the sciences. Similarly, family pressures can take them away from research before they have reached their peak productivity. There may also be differences that are not immediately evident from publications alone. For example, there is some evidence that informal communication between male and female researchers may be more limited than within solely male or female groups. This may affect such matters as collaboration in research. In terms of amount of collaboration, as reflected in multiauthored articles, women do not differ greatly from men. But there may be differences in the nature of the collaboration. For example, one U.S. investigation found that over 50% of the male junior academics studied had coauthored articles with senior professors, as compared with 25% of the female.[55] In subsequent promotion from assistant to associate professor, 62% who had such coauthored articles were promoted, as compared with only 13% of those who had not.

The position regarding women in research has some similarities to researchers in developing countries: numbers are generally increasing, though differentially across different fields, but problems relating to recognition remain. The overall position for both male and female researchers in these countries is worse than in Western countries. This partly relates to deficiencies in material resources or to limitations imposed by bureaucracy, but lack of communication, both formal and informal, is also significant.[56] Abdus Salam, who received the Nobel Prize for physics in 1979, left Pakistan for the UK in 1954 with the comment that not one library in his own country had received any journals since the Second World War. So, though there are a number of high producers from developing countries (Salam had published some 200 articles by the time he received his Nobel Prize), several of the best known reside abroad. This is particularly true of scientists. In the humanities, the balance may be different. A Sanskrit scholar in India obviously has advantages, as well as disadvantages.

Productivity patterns for researchers in developing countries have rather similar characteristics to those discussed previously, both as regards distribution across different authors and throughout a single author's lifetime. The key difference lies in the number of publications produced by each researcher, which is below the levels of leading research countries. This difference can also be discerned in some small developed countries. It may relate to the need for a "critical mass" of interacting researchers if research is to take off and lead to a stream of publications. The situation is somewhat confused by the number of researchers in developing countries who have trained abroad. In top academic departments in such countries, as many as half of the staff may have received training abroad, mostly at the Ph.D. level. They often maintain their research links, so their publishing activities may be transnational. In a country such as Saudi Arabia, which has a number of expatriate staff along with many Saudi nationals who have been trained abroad, the range of research links external to the country may be of the same order as the level of internal collaboration.

Overseas training can lead to a different research style. Many developing countries tend to stress rote learning in their education, with a corresponding emphasis on learning from the printed word. As an Indian scientist commented: "One tries to learn much more from books if you're Indian, whereas they [the Americans] learn much more from talking to each other."[57] There is also often a preference for absorbing information rather than publishing it, for theoretical rather than practical work, and for carrying out research alone rather than in collaboration. These attitudes are not necessarily detrimental to research in the humanities. They are less helpful in the social sciences and still less in the sciences. Apart from creating tension between those trained abroad and their home-trained colleagues, such differences in attitude affect productivity. Different productivity levels between developed and developing countries lead to something rather similar to the Matthew effect for individuals.[58] Contributions from the leading research countries become overcited, whereas those from the remainder are even less cited than might be expected. Clearly, this is a factor that can depress still further the likelihood of researchers in developing countries becoming widely recognized.

Publications produced by amateur researchers often complement, rather than compete with, those produced by professionals. For example, an historian interested in a particular theme may well call on information unearthed by local historians who are amateurs. Where overlap occurs, amateurs may, within their restricted fields, be able to talk on level terms with professionals. A professional biologist remarked concerning taxonomy that there is: "no distinction, in terms of ability, between good amateurs and professionals. Many of the accepted authorities on species, to whom professionals would turn for advice, are amateurs."[59]

It is possible to discern categories of eminence within the amateur community, as within the professional community. The difference is that, for amateurs, it is based on who can give advice, as much as on publications (i.e., on informal, rather than formal, communication). This is reflected in one suggested categorization of members of amateur societies into three types—the apprentice, the journeyman, and the master.[60] The apprentice is a learner; the journeyman is a knowledgeable, reliable practitioner, who can work independently; the master actually contributes to the subject. In terms of advice, the masters are invoked by the journeymen when they stand in need of assistance, and both groups help apprentices. This categorization ties in with the emphasis among amateurs on practical work that involves hands-on skills, as compared with the theoretical emphasis of professional research that is linked more closely with publications.

Amateur societies can act as a link between professional researchers and the general public, both by recruiting members from the latter group, and, more broadly, by disseminating ideas via the media. It is the better qualified amateurs—those categorized previously as "masters"—who typically contribute most to local media. At the national level, it is usually professional researchers who figure in the media, though this may be less true of the humanities. Again, the professionals involved are typically eminent in their field of research.

There is an important proviso to this picture. The main concern of the media (especially radio and television) is that the people they approach should have good presentational skills. Unless researchers can talk about their work in a way that appeals to a general audience, they are unlikely to figure greatly as media presenters, however eminent they are. Other factors are also at work. For example, since the media are especially interested in controversy, they like to involve in their presentations people who, in research terms, are mavericks. Despite this, when it is a question of where media professionals turn for expert advice, the answer is mainline and usually senior researchers. Media reporters and producers, once they have found a helpful and reliable researcher, often turn to them for their reactions to any topic that is even loosely related to their area of expertise. The general effect of such repeated exposure is to underline the image of researchers mentioned previously—the "great man," or, less frequently, "great woman," syndrome.

Collaboration

In the early days of research, lonely, eminent researchers certainly existed. Though they required contact with their peers in order to discuss ideas or to obtain feedback on results, their actual research was often carried out in isolation. Even so, some collaboration existed from the start. For example, the Royal Society in its early days saw cooperative effort as one way of promoting new investigations. Collaboration between equals has continued ever since. When Francis Crick and James Watson wrote their famous note on DNA in 1953, they collaborated as equals in the research. One fascinating example of this kind of collaboration is provided by the works of Nicolas Bourbaki. A major volume on mathematics appeared in 1939, with the author named as Nicolas Bourbaki. More volumes followed in succeeding years. *Bourbaki* actually proved to be a pseudonym adopted by a group of mainly French mathematicians, who collaborated over many years in producing the work.

The Bourbaki group was concerned with examining mathematics from a particular viewpoint. This is a characteristic of what is often labeled a research "school," though a school may well extend over more than one generation of researchers. An example of this also from France, is the *Annaliste* school of historians. This school both examined history from a particular viewpoint and extended over a considerable time: it first appeared in the 1920s and still has adherents today. The activities of both the Bourbaki group and the Annaliste school were aimed at producing publications. The same was true of the famous school of organic chemistry set up by Justus von Liebig at the University of Giessen in the first half of the nineteenth century. In this case, the work of the school was commonly published in a particular journal—the *Annalen der Chemie und Pharmacie*—which had Liebig as its editor.

Liebig's activities pointed to the way that future collaboration would increasingly take—less collaboration between equals than hierarchical cooperation in teams. Though a number of Liebig's students subsequently carved out research careers for themselves, they began by working as junior colleagues on the research program that Liebig had devised. This idea of teamwork as a guided activity advanced in the first half of the twentieth century, when scientific groups containing research assistants, research students, and technicians, led by a senior researcher, began to appear. Its real development, however, came after the Second World War, in such fields as nuclear physics and space science. As these latter two examples underline, it is large-scale experimental or observational projects that particularly demand teamwork. Theoretical studies are usually less demanding of such a high level of cooperation in teams. Mathematics, for example, is less conducive of teamwork than most sciences (Table 22).[61] Even so, small collaborative groups are now commonplace in "little" science, and teamwork can also be found across a range of the social sciences (e.g., survey work) and humanities (e.g., archaeology). The basic reasons for teamwork can be found in the growth and specialization of research. Carrying out an experiment, for example, now typically requires a range of skills and access to considerable resources (in terms of personnel and finance) that are beyond the capabilities of an individual.

Teamwork has a major impact on both formal and informal communication. In small groups, or in collaboration between equals, all the participants may have a reasonable overview of the research project. In large teams, ordinary members may be part of smaller groups within the overall structure and have a detailed knowledge of only part of the project. In such teams, the team leader, often working with a core of senior colleagues, has the job of

Table 22

Proportions of Scientists in Various Subjects Involved in Different Types of Cooperative Working

Subject	Working with graduate students (%)	Working with staff colleagues (%)	Working with technicians (%)
Mathematics and statistics	42	25	12
Physics	93	50	43
Chemistry	88	15	35
Experimental biology	83	21	75

organizing and integrating all the activities. Teams of this sort have been commonplace in industry and government research establishments for some time. Their research work has normally been mission-related, rather than the interest-related research which has typified the academic world. The scale and nature of some present-day academic investigations, along with current pressures encouraging applicable research, mean that universities are increasingly concerned with projects that are of the mission-related type. Correspondingly, the amount of teamwork is increasing. There is evidence that the more integrated and coordinated the team, the higher the quality of its performance.[62] The person providing that integration and coordination—the team leader—becomes the most visible researcher: an exact antithesis of the traditional lone genius.

Literature generated by collaborative research shows significant differences from that produced by individual researchers.[63] As would be expected, the degree of collaboration, whether in different disciplines or in different countries, is linked to the level of financial support. Less expectedly, collaborative research appears to be more widely visible (as measured, for example, by citations) than individual research and also tends to be of higher quality. The most-cited papers in a discipline are coauthored more often than would be expected, and they often involve the most productive and eminent researchers. To put it another way, the high producers discussed earlier are more likely to be frequent collaborators than their peers who produce fewer publications. The general link between the proportion of multiauthor publications and overall productivity is reflected in Table 23, which provides data from samples of researchers in five different subjects.[64]

Multiauthor publications offer some problems for the definition of productivity. For example, if a journal article has three authors, should it be counted as a third of an article for each? Equally, the authors listed on the publication do not necessarily tell the whole story regarding the collabora-

Table 23
Multiple Authorship and Relative Number of Publications
in Different Subjects

Subject	Multiauthor publications (%)	Average number of publications
Chemistry	83	6.1
Biology	70	5.7
Physics	67	4.9
Mathematics	15	4.0
History	4	0.5

Table 24
Multiple Authorship in the Social Sciences

Subject	One author (%)	Two authors (%)	Three authors (%)	Four or more authors (%)
Economics	83	16	1	–
Social work	75	20	4	1
Sociology	75	21	3	1
Psychology	45	36	15	4
Biochemistry	19	46	22	13

tion, for not everyone is necessarily included, and sometimes people who were hardly involved are named. However, the correlation between multiple authorship and collaboration in research is sufficiently strong for it to be useful as a guide to changes in research collaboration as a function of time. In physics, for example, the proportion of single-authored research articles dropped from 55% in 1952 to just over 30% in 1983 as the level of collaboration increased.[65] (These are average figures: for particular subfields of physics, the actual proportion can vary from a majority of single-authored articles to hardly any.) Multiple authorship can also be used as an indication of differences in the level of collaboration in different subjects. Table 23 contrasts history with the sciences. Table 24 provides a similar comparison between the social sciences.[66] Though collaboration is highest in the sciences and lowest in the humanities, the overall trend is towards increased collaboration across the board. This trend is not limited to academic research. Table 25 provides data on multiauthor articles published by researchers in European and Japanese firms during the 1980s.[67] There are again differences from field to field, but, overall, an increase in collaboration.

Table 25
Increase in Collaborative Publication by Researchers in Industry

Industry	Collaborative articles in 1980 (%)	Collaborative articles in 1989 (%)
Pharmaceuticals		
Europe	38	54
Japan	21	38
Electronics		
Europe	20	44
Japan	19	28

The Impact of New Technology

This picture of research activity and productivity reflects the position in a research community using traditional modes of working. Will the growing use of information technology affect any of the conclusions? There have been numerous surveys, all of which show rapidly increasing access to computers in many countries. However, use of networked computers can vary with the distinctive social, economic, and regulatory characteristics of each country. For example, computer usage in the home is now commonplace in both the United States and UK, but the type of use reflects national differences. There is less networked use from home in the UK because it is more costly to use telephone lines (a factor that applies to Western Europe as a whole). This explains why a study of behavioral research groups in the United States, the UK, and the Netherlands found there was not much difference in the patterns of usage except for the greater U.S. use of electronic mail from home.[68]

The policy in most research institutions is toward provision of networked computers for all researchers. Blanket implementation is, however, another matter. Information technology is developing so rapidly that hardware, software, and networks need to be updated at frequent intervals. Unless this is done, information handling is impaired. For example, any institution that could not quickly upgrade facilities to handle Web-based communication in the mid-1990s put its staff at a disadvantage. Such response is not equally feasible for every institution. In the United States, for example, the large, research-oriented universities can make better provision for their staff than the smaller universities and colleges. Continuing change can therefore mean continuing differences in access to electronic communication between institutions, though the nature of the differences changes with time.

Given adequate access to information technology, what is the motivation for researchers to use it? The discussion of motivation at the beginning of this chapter effectively identified two key factors—intellectual curiosity and career prospects. An increasing number of research topics can no longer be properly investigated without using information technology. Part of the reason is that there is simply too much information in circulation for it to be handled in any other way. Satellite data, for example, is collected in vast quantities each day and can only be assimilated by technological means. The other part of the reason is that there are many topics today—ranging from meteorology to linguistics—where the actual research may require use of a computer. Looked at another way, information technology is opening up new research opportunities. Many are seen as being of great importance and so are attracting keen researchers. Consequently, computers are becoming an important factor in deciding which research topics attract most interest. (Indeed, there may be a danger that they will come to have too much influence in determining which research topics are examined and in what way.) From the individual researcher's viewpoint, this is all a major motivation for being computer literate.

An ability to use computers and networking is thus becoming essential for all new entrants to the research scene. However, the amount of computing knowledge they should seek has to be carefully balanced. Too little can hinder research activities, but too much may divert its possessor from mainline research to a technical computing role. For example, much research depends on the development of suitable software; but the person who develops it is rarely one of the senior researchers. There is a basic principle at work here concerning rewards. Most important rewards for research, from promotion to the award of a prize, still do not depend on an individual's knowledge of information technology. What they require is a knowledge of when and how to bring it into play. In these terms, it is no different from any other tool used by researchers. The precomputer picture of teamwork is still valid, but the team must now include expertise in the handling of electronic data.

It might be expected that older researchers, who have not grown up with information technology, would find more difficulty in coping with it than younger researchers. Surveys of information usage as a function of age seem to confirm this. In the mid-1980s, two-thirds of humanities scholars who had started teaching in U.S. universities after 1980 used computers, as compared with less than half of those who began their teaching careers before 1970.[69] Similarly, a survey of British scientists in the early 1990s found that senior staff in higher education, industry, and research establishments were generally less in favor of the new technology than their juniors.[70] However, such survey data have to be treated with care. In the first place, senior researchers often delegate technical activities to junior staff. As a result, surveys may underestimate the reliance of senior staff on computers. In addition, senior staff, more than junior staff, suffer from information overload. Consequently, networked computers—which allow large quantities of new information, especially electronic mail, to come to them—are not universally popular, even among computer-literate senior staff. It follows that differences in computer literacy with age can be less significant in terms of outcome than the results of some surveys might imply.

One of the most widely recognized properties of communication via electronic networks is its tendency to even out differences between different levels of users. It is often difficult when exchanging electronic information to detect the status of the person at the other end of the line. In terms of acceptance, this can mean that research students, or junior researchers, are more on a par with senior staff than they are when using traditional modes of communication. At the same time, transmission via networks can make research knowledge available to a much wider audience more quickly than is possible via traditional channels. These differences, combined with the greater computer skills of younger researchers, tend to reduce the previously well-marked differentiation between levels of researchers. Messaging via networked computers thus introduces a kind of semi-anonymity, disguising differences between users. It might be expected that this would help female researchers, for example, to participate more readily. The situation, unfortunately, is not as simple as this would suggest. Computing has been a male-dominated activity since its birth, and this still influences communication habits. The semianonymity of computer communication can, for example, encourage users to be a good deal blunter and more adversarial in their comments than they would normally be. The democratizing effects of computer networks can consequently represent a leveling-down of communication, as much as a leveling-up.

Since a prime requirement of computers and networks is that they should handle increasingly large amounts of information, it might be supposed that their use would lead to greater research productivity. As has been remarked previously, this is often true. Automated measurement, whether of astronomical objects or literary texts, produces far more results per unit time than older manual methods. But it depends on the reason for using computers. If it is for tackling a new type of research problem, rather than aiding an existing type of investigation, it does not necessarily lead to an immediate increase in productivity in terms of published output. What happens depends on the need for human involvement. Where such intervention is required— for example, in formulating the original project or in writing up the results— the production process is held up. Such bottlenecks mean that productivity may still ultimately depend on the number of researchers available.

It is clear that access to networks encourages teamwork. The ability for everyone to access the same data and to interact easily in their use aids joint endeavors. At the same time, networking can help in integrating the group. Indeed, it may help to extend the group's influence both in terms of numbers and in geographical spread. The traditional area for computer application has been in quantitative research. Where this has developed—in subjects ranging from physics to history—collaborative research groups have become commoner. Computer applications to areas of qualitative research are now appearing. It remains to be seen whether this will lead to more collaboration in fields where teamwork has occurred less frequently.

In principle, a move to electronic communication should offer considerable advantages to researchers in developing countries. They can, for the first time, interact informally with researchers elsewhere on equal terms. Moreover, in terms of both formal and informal electronic communication, they are operating in the same timeframe as researchers in developed countries. The value of all this has been demonstrated in recent years in Eastern Europe. Due to chaotic financial conditions, acquisition of printed material has often been impossible. For East European researchers, access to networked information has proved to be a vital lifeline. The positive factors are obvious: the negative may be more subtle. For example, enhanced electronic collaboration may lead to an emphasis on the sorts of research problems that interest researchers in developed countries. It certainly demands a willingness to communicate in one of the major world languages and could encourage a greater reliance still on foreign publishing.

One final point of interest relates to the ability of networked communication to transfer not only knowledge but also some kinds of skills. For example, an experiment in Norway allowed doctors in remote places to treat their patients while receiving networked advice from specialists elsewhere.[71] It was found that repeated interaction enhanced skills, as well as knowledge. Amateurs are already interacting with professional researchers via networks, and there are signs that this is enhancing amateur–professional collaboration. Indeed, since the boundary between specialist networks and the mass media is becoming increasingly fuzzy, it may be that computer-based collaboration with the general public (e.g., in environmental studies) may become a research option of growing value in the future.

4

Channels for Communicating Research

Between researchers and their audiences come the channels by which they communicate. Some of the channels may be taken for granted. For example, a face-to-face discussion employs the earth's atmosphere as a channel for the exchange of speech, but it is rarely necessary to remember this when looking at the problems of conveying oral information. Other channels employ media whose characteristics cannot be ignored when looking at the transmission of information. In this category lie the printed page and the computer network.

Whatever channels are used, the provision and absorption of information depends ultimately on the human senses. So far as research communication is concerned, such senses as smell, taste, and touch play little part in transferring information. There may be occasional minor differences—for example, some people find the move from paper-based to electronic-based communication more difficult because of the lack of tactile contact—but they are rarely significant. A study of communicating research loses little by concentrating exclusively on sight and sound. Speech is mainly important for informal communication: by telephone, as well as face to face. Informal communications are, by definition, ephemeral, and this is generally true of information transmitted by speech. (There are exceptions—for example, when speech is captured on tape or disk.) Formal communications, such as books and journals, have a long-term existence, and they rely essentially on vision. It is therefore the sense of vision that is basic to much of the discussion in this chapter.

Design for Reading

The essential question then comes down to this: how can a particular channel be employed so as to convey visually, with maximum impact, information from a researcher to others? To answer this requires first a knowledge of how people, more especially researchers, read. "Reading" here includes how they look at tables, diagrams, and pictures. At the most basic level, this implies observing how readers" eyes move around the printed page or computer screen.[1] In terms of text, the commonest method of reading is for the eye to proceed along the lines in a series of jumps. The eye transmits to the brain what is seen at each point and then jumps on. The layout of the text—for example, appropriate spacing between lines—helps the eye to make these jumps accurately.

This discontinuous absorption of information interacts with the intentions of the person who is reading. Readers are not only trying to make sense of the text, though that, of course, is a prime purpose. They often have a specific motive for reading the text, and this will guide how they move through it. It is seldom necessary to read every word in order to absorb what is needed. In most texts, the language shows a fair degree of redundancy, so that extrapolation between sample words, or sentences, can give a good enough idea of the message being conveyed. The motivation drives the sampling process. Thus if the concern of the reader is simply to obtain an overview of a document, he or she will skim it rapidly, perhaps ignoring whole paragraphs, or even sections.

Tabular material and diagrams cannot be treated in the same way as text, since their level of redundancy is usually low. With tables, the eye generally fixes first on the words explaining the contents. Similarly, diagrams may have an obvious starting point from which the eye is led on. A picture, such as a photograph, unless it explicitly draws attention to features (e.g., via arrows) does not provide an obvious starting point. The eye must therefore construct its own framework. For example, it typically begins by seeking out places where the contrast is highest. Unlike printed text, which, in the research world, is almost always black on white, printed pictures may also be in color. This normally enhances the amount of information compared with a black-and-white image but also increases the effort required to absorb it. The eye now tries to follow both contrast and color differences.

A proper discussion of reading thus requires knowledge of the individual readers and their motivations, as well as of the texts being read.

Nevertheless, it is still possible to point to features intrinsic to a text that can help, or hinder, a reader. An obvious example is whether it is actually possible to read the material. If a text is printed in letters that are too small or which blur into each other, it can become literally unreadable. Even if the letters are discernible but require some effort to read, the average reader will soon lose interest. Such problems are said to be a matter of "legibility."[2]

Since the eye is a flexible instrument, a fair range of typesizes can usually be discerned without too much difficulty. For a given size, the relative ease also depends on the nature of the typeface. Most typesizes and typefaces in modern books and journals assist easy reading. By way of contrast, the Gothic typeface used in older German books and journals was guaranteed to slow down the reader. To a lesser extent, this is also true of large slabs of text set in italics. It is customary to employ differing typesizes and typefaces in order to distinguish different parts of a text. The choices made are not always optimum for ease of reading. For example, the abstracts attached to journal articles were frequently printed in a smaller typesize than the main text and sometimes in italics. In consequence, the part of an article that is most often looked at by readers was set, inadvertently, in such a way as to slow down reading. Fortunately, most publishers today have realized this, and use normal typesizes and typefaces for abstracts. They may even give additional emphasis by printing them in a bold typeface.

Letters can be too large for easy reading, as well as too small. (Imagine a newspaper printed entirely as headlines.) Similarly, the line of a length of text can be too long or too short for the eye to comprehend readily. This is why, for larger sizes of paper, the text is often split into columns. For speedy reading, the eye has to be able to flick back to the beginning of the next line and pick it up immediately. Consequently, the left-hand end of each line needs to lie on the same vertical axis—"left justified" in the printer's jargon. (It is less important for the right-hand ends to line up, so a number of scholarly publications, particularly journals, leave the right-hand ends ragged.) In a parallel way, readers find short paragraphs with spaces between them easier to read than long paragraphs.

There is a problem here for publishers. These requirements for easy reading act to limit the number of words that can be put on a page. However, publishers, and especially journal publishers, are faced with the need to keep down costs. That can be assisted by cramming as many words on each page as possible. Cost has significantly affected design down the years. Italics were introduced in the sixteenth century partly to save space and so save costly paper. In the nineteenth century, when paper was cheap, compositors were usually paid in terms of the number of lines they set. They naturally used up as much space as possible so as to increase their pay packets. Some of their practices continued into the twentieth century, even when paper became more expensive. The same kind of dilemma of cost versus design arises when the paper is purchased. Thinner paper costs less both to buy and, as part of the subsequent distribution, to mail. But, if it is too thin, the print on one side will show through on the other. This can reduce the ease of reading. A similar sort of dilemma relates to the paper surface. Matt paper is both cheaper and better for reading text than glossy paper. (Glossy paper can produce unwanted light reflection.) However, photographs reproduce much better on glossy paper, which must therefore be used for subjects, such as biology or the history of art, where good color reproduction is often essential. The result of all these conflicting pressures is that the average research publication is usually designed to be quite easily readable, but not necessarily to the optimum extent.

Such points as using a different typeface for abstracts, restricting paragraphs to a reasonable length, and so on, reflect an important design aspect of research publications: the way they are laid out to help guide the reader through their contents. The more necessary it is to extract information rapidly and efficiently, the more essential it is for the information to be presented within an appropriate structure. Factors such as typesize, typeface, spacing, and layout can be used to help a reader navigate through the text. This structuring ultimately depends on how it is expected readers will use the text. If the text is an essay-style discussion of a topic, the structure may be fairly loose, with chapters providing the main markers. (Any scholarly book is also expected to have an index to help examine its contents for specific topics.) At the other extreme, a densely argued monograph may be highly subdivided—by chapter, section, and subsection—to help readers absorb the discussion stage by stage. The sections may even be numbered to allow reference backward and forward as the argument develops. Journal articles have developed their own structure. The sequence—title/author name(s) and affiliations/abstract/body of text/references—is common to articles in most disciplines. Specific disciplines may require additional structure. Thus the body of the text in an article on an experimental topic may be structured along the lines: introduction/methodology/instrumentation/results/discussion/conclusions.

Good navigation refers to more than text alone. Tables and graphics have to be integrated in with the text. This is often harder than structuring the text alone. For example, captions to photographs are not always well positioned or particularly helpful. Yet, as noted, readers may need most help with photographs. Nor is it only at the article or chapter level that navigation may be suboptimum. An obvious requirement for the cover of a book or journal is that it should be easily visible and convey enough information for readers to be able both to distinguish it from others and to determine what it contains, without difficulty. Publishers try to design covers, often using color, to help this process. Sometimes they get it wrong—for example, employing one pale color on another with resultant loss of contrast. At the next stage, contents pages play a vital role in tracking down the information contained in books and journals. Some publishers have been slow in following best practice as regards layout for these, with more work consequently being placed on the reader.

Overall, structuring of scholarly publications has improved down the years. Compare, for example, the citation by authors of other scholarly material as it is done now and as it was done two hundred years ago. In the first place, an appreciable proportion of the material published then contained few or no references at all. Where they were given, they often appeared in the text, or in footnotes, not collected together at the end, as is commonplace now. There was no standard method of citing references. Sometimes, the work would be cited purely in terms of the person who had been responsible for it, without further information. Hardly surprisingly, readers were occasionally hard put to identify the publications concerned.

The move toward standardization of presentation, as remarked previously, reflects the growing pressures on research communication, more especially as a result of its rapid expansion. This has made it more difficult for readers to find relevant information. Standardization helps with this. As a channel for conveying research information, printed books and journals have therefore changed appreciably with time. The way they look now depends on the nature of research and the history of the research community. It, therefore, embraces a mix of factors ranging from the expectations of the community to developments in printing technology. An obvious example of the latter is the way reports of research have come increasingly to be supported by illustrations. For many years, illustrations of the type that researchers wanted could only be produced in a printable form by highly skilled engravers. Since most researchers did not have the necessary skill, they had to instruct the engraver in what they wanted. The whole activity was costly and time consuming: even so, the end results were not always satisfactory. (Hardly surprisingly, when a good engraving was produced, it might be used to illustrate more than one research publication.) In the nineteenth century, new processes became available, reducing the skill that was necessary to make a reproducible illustration, and, by the early twentieth century, even photographs could be reproduced in books and journals. The difference this makes can readily be seen by comparing journal articles from two hundred years ago with their present-day equivalent. The number and range of the illustrations are now greatly increased. More importantly, they have come directly under the control of the researcher, who may well have produced them all personally.

Readability of Text

The question so far has been how the information channel provided by print-on-paper can be organized in such a way as to aid the user. The design process for books and journals recognizes that extracting information is a compromise between the properties of the medium and the perceptual requirements of readers. The same kind of interaction also occurs with content. What readers absorb from a book or article depends partly on the way it is written and partly on the prior knowledge possessed by the reader. Again, some kind of compromise is usually necessary—in this case, between presenting information in the most easily digestible way and doing justice to its nature. For example, a range of readability formulae have been devised to test in a quantitative way how difficult a piece of text is to read.[3] These formulae have various limitations. One that affects the present discussion is that they have mostly been produced for such material as school textbooks or newspapers rather than research publications. Nevertheless, if the formulae are applied to research material, they certainly suggest that it must be much harder to absorb than the average reading matter of even well-educated readers. (There are exceptions: for example, history books may be written for a wider public than scholars only, and their "readability" then improves.)

Reading formulae are typically based on sentence lengths and the complexity of the words employed. There is evidence to suggest that increases in either of these make it more difficult to absorb information from the printed page. During the past hundred years or more, sentences in scholarly publications have tended to become more difficult in these terms.[4] The sentence lengths depend partly on the complexity of the argument being conveyed and partly on the style of writing. The latter is looked at again in the next chapter, but it should be noted that the passive constructions and related stylistic factors typically used in scholarly contributions add to the difficulty of reading. This is due not only to their structure and greater verbosity, but also because they may introduce an ambiguity the reader has to resolve. Consider the sentence: "Lung cancer death rates are clearly associated with increased smoking." There are a whole series of questions that can be asked about this.[5] Does "associated with" imply a cause or a correlation? Does "increased smoking" mean that people smoke more or that more people smoke? Does "lung cancer death rates" refer to how many people die or to how quickly people die? This is a lot of ambiguity in one apparently innocuous sentence for a reader to resolve.

Though long sentences are certainly harder to read, the problem of absorbing the contents of a sentence is thus a more complicated matter than the length of the sentence alone. The same holds for the problems presented by individual words. All special interests develop their own vocabularies. To a nonaficionado, the sports pages of a newspaper may be mostly incomprehensible. Jargon develops as a shorthand way of describing what is happening. For the jargon to work, it must provide a vivid and illuminating description for the specialist. For example, to most people the names of complex chemical compounds are both meaningless and unmemorable. To a chemist, they immediately throw light on the nature of the compound under discussion. When text is analyzed in terms of the frequency with which different words appear, a distribution, reminiscent of Lotka's law (discussed in the previous chapter), is found. If the words in a reasonably long piece of text are counted and ranked in the order of frequency of their occurrence, this proves to be proportional to the rank order. For example, a word ranked tenth in terms of frequency is used one-tenth as often as the word ranked first. This correlation is known as Zipf's law, but George Zipf, an American philologist, also noted a further correlation.[6] The words that appear most frequently are also, on average, the shortest words. Longer words are therefore both more difficult to absorb and less frequently encountered in text. Even specialists prefer shorter words, if possible. Biochemists use *DNA* rather than *deoxyribonucleic acid* because it saves effort when they are referring to the compound all the time.

The equation of short words with easy reading is only part of the story. Researchers have a great tendency to form new nouns from existing verbs or adjectives. For example, in the days of vacuum valves it was customary to use a chemical substance to remove the final traces of gas from the valve. Since its job was to get hold of the gas, the substance was labeled a "getter"—a verb being used to create a noun. (In this case, the linguistic process went on. A valve so treated was referred to as a "gettered" valve, and the activity was called "gettering," so producing a new verb from the noun.) The nouns produced in this way are often combined with others to form a meaningful cluster: an example has already been quoted—"lung cancer death rate." Though each word in this cluster is short and simple, the reader has to absorb the cluster as a whole. That can be difficult.

Noun clusters illustrate another characteristic of scholarly prose that makes it difficult for a reader to take it in—the high density of the information conveyed. A related problem is the demands that specialist words may make on a reader's mental resources. Understanding and using them properly often requires extensive theoretical underpinning. For example, physicists say that fundamental particles have a property that they call *charm*. The word looks straightforward enough, but to understand its meaning in this context requires an extended theoretical introduction. When the French scientist, Antoine Lavoisier, introduced a new way of naming chemical compounds at the end of the eighteenth century, it required a simultaneous change in theoretical outlook.

> while I thought myself employed only in forming a nomenclature, and while I proposed to myself nothing more than to improve the chemical language, my work transformed itself by degrees, without my being able to prevent it, into a treatise upon the Elements of Chemistry.[7]

The extent to which words and phrases are theory laden depends partly on the subject matter. Research publications dealing with theoretical approaches, whether in physics or literary criticism, naturally tend to have a higher proportion of such words. At a more general level, words are increasingly difficult to absorb in proportion to the number of other entities that have to be defined first. This sort of problem extends beyond words or sentences to entire articles or books. The more abstract or technical a piece of text is, the more difficult it is to follow. This is a major reason why scientific or technological research articles are often more difficult for the reader than humanities articles. The logical style of the former, with its tendency to refer to abstractions, contrasts with the narrative style of the latter, and its emphasis on concrete events and personalities. But the difference is not clear-cut. A philosophy text, for example, may prove more difficult to follow than a science text.

The Act of Reading

Researchers thus bring their backgrounds with them to any text they read. Equally, they bring their own intentions to each reading. They may be looking for particular data, or for general interest, or for references to other work, and so on. Considering a research publication as an information channel, it must, if it is well designed, satisfy the whole range of purposes that readers may have. The readers can then adapt their approaches to the text so as to provide the type of feedback that is appropriate for their particular purposes. One reader, for example, may obtain a general overview of an article by rapid and selective scanning of the text. Another, who is looking for specific data, may concentrate on the sections of the article most likely to contain them. A third, who wants to use the contents for further research, may go through the entire text in detail, taking notes and, perhaps, rereading key sections. Even an individual researcher can decide to examine a specific article in more than one way—perhaps scanning for general understanding first and then reading for detail afterward. Indeed, the researcher may return to the same article again at a later time with different requirements. If so, there is likely to be some change in the accessing methods employed. The form of the printed material must satisfy them all.

A similar range of techniques can be discerned when researchers read whole issues of journals or books. Most readers first scan the contents list, which is why this is usually prominently displayed. If they are dealing with a journal, they may then flick through the entire issue looking for anything that catches the eye. Alternatively, they may turn to a particular article and read the abstract. If this produces all the information they need, they may then move to another article. If not, they may look at section headings, diagrams, and tables within the article. Again, this may give them sufficient information, or they may settle down to read the article more thoroughly. This browsing process allows a researcher to "de-gut" a publication very efficiently. The whole operation is facilitated by the standardized layout and written style of the text.

This raises a vexed question in discussions of reading. Consulting an article or book can mean anything from a casual glance at the contents to a careful reading of the entire text. Should these all be counted as a "reading" of the publication, or ought a line to be drawn somewhere? Surveys of journal readers suggest that, of those who go past the title and abstract, perhaps a third might read half or more of an article.[8] This latter amount can reasonably be used as a definition of a "reading." In these terms, the average mainline U.S. journal article in the sciences and social sciences is read over a hundred times. In some subjects, such as engineering, it may be read several hundred times.

Survey responses of this kind typically relate to the better-known journals, which are naturally the most thoroughly read. As with other information activities, journal reading is statistically skewed, with a limited range of journals attracting most attention. The same is true of articles within journals. Some are extensively read, whereas others receive much less attention. Nevertheless, the quoted number of readings contrasts with the often-heard claim that the average journal article is never read. Sometimes this claim is based on a confusion between reading and citation. It is true that many research publications are never cited, but it cannot be deduced from that, that they are never read. Looked at another way, dismissing readings that take in less than half the contents is surely too rigorous. Readers extract the information they want: if that entails covering only part of an article, it does not make the information less useful. For example, chemical articles are typically short, and chemists quite often find that the abstract of an article contains all they need to know. However "reading" is defined, it is apparent that significant journals (and major monographs) are well read and represent major sources of information.

The process of reading has been discussed in detail because researchers devote so much time to the activity. A study of biological researchers, for example, found that about half spent more than four hours a week reading relevant literature, and other surveys have found longer times still.[9] (The range for different individuals in the same research field is great, so average values have to be treated with caution.) Up to half the time is devoted to journals, and the remainder to books, reports, etc. There are differences from subject to subject, with humanities researchers typically devoting more time to books. The average length of time spent on the journal articles that are deemed worth reading in detail varies from half an hour upward. Again, there are systematic differences from subject to subject, with mathematics articles requiring the lengthiest reading, presumably due to their level of complexity.[10] These estimates refer to researchers whose native language is English and who are reading English-language literature. The amount of foreign-language material that English-language researchers read tends to be small (except in the humanities), and it naturally tends to take longer to read. Equally, researchers in countries where the native language is not English require longer reading times in order to cope with English-language material.[11]

One thing apparent from looking at reading activities is that some researchers are much more information-active than the average. These committed readers are often also more research-active, so both their consumption and production of information is above average. Their hyperactivity can sometimes be disguised because they are using so many channels to access information. For example, they may use libraries less than other researchers who are less information-active. This does not necessarily reflect a lower level of information usage. Such people often receive personal copies of more journals than the average or hear about developments in the literature to a greater extent from their research students and staff, so they have less need to visit the library. In any case, most researchers do a fair amount of their reading at home. One survey found that, for those who reported reading outside of office hours, 65% of their browsing through journals, and 85% of their careful reading of journals, was done mainly at home in the evening.[12] (When traveling was another, but much less popular, time.) Longer documents, such as books, are even more likely to be read at home, though humanities scholars also do more reading in libraries than their scientific colleagues. The balance between time spent on books and on journals varies with the subject, but these two sources generally outweigh—for academic researchers, at least—other formal sources of information.

Publishers

Reading journals and books corresponds to the output end of the print-on-paper communication channel. At the input end is the author; between authors and readers come two groups whose task is to organize the transfer of information as efficiently as possible. The first of these groups is the publishers. Their job is to take the authors'' work, put it together in a way that is acceptable to readers, and then disseminate the results. The second group consists of librarians and information staff. They codify and store the material coming from publishers so as to make it accessible to readers. This basic division of the print communication channel between the production and the organization of the material has been there from the early days of research communication, but it has become increasingly sophisticated with time.

Looking at the first group in more detail, it is apparent that publishers are involved in three main types of activity. They must first interact with authors to make sure that their material is suitable for publication and is written acceptably. For scholarly publications, assessment of suitability is carried out mainly by the research community itself. This process is discussed as a part of "quality control" in the next chapter. The next stage is the physical production of the book or journal: at this point, questions affecting layout and legibility are decided. In the early days of publishing, publishers and printers were often the same people. In some cases, this combined activity continued into the twentieth century, but publishers and printers are now usually distinct entities, so production entails cooperation. The final activity—dissemination—involves marketing, as well as the actual physical distribution of the printed products. The concern of marketing is that all potential purchasers are aware of the existence of the publication concerned. Physical distribution often involves the publisher with other intermediary groups, more especially bookshops and subscription agents.

As we have seen, the main products of scholarly publishing are journals and books. Journals, as distinct from magazines, have a history rooted in scholarly interests and are dominated by them. In terms of sales, scholarly books do not correspondingly dominate the market for books, though they contribute significantly in terms of the number of titles produced. (The difference is due to the fact that the average scholarly title is produced as a short run.) Three main types of publishers are involved in the provision of scholarly books and journals—commercial publishers; university and other institutional presses; learned and professional societies and associations.

Commercial publishers with a scholarly output come in various shapes and sizes. The larger ones, such as Elsevier or Springer, spread themselves across both books and journals, and across a wide range of fields. Their predominant concern is scientific, technological, and medical (STM) publications. STM books and journals can be priced more highly than those in other fields, and they have higher sales, not least because they have an international public. Smaller commercial publishers tend to select particular niches and concentrate on them. They, too, have some preference for STM or professional (e.g., legal) subject matter, but some have specialized successfully in the social sciences and the humanities. Books in these latter areas do occasionally have the potential to generate general interest, which can lead to major sales.

The prototype university presses are traditionally those of Oxford and Cambridge in the UK, but, these two apart, it is in the United States that university press publishing has been most important. Unlike commercial publishers, many university presses pay special attention to producing books in the social sciences and the humanities: in these fields they are often a dominant influence. University presses were set up to provide outlets at universities for scholarly research that would otherwise be difficult to publish. This reflected the situation in countries like the United States and the UK, where universities are major generators of research. In some countries, research is dominated by work at special institutes rather than in universities. In such countries, university presses are typically less important and may be replaced by other institutional presses. In France, for example, CNRS, which controls a number of research institutes, also acts as a scholarly publisher.

Many learned and professional societies publish books, as well as journals. Indeed, some of the larger societies, such as the American Institute of Physics and its British equivalent, have significant book publishing programs within their fields. In addition, there are some societies, primarily in the humanities, that were created specifically in order to produce books. For example, two new societies were formed in London during the 1860s. One, the Early English Text Society, was concerned with producing scholarly editions of old English literature. The other, the Harleian Society, was devoted to editing and publishing manuscript material relating to genealogy, family history, and heraldry. Both became important sources of information in their chosen fields. However, it is in the journal publishing field that societies are most significant. Their domination is not in terms of number of titles. A typical research library in North America or Western Europe will subscribe to more titles from commercial publishers than from learned societies. But the prestigious journals to which the research community gives most weight are particularly to be found among the learned society titles.

The in-house operations of scholarly publishers require personnel with a range of specialist skills. Editors are needed for a number of purposes—to commission new material (for books, rather than journals), to assess content, to prepare material for the printers, and to assist with the business and marketing activities. At a large publishing house, each of these activities may be assigned to different people; but small publishers will expect an editor to cover a range of these jobs. One difference from much general trade editing is the need for subject background. Scholarly editors must know enough of their field to be able to edit and correct material intelligently. They must above all be able to cooperate with their research community. Thus a commissioning editor must be acquainted with a wide range of researchers and be able to converse with them about the publisher's requirements. Expert advice is essential in scholarly publishing: fashions in research can change, and the gestation time for scholarly books may be long. (University presses relish stories of elderly professors who bring along manuscripts contracted for in their youth.) These various demands mean that in-house editorial staff have often had some kind of training in the general subject area of their work. Editorial staff on journals naturally have to deal with many authors, but so do editors of the multiauthor books, book series, and conference proceedings that are commonplace in the scholarly world.

In all these cases, there is likely to be an in-house editor together with an external editor who is a specialist in the research field concerned. The overall effect is to produce considerable interdependence between the publishing house and the scholarly community.

Scholarly publishing was traditionally a national activity. Markets elsewhere were obviously recognized, but they were rarely systematically exploited. In the past fifty years, this situation has changed. The growth of research—more especially of STM research, which is potentially of worldwide interest—and the increasing use of English for communication has led to an internationalization of scholarly publishing. Leading STM journals often have a considerably higher proportion of their sales outside their country of origin than within it. Learned society publishers have, on the whole, retained their separate national identities, although several have set up links with each other. One example of this transnational trend is the designation of some journals in Western Europe as "Eurojournals." A considerable number of societies have contracts with commercial publishers—not necessarily in their own country—to carry out activities (e.g., negotiation with printers and distribution) where they are not confident that they have the necessary in-house expertise. In contrast with the relative stability of learned society publishers, the recent history of commercial scholarly publishers has been a good deal more turbulent. Many have been involved in mergers and acquisitions as they have tried to position themselves within the international market. The obvious example is the acquisition of Pergamon (the second largest producer of journal titles) by Elsevier (the largest producer). This jockeying for position is not over yet: it is being exacerbated by current uncertainties regarding electronic publishing.

The position for scholarly books is rather different, not least because English-language scholarly books are less dominant internationally than English-language journals. There are various reasons for this, ranging from the problems of reading long stretches of text in a foreign language to the fact that many scholarly books relate to topics in the social sciences or humanities that do not travel well. The main market for English-language books is the United States, and it also dominates the export trade in scholarly books. In 1984, the United States exported nearly 34 million copies of STM and professional books (topics that tend to travel well) with a value of $154 million; by 1991, this had increased to 72 million copies worth $466 million.[13] In the years since the Second World War, it is these types of books that have shown the most rapid growth of sales within the United States, as well as for export. Hardly surprisingly, scholarly publishers from elsewhere, more especially

Europe, have tried to establish a presence on the North American scene (while U.S. publishers have naturally looked in the reverse direction). Initial attempts to establish a presence in a foreign country have often involved setting up an office there, but with policy still directed from the home country. In some cases—Oxford University Press is an early example—the office has evolved into a quasi-separate publisher, formulating its own policy. This latter approach is reflected in the more recent popularity of gaining entry by acquisition of, or merger with, a company within the country concerned. The process has gone on to the extent that most researchers are now thoroughly confused as to which publishing company is owned by whom.

Publishing scholarly books presents particular problems for countries where the indigenous language is not widely spoken elsewhere. Japan, with its large, well-educated population and well-established publishing industry, can provide its own scholarly publishing infrastructure. India, too, has a fair publishing infrastructure. It faces the different problem of having a range of indigenous languages, which are mutually incomprehensible. As a result, though only 2% of the population can read English, about half of the books are published in that language. At least with scholarly publishing there is the advantage that most researchers can read English. The corresponding disadvantage, of course, is that Indian publications may be in competition with those from English-language countries. However, the position in India is better than in some developing countries. These face similar difficulties, but with little by the way of a publishing infrastructure and less tradition of research training in a major world language. One consequence is that many of these countries have a program of translations. Even in Japan, many more scholarly books are translated into the Japanese language than out of it. For most developing countries, one drawback of this approach is the need to pay the original publisher, often in hard currency.

Libraries

If publishers come first in terms of influencing the flow of scholarly material through the print-on-paper communication channel, libraries come a good second. They are the most important purchasers of scholarly publications, both books and journals, so their decisions affect publishers, as well as readers. In the UK, for example, university libraries purchased nearly 2,700,000 books during the academic year 1994–1995, together with some 600,000 journal titles. This may be compared with all the special libraries and information units in the UK, which acquired over an equivalent period nearly 1,200,000 books and just under 600,000 journal titles. (*Special libraries* here designates the information units that service industrial and commercial enterprises, government departments and establishments, hospitals, professional societies, museums, etc.) By no means were all the books purchased related to research or development work, but it is safe to assume that most of the journals were. Special libraries are primarily concerned with acquiring STM and professional material: acquisition of material in the humanities and social sciences mainly falls to the lot of the universities. This, along with the purchase of student course material, is the main reason why journal purchases were similar between the two groups, but book purchases differed greatly.

Special libraries and universities are the most significant purchasers of scholarly books and journals, but some other institutions—more especially national libraries—maintain extensive collections. Owing to the growth of scholarly publishing during the twentieth century, few libraries, other than national libraries, can hope to have reasonably complete coverage of relevant research publications. In consequence, both university and special libraries seek to support their own purchases by borrowing from other libraries. Because of the size of their collections, national libraries are often important contributors to such interlibrary lending schemes. In the UK, for example, the British Library has a Document Supply Centre. In 1993–1994, this Centre received nearly four million requests for material. Of these, nearly three million were requests from other institutions within the UK, far more than all other interlibrary loans in the country. Some two-thirds of the material requested from the Document Supply Centre actually related to journals. Most of this was supplied in the form of photocopies rather than physical loans. Publishers have long been afraid that such provision of material must affect the sales of their publications, more especially the number of journal subscriptions. In fact, most studies down the years have found that document delivery services tend to supplement rather than replace existing journal purchases. Given an appropriate charging system, they can therefore form an additional source of income for publishers. The interesting question now is whether publishers and document delivery services might cooperate in a similarly advantageous way in the provision of electronic publications to readers.

Libraries have two basic functions—to archive publications and to make them available to readers. These functions are obviously related. Unless the publications are properly stored and organized, they can hardly be made readily accessible. Acquiring material begins with the selection process. This typically involves negotiation between library staff and research staff in their institutions. In some institutions and countries, decisions are taken with little reference to library staff, whereas in some others, library staff may dominate the discussion; but where research material is concerned, researchers almost always have the final word on acquisitions. The actual process of acquisition may be handled in various ways, depending on the size and complexity of the operation. A small information unit may purchase its books and journals directly from the publishers. Larger libraries are more likely to turn to intermediaries—subscription agents for journals and wholesalers for their book supply. These intermediaries take over the strain of negotiating with numerous publishers scattered over a range of countries. Though they must obviously be paid, there is a corresponding saving on in-house labor in the library.

The agents may also assist with the next stage, which involves classifying and cataloging the incoming material. These processes have to mesh with the way researchers think about knowledge and so guide them both conceptually and physically to the publications they need. Until quite recently, individual libraries tackled this task according to their preferences. Now, in countries with well-established electronic networks, they are more likely to link with each other, and with intermediaries, to carry out joint cataloging, so that overlapping parts of collections do not need to be treated many times in different libraries.

One advantage of cooperation is that it can speed up library operations. It takes time to acquire publications. Overseas purchases, in particular, may suffer long delays between ordering and arrival. There is then a further wait while publications are cataloged before they reach the library shelves. Cooperation can shorten this delay. New books are often displayed on special shelves for a short period before they are borrowed or go into the main collection. Similarly, new issues of journals are usually put on separate display, until the next issue arrives. Generally, new journal issues are more noticeable (they are put cover up, whereas books only have their spine on show) and they stay on display longer (since most appear monthly, or at longer intervals). Consequently, browsing through new journal issues can be easier than browsing through shelves of new books.

From this point on in the progress of the material, much of the library assistance to readers is routine. Such activities as issuing books or restoring publications to their proper places on the shelves are straightforward. However, they illustrate one of the fundamental features of information handling: delays or inaccuracies at a low level can be more frustrating for researchers seeking information than many problems at a higher level. Thus a misplaced book can effectively be lost for months. Another routine activity is binding, typically of a set of journal issues into a single volume. If it is carried out at the wrong time, it can remove from circulation material that researchers want to consult urgently. Hence, simple, behind-the-scenes operations in libraries can offer a significant barrier to information transfer unless they are efficiently planned and executed.

Most research-oriented libraries try to cater for the needs of their users by having subject specialists on their staff. This is a straightforward operation for special libraries, since they only cover a limited range of subjects. For example, pharmaceutical firms normally expect their information staff, like their research staff, to have backgrounds in chemistry or biochemistry. University libraries, however, must cover all the subjects provided at their universities. Applicants for posts in university libraries are most likely to have backgrounds in the humanities or social sciences, which can lead to problems in providing close support for scientists and engineers. It does mean that university libraries usually have staff who can cope with foreign-language material in their collections. However, financial restrictions in recent years have led to cutbacks in such material, especially in STM subjects. This increasing tendency to acquire publications in the national language plus English (if not the national language), means that readers can usually handle much of it themselves.

A prime function of libraries is to act as depositories so that researchers have access to information published in the past, as well as that currently appearing. This immediately raises queries about storage space. The growth of research literature chronicled in Chapter 1 means not only that a research library must have an increasing amount of storage space available as time passes but that it must become available at an increasingly rapid rate. Various methods have been devised for cramming more publications into the same space, often by storing less-used material separately, but that hardly offers a complete solution. A further problem relates to the conservation of the stored material. To keep it in good condition requires a controlled environment. In some cases—for example, books printed on acid paper—it entails individual attention to each item. A library that possesses a large collection must devote considerable funding and staff time simply to maintaining what is there. Inevitably, this leads to increasing pressure to limit the size of the collection, typically by weeding out little-used material. Such disposal is a regular feature in most special libraries. In university libraries, it is often more difficult to carry out because future research needs are more diffuse. In either case, disposal is based on the assumption that interlibrary lending will supply the missing items, should there be a subsequent demand for them from readers.

In many developing countries, questions of library space are less urgent. Collections are often limited in extent and are growing less rapidly than those in developed countries. Conservation, on the contrary, is more important. Developing countries often have a climate that exacerbates the deterioration of printed material, and control of library environments is not always feasible. In any case, the libraries often suffer from more immediate problems. Not all material ordered is delivered: some may be lost in transit, either by theft or defects in the delivery service. Even if they arrive, deliveries from foreign publishers can take a long time in transit. When they finally turn up, librarians may see no reason for urgency in processing them for readers. Indeed, librarians in many developing countries tend to see their work in traditional terms, as conservers of knowledge, so their interaction with researchers is often less fruitful than in developed countries.

Oral Communication

The need for some degree of informal interaction between librarians and their readers is a particular instance of a more general rule. For efficient communication of research information, formal printed sources must be complemented by informal (usually oral) sources. We can note first some of the disadvantages of oral communication. As a method of conveying research information, talking has more limitations than writing. Speech can be produced more quickly than writing, but written information can be absorbed more speedily. Reading an article will provide more information in less time than listening to a talk on its contents. Visual aids are used with talks partly to increase this throughput of information, but also partly to counteract another deficiency of spoken communication—the problems it encounters in trying to transmit systematic information of the type found in tables or diagrams. Since the amount of such information is subject dependent, some research is harder to present orally than others. A talk on physics, for example, will normally require considerable visual assistance.

Readers can jump backward and forward when absorbing textual material, rereading parts that are particularly difficult to follow. Speech presents information in a strictly linear way. Unless a talk is being recorded, there is no method for backtracking. For this reason, talks require a higher level of redundancy than articles: saying the same thing in different ways substitutes for nonlinear reading of text. This is the basis for the traditional advice to lecturers: "Tell 'em what you're going to tell 'em, then tell 'em, then tell 'em what you've told 'em."

Speech also suffers from problems parallel to those of legibility and readability in printed texts. A speaker whose voice can hardly be heard is on a par with a text whose letters are too small to be read. Similarly, a pronounced accent—regional or due to speaking in a foreign language—is a little like a typeface that differs too much from the normal for easy reading. It is more difficult to draw parallels with readability. It is true that large numbers of complex words offer the same problem to listeners as to readers. The equivalent to sentence length is less obvious. There is no marker in speech like a full-stop in writing: even pauses are not always logically placed.

As Table 26 indicates, speech is appreciably less formal—that is, more like ordinary communication—than written presentations of research.[14] The extent of the difference depends on the type of oral presentation: a research lecture uses more formal language than a casual conversation. Spoken presentations of research do not usually attain the same level of integration as written presentations, nor do they normally seek the same level of detachment. Again this can vary, depending on the subject matter. Narrative material, for example, can usually be presented more informally than a sequence of logical arguments.

The difficulties of spoken presentation are clear enough: what about the advantages? A major one is that the research is presented by its originator, who can draw attention to items of particular importance or difficulty in a more helpful way than is possible via a written text. The overwhelming advantage, however, is that spoken presentations allow for feedback. It is customary with talks to allow time for questions at the end, and it is also often possible to speak with the lecturer after the talk is over. In fact, the value of feedback becomes increasingly evident as contact becomes more

Table 26
Differences between a Conversation and a Scientific Text
(Expressed in Frequency Counts per 100 Words)

	Passive constructions	First- and second-person pronouns	Word contractions
Conversation	0	10.2	5.1
Scientific text	6.8	0	0

informal. As compared with books or articles, discussion has a number of virtues. These might be summarized as: immediate feedback, information adapted to the recipient, implications spelt out, and "know-how" transmitted along with conceptual knowledge. It is hardly surprising that surveys of researchers' use of communication channels find that discussion with colleagues ranks along with journals and books as a prime method of acquiring information.

We are saying that speaking, like reading, is an interactive process, so some of the same points must apply. More particularly that what is gained from a discussion depends on what is brought to it. The difference is that a face-to-face discussion involves a social relationship, whereas interaction with the printed page does not. Anyone can try to make sense of a research article, but it takes a modicum of courage for a research student to strike up a conversation with an eminent researcher. Even within a cohesive research group, discussion is not entirely unstructured. The potential limitations are reflected in the following description of life at a research institute.

> It is an unwritten law that everyone attend morning and afternoon tea in the cafeteria. This ritual is seen as having a socially binding effect, encouraging people to see themselves as a part of the Institute, and not just their Unit or Laboratory . . . . The first year trainee technicians are simply never seated at the same table as the Manager, Instrument Officer and long-serving senior technicians, who usually take their tea together. Whilst the technicians tend to sit with one another, they can also be seen at tables made up of the scientific staff of their own Laboratory—which is the commonest arrangement among the scientists themselves. There is also a temporal and spatial distribution. Thus the lower ranking social groups (who start work earliest) arrive first and sit at the rear of the room. Next come the technicians working in animal and service areas, again sitting at tables toward the rear, followed by the laboratory technicians. Their arrival overlaps with that of the scientists taking the opportunity to button-hole people working in other Units. However the social structure of the tea room is rigid enough for people who don't fit neatly into any of the groups to find the tea ritual a most uncomfortable experience. Only the Director has no home base, moving from table to table with ease.[15]

As this scene suggests, discussions naturally occur most readily when researchers congregate together. Thus one study found that exchanges were especially likely to occur around the middle of the day and also around the middle of the week.[16] The former tendency can be linked to the lunch break. The latter may tie in with the holding of seminars, since Wednesday is a popular day for these. (According to academic legend, this is in order not to break into either of the weekends.) Unlike reading, which is often preferentially done at home in the evening, discussion is obviously easier in the workplace and so is more likely to happen during the day. As with reading, some information is picked up from the general discussion (the equivalent of browsing), whereas some comes from specific questioning, often formulated in outline beforehand. Oral communication has greater flexibility for information-gathering purposes than written communication: it can also be used for a greater range of actions, such as planning for future research or encouraging the work of others.

Conversation does not have to be face to face: it can be via a telephone. Discussion of research on the telephone is commonplace but usually considerably less important than face-to-face discussions. A survey of British biologists found that over 90% involved themselves in direct discussion of their research with colleagues, but less than 50% made a similar use of the telephone for research discussions.[17] A study of U.S. biologists concluded, moreover, that although extensive use of the telephone led to an increased success in tracking down information, it led to no appreciable growth in productivity.[18] This lesser popularity and value of telephone conversation may be partly because it is unable to transmit nonverbal communication. In ordinary conversation, successful interaction depends on interpreting the body language of the participants. The British biologists were asked about their use of informal communication channels. Table 27 indicates the proportion who had used the various channels for the communication of research information during the previous year.

Table 27
Use of Informal Communication Channels for Research Information by
Biological Researchers

Channel	University agricultural faculty (%)	University biological faculty (%)	Research establishment (%)	Pharmaceutical laboratory (%)
Face-to-face discussion	95	92	88	89
Telephone	51	42	43	44
Fax	43	38	35	34
Correspondence	53	30	35	16
Electronic mail	15	21	17	32
Conferences	11	10	4	10

Conferences

Conferences are the epitome of informal interaction. Oral interaction ranges from a talk presented before a large audience to casual conversations at coffee breaks. Attenders at conferences often claim that they come not to attend the scheduled presentations but to talk to colleagues. Nevertheless, most people attend at least a few of the talks, though not necessarily purely for their content. It is, for example, one way of identifying and assessing contributors, who may then be approached informally outside the lecture theater. One reason for not attending lecture sessions is that the researcher already has a general idea of the work to be reported. This arises from previous oral dissemination to smaller gatherings, such as research seminars, or written dissemination, as via reports or theses.

There seems to be a balance of activities that depends on the scale of the conference, with larger conferences involving more discussion outside the lecture theater, and less attendance within. This is not altogether surprising, since the larger conferences are national or international in scope and give the opportunity to meet geographically distant colleagues. An international research union may only have a general meeting once every three years, which makes it a major landmark for informal exchanges in the subject. Smaller conferences, sometimes restricted to invited participants only, can be much more focused, and the scheduled sessions then become more important.

The more frequently researchers attend conferences, the less likely they are to gain something new from them. Frequent attenders tend to be senior researchers, who are most likely to know already of new developments in their subject. Their presence may be because they are society officers or have been invited to give talks, rather than from a particular keenness to attend the conference. The material contained in conference talks is usually up to date, stemming from research that has been completed not too long prior to the conference. The people who usually gain most from listening therefore tend to be junior researchers, who are less likely to have prior knowledge of the research. At the larger conferences, a significant proportion of the audience also consists of more senior researchers who are hoping to learn of developments in specialisms that are tangential to their own interests. Attenders at conferences may plan to make particular contacts beforehand, but also often make unexpected, but useful, contacts during the course of the conference.

In general terms, perhaps half the attenders are likely to pick up useful information outside of the scheduled sessions.[19] Some 20% of attenders meet new acquaintances who provide worthwhile information subsequent to the conference. The commonest kind of information provided (other than transcripts of the talks) is either "know-how" or stimulating ideas.

A major problem with many conferences is the excessive number of talks that are given. Part of the reason is that, for employers as a whole, payment of funding to participants has, in recent years, often depended on the applicant giving a talk. This not only introduces an information overload for listeners, it also leads to a reduced time for the presentation of each talk, so affecting their comprehensibility still further. Experiments have been tried to increase interaction between the presenters of talks and their potential audiences: a popular one in recent years has been the introduction of poster sessions. In these, the presenters do not give talks, but pin up printed synopses of their research on boards, by which they then stand. Other participants at the conference walk around scanning the boards and, if they wish, discussing the synopses with their authors. The great advantage of such sessions is that participants can concentrate on the contributions that particularly interest them and follow them up immediately with face-to-face discussions. One drawback is that the value of poster sessions is higher for some subjects than others. They work best where the subject matter is practical and graphics oriented: for example, they are popular at biochemical meetings. There is also sometimes a feeling that this kind of presentation is only second best, since poster sessions at conferences are often combined with a traditional program of talks. Nevertheless, they have proved a successful way of exposing new researchers to information activities at conferences.

Most researchers, including many in developing countries, go to conferences at least once a year. The consequences in information terms are significant. A survey of British scientists found that over 90% had obtained useful information from attending conferences in the previous six months.[20] Even more had acquired information from the published proceedings of conferences. Talks at conferences and sometimes the subsequent discussion of them, frequently appear later as collected publications, either in book form or as a special issue of a relevant journal. There has been considerable criticism of such publications, usually on the grounds of the quality of the reported work. The truth of this claim depends on the nature of the conference. A prestigious meeting with carefully refereed contributions can rank high as a source of information. The same can be true of a smaller conference devoted to a particular theme with invited speakers. Lightly refereed, general conferences can provide material of a more variable quality.

In part, the value of published conference proceedings depends on whether the research discussed at the conference will subsequently be published elsewhere. Perhaps half of the research reported at conferences eventually appears via other outlets. The extent depends on the people involved and the field. Academics, for example, are usually keener than (say) industrial researchers to see their work in print. So they may pursue publication in journals, as well as, or instead of, in a conference publication. In a professional field, such as engineering, articles in refereed conference proceedings rate alongside journal articles in importance. So engineers are less likely to seek publication via other routes. Publishing conferences proceedings can take some time, so they are less useful in rapidly changing fields. (Against this, publishing through other outlets after the conference can sometimes take even longer.) Many conferences provide attenders with collected abstracts of the talks or even with complete manuscripts. So even if they do not go to the talks, attenders can have an adequate knowledge of what was going on.

Human Networks

Researchers thus have available a variety of opportunities for oral exchanges concerning their work, ranging from discussions with a colleague in the next room to contact with foreign researchers at international conferences. The extent and frequency of such contacts tends to have a skew distribution across researchers. Eminent researchers typically act as important foci for informal information exchanges, just as they do for formal exchanges. Thus studies of who obtains information from whom typically find that a few names are mentioned more often than the remainder.[21] The eminent researchers themselves especially favor contacts with other eminent researchers in their field. In the academic world, most of these latter will be in other higher education institutions both at home and abroad. The picture of informal communication that this suggests is essentially hierarchical, with the leading roles taken by groups of well-known senior people in each speciality.

> The people in such a group claim to be reasonably in touch with everyone else who is contributing materially to research in this subject, not merely on a national scale, but usually including all other countries in which that speciality is strong. The body of people meet in select confer-

ences (usually held in rather pleasant places), they commute between one centre and another, and they circulate preprints and reprints to each other and they collaborate in research.[22]

Such groupings have been variously labeled—invisible colleges, social circles, and so on. These terms are not identical in meaning: they reflect differing views of how the system works. However, they are all applicable to a picture of informal communication based on a preferred set of contacts. The commonest picture envisages a two-stage process—informal communication between individuals and research groups and informal communication within research groups. Information-active researchers—often the same people as the highly productive researchers of the last chapter—are the central actors in research groups. They play a leading role in communication both within and between groups. Their contacts with other groups are with the leading researchers there. These are the people who are usually in mind when an "invisible college" is mentioned. As one investigation of a research specialism observed:

> From the viewpoint of communication, these key scientists are nodal points for the dissemination of information. On average, they are in contact with five times as many scientists as others and account for 83% of the contacts between research centers. Information transmitted to central scientists is so situated that it could be transmitted to 95% of the scientists in the network through one intermediary or less.[23]

Though this type of picture is a useful guide, it rarely reflects the entire situation. For example, the relative amounts of internal and external communication, and who is involved, will depend on such factors as the size and composition of the group. A large research group usually generates many of its research exchanges internally. A small research group may not generate an acceptable flow of research information internally, so members look outside the group for information exchanges. At the same time, most researchers have an upper limit to the number of people with whom they can maintain regular exchanges of information. The original estimates of the likely size of an invisible college suggested this upper limit might be a hundred people. However, it is unlikely that many researchers are in frequent contact with this number. Judging from the behavior of teams working in a variety of fields, close contacts are not likely to exceed some twenty people for most researchers. Along with this inner group, there will be a much larger range of looser contacts, which may well reach a hundred people or more.

The number and nature of contacts can vary with group composition.

Thus a group consisting of older, more experienced researchers is likely to have a different pattern of communication from one mainly made up of younger researchers. For example, more members in the former case are likely to have their own set of external contacts. In terms of information collection, the larger the number of contacts, the better. Hence, in principle, links between members of an invisible college should look like a fully interconnected network for optimum information transfer. In practice, such total linkage is unwieldy and may be wasteful, in the sense that the really significant information can be gathered via fewer contacts. Hence, there tend to be groupings even within an invisible college structure.

The communication network within a single research group is different. It typically resembles either a star configuration with the group leader as the main dispenser of information, or a tree configuration, with the leader at the apex. This is an efficient way of disseminating information, but the group members (other than the leader) are typically less happy with this type of information transfer than with a more densely connected network. The resultant problems may be reflected in the disputes that can break out within large research groups (as has been recorded, for example, in high-energy physics[24]).

Table 28 compares ratings of the barriers to informal communication, as seen by the heads of research units and by their staff.[25] In general, the agreement is good (though heads, hardly surprisingly, are more worried about time constraints). The importance attached to differences in educational background seems to relate to the different sorts of language and knowledge deployed by different groups within the units (e.g., "researcher speak" versus "technician speak"). The promotion and reward system tends to act as a con-

Table 28
Barriers to Informal Communication in Research Units

Factor involved	Rating by head of unit	Rating by member of unit
Difference in educational background	1	2
Promotion and reward system	2	1
Time pressures	3	6
Hierarchical structure	4	3
Poor social relationships	5	4
Professional rivalry	6	5
Physical distance from colleagues	7	6
General mistrust	8	7

trol on what, and how much, information is exchanged. The fact that professional rivalry ranks well below reward as a barrier implies that, without the competition engendered by a desire for promotion, information would be interchanged more freely. The problems associated with a hierarchical structure and with poor social relationships seem to go hand in hand. They, along with any feeling of mutual mistrust, can be linked to the sort of communication patterns within the unit that its head allows to develop. The physical distance from colleagues is not rated highly here, perhaps because most members of the units surveyed were housed together.

As geographers have long since demonstrated, contact between groups typically falls off as the inverse square of their distance apart. Consequently, interaction between research groups situated in different buildings some distance apart may be much less than when they are housed in the same building. Indeed, there is evidence that vertical distance is an even more effective barrier than horizontal distance, so that two groups in the same building, but on different floors, may communicate appreciably less than when they are on the same floor.

Studies of informal communication in different research specialities have shown that they can have widely varying communication structures. Even where something like an invisible college structure is discernible, the main participants are likely to have as many regular research communicants outside this structure as within it. In general, an invisible college framework is likely to be favored where there are well-established research groups situated in a limited number of institutions. These should contain leading researchers who have a long-term commitment to the specialism and who recruit new researchers to continue work in the field. Though such conditions are most obviously satisfied by a scientific specialism, such as high-energy physics, they can also be found in some areas of the social sciences and humanities. (An example is the French-language grouping devoted to the study of "bibliologie.") Though a number of the invisible colleges are international in outreach, there are some limitations on this, not least because research resources and environments differ. Such communication factors as language can also play a role. Where, as with the old Soviet Union, both the political environment and the language told against international interaction, informal communication of the invisible college-type was limited.

One factor that is important, even within a single country, is the need to acquire informal information efficiently. In a rapidly changing field, it is necessary to be aware of new developments as soon as possible. Communication via invisible colleges can be an effective way of providing the necessary information. A particular specialism rarely grows at a constant rate. Correspondingly, an invisible college communication structure may be appropriate at some stages in the lifetime of a specialism, but not at others.

Invisible colleges and similar types of groupings are probably best viewed as differing methods of organizing interaction. They may change as the nature of the research and its environment change. To the extent that such groupings are concerned with informal communication, they suggest that three basic principles are at work.[26] Lower status researchers are more likely to seek information from higher status researchers than conversely. Higher status researchers are more likely to seek information from other higher status researchers than from lower status researchers. Higher status researchers are particularly active in information exchange. All these are tendencies, rather than absolutes, and depend on such factors as the information being exchanged. For example, (higher status) supervisors may rely on their (lower status) research students for information on new publications of interest.

Information Flows

One common way of investigating communication within a group or organization is to examine who consults whom when they stand in need of information. Such an investigation usually leads to the identification of a limited number of people who are particularly active as information foci. Who they prove to be can depend on the nature of the information. For example, a departmental secretary may be an important focus for general information, but not for research-related information. The researchers previously labeled "high producers" almost always figure on the list, but it is often not confined to them. In industry, for example, research administrators may be important sources of information. Various terms have been used in the literature for such communication foci. One frequently encountered word is *gatekeeper.* This description is intended to conjure up a picture of someone standing amid a flow of information. As each enquirer comes along, the gatekeeper opens the gate to allow through those items of information that are relevant to the particular enquiry. A gatekeeper must obviously have access to a range of information sources both within and outside the employing institution. The sources may be both formal and informal, but the information transfer from gatekeeper to enquirer is via informal channels. It should be added that a very broad definition of gatekeeper is being used here. More restricted definitions (along with other terms) can be found in the literature.

At the other end of the scale, investigations of group communication typically unearth information *isolates* (i.e., people who are rarely, if ever, approached for information). Such people are not usually found within cohesive research groups, but are common within larger organizational groupings. Isolation may be due to personal choice—for example, because the person concerned has a greater interest in teaching than research—but it can also be due to external factors. Thus if a university department has only one specialist in a particular research field, he or she may have reduced opportunities for informal contacts with fellow-specialists. This leads to fewer opportunities for collaboration and, often, less recognition from peers in the same field. How serious being an isolate of this kind is depends on the research field. The more important research groups are, the more serious geographical isolation is likely to be. Hence, isolates in science are likely to have their research activities more affected than isolates in the humanities.

Both gatekeepers and isolates are minority groups. The majority of researchers in any organization both ask questions of a moderate number of their colleagues and receive a moderate number of queries in return. Moreover, the picture is not static. It partly depends on organizational structure. Thus a gatekeeper who is transferred to another position within the organization may cease to be a gatekeeper. Yet it is also a personal attribute. People who do not obviously occupy a gatekeeper position in an organization may be so information-active that their colleagues turn to them for information. As this suggests, there may well be a mismatch between the formal structure of an organization and the flow of information. The formal information generated (e.g., via memos) is usually distributed in a way that reflects the hierarchical structure of the organization. Though the informal information flows may have some links with this hierarchy, they rarely show an identical structure.

Various ways of modeling information flow through groups or populations have been proposed. Most look at what happens when a new item of information appears. (They are often generalizable to formal, as well as informal, information flows.) The simplest model sees information transfer as a diffusion process. When a lump of sugar is dissolved in a coffee cup, the sugar, as it dissolves, gradually diffuses outward through the coffee. The time taken to reach any point in the coffee depends on its distance from the sugar lump. The analogy for information is that, when new information is generated, it will be picked up quickly by those researchers most immediately concerned, then more and more slowly by those whose research interests are increasingly divergent. For example, Shannon's classic work on information theory in communications engineering appeared in 1948. It was referred to by psychologists in 1949 and by researchers in biology, linguistics, physics, physiology, and sociology a year later. By 1955, the work had been mentioned in at least 17 major research fields spread across the sciences and social sciences.[27]

Diffusion looks at information transfer as a global process. It can also be modeled at a more individual level. For example, the transmission of research information has been compared with the progress of a disease through a population. At any one time, the population will contain three groups of people—those with the disease, who can infect others; those who have had the disease, but are no longer infective; those who have not yet been infected. Substituting *information* for *disease* leads to three parallel groups— those who have information on a research topic and are able to impart it; those who have the information, but are not available (e.g., due to a change of location or research interest); those who have yet to receive the information. The extensive theoretical modeling of epidemics can therefore be applied to this situation. It has been used, for example, to explain changing levels of interest in a particular research topic.[28]

Such quantitative models can be helpful as aids to thinking about some types of communication activity. The situations to which they can be applied with confidence tend to be limited in number. Thus epidemic theory supposes that all "infected" people are equally likely to transmit information. In fact, as we have seen, some members of a research community are much more likely to provide information than others. There are, similarly, a large number of nonquantitative models that can be applied to the informal communication of research. Many of these have been developed to help understand mass-media communication and so require some modification for application to the research community. For example, several models present ways of looking at the gatekeeping function, emphasizing the way in which gatekeepers and information channels interact.[29] Again such sociological models are helpful for concentrating the mind on specific aspects of information transfer, but cannot be applied too widely.

Eminent researchers tend to attach themselves to the informal communication networks in their fields from early on in their careers.[30] The commonest way is by gravitating toward the research centers where the most important advances are being made. In such places, not only is there more informal communication internally, but also established researchers pass on information from elsewhere, and meetings with visitors allow junior researchers to create their own networks. Conversely, for researchers who are isolated from such centers, establishing informal communication networks is more difficult. This is a particular problem for researchers in developing countries, which may contain few internationally recognized research centers. They find it difficult to establish and develop research contacts both nationally and internationally. In developing countries, the communication infrastructure (e.g., telephones) may be unreliable, and long-distance travel may be limited by finance or location. Moreover, the organization of the research community may not encourage informal communication: for example, funding for travel and attendance at society meetings may be limited to senior staff whose work has become mainly administrative. International contacts can sometimes be established at international conferences held within the developing country (though most conferences are held elsewhere). The problem is that such meetings usually rely on funding from outside the developing country.

The same is true of a significant proportion of the visits made for research purposes between developed and developing countries. Though some of these visits are one-off affairs aimed at getting advice, most funding agencies have found by experience that continuing interaction is the best way of developing a research environment. Visits, or staff exchanges, need to be organized directly between the institutions concerned, since frequent visits with limited objectives are more likely to encourage joint research. The drawback of such continuing support is that it can usually only be afforded for a limited number of institutions. The hope, of course, is that such contacts will become self-supporting. The greatest likelihood of this often occurs when younger researchers are dispatched to internationally known research centers for doctoral or postdoctoral work. The contacts they establish within and via their host institutions often remain important for informal communication after they return home. The main problem with this approach in the past has been that a significant proportion of these researchers have opted to extend their careers abroad, leading to a "brain drain" from the developing country. More recently, financial pressures in developed countries have limited the opportunities available for further work there and so reduced the importance of these losses of trained personnel.

The same pressures have led to some restriction on access to informal communication channels, even for Western researchers. A study of biological researchers in the UK found, for example, that a quarter were experiencing major restrictions on their travel to conferences, and 10% were being significantly limited in their use of long-distance telephone calls.[31] The people most affected were junior researchers. Now there are relatively more women than men in junior research posts in most subjects. This means that female researchers are affected more, on average, by these sorts of restrictions than are male researchers. It seems that gender differences in informal communication are probably better explained by such status differences than as direct evidence of discrimination. It is true, however, that many female researchers feel they are less involved in informal networks than male colleagues of similar status.[32] The extent to which such feelings arise seems to depend on the male–female balance in the subject: the fewer the females, the more difficult it is for them fully to exploit informal communication channels. Some anecdotal evidence for seeing gender imbalance as a barrier comes from male researchers working in feminist subjects, where they form a minority. They can similarly feel marginalized in terms of informal communication.

Amateur researchers are also, in a sense, marginalized relative to professionals, but their situation is more complex. Most amateurs are in touch with others in their locality, often via society meetings, evening classes, and so on. The most enthusiastic amateurs in each locality are usually in contact with their peers at the national, or even at the international, level. At the same time, a few professionals may belong to local societies, and more will mix with amateurs at the national level. In subjects where amateurs play a significant role (such as ornithology or literary and historical studies) professionals and amateurs may have national societies to which they jointly belong and where they can exchange information informally. Even where there are separate amateur and professional societies (as in astronomy or geology), some amateurs will belong to professional societies and vice versa. As a result of these overlaps, amateurs are often involved in two informal communication networks—their own and, either directly or at second-hand, the professional network.

Both amateurs and professionals may be called on by the mass media to assist in reporting research activities to the general public. In part, this reflects the normal media procedure of consulting experts, but external expertise is also necessary because the number of media professionals who specialize in the presentation of research is small. If it is to be reported as news, research must compete with all the other items that the media handle. From this viewpoint, research suffers from some drawbacks. For example, news has to be current. Much research takes a long time to complete and so may fail this criterion (though currency can be added by fixing a date for the public unveiling of the research). However, research does not appear in the media solely as news items. A good deal is presented as specially prepared articles or programs, often devoted to a particular theme. Some may receive a mention in programs devoted to other topics: for example, a discussion of an exhibition of pictures may involve reference to research in art history. Recent research developments may also receive mention in educational programs on radio and television.

The mass media embrace newspapers, radio, and television. The different channels cater for overlapping audiences, but each typically breaks their audiences up into socioeconomic groups. For example, newspapers vary from the up-market broadsheet to the down-market tabloid. Hardly surprisingly, it is the newspapers and radio–television channels aimed at the higher socioeconomic groups that contain most information about research. Magazines tend to be more specialized in their contents. As a result, they can attract a readership that covers professionals and amateurs, as well as the general public. For example, 60% of the readers of the British magazine *New Scientist* have some kind of science qualification, and 40% describe themselves as professional scientists.[33] All the mass media have been expanding their information output in recent decades (more pages in the newspapers and more channels on radio and television). However, the output of research has increased even more rapidly, so the problem of selection has not been eased.

The way selection works depends, in part, on the physical properties of the medium. For example, television is naturally attracted to topics that provide good visual images. Speech transmits information more slowly than it can be conveyed by the printed word. An article in a newspaper can therefore usually provide more detail than an equivalent presentation on radio or television. The differing nature of the channels also affects the way information is provided. Thus radio programs present items of information one after the other: so if an item is missed, it is lost. Such serial presentation must therefore be very clear and, like any oral communication, must be reinforced by reminders of what is happening. This is why radio announcers often summarize the items yet to come or that have previously been said. By way of contrast, newspapers are not serial transmitters of information. A reader can move backward and forward through the contents and can reread items that are not clear the first time round. A newspaper is therefore laid out in such a way as to call attention (via headlines) to the main topics it contains. Readers can then select and read topics in whichever order they prefer. Television is more like radio, but simultaneous oral and visual presentation allows greater flexibility. While the "voice-over" is providing one type of information, the visuals may give additional or alternative information. In a weather forecast, for example, the presenter may give a general outline while the weather chart in the background gives further details. Because the mass media do have these differing properties, users often access more than one of them in order to acquire supplementary information.

Electronic Channels

Just as mass-media channels have differing characteristics, so, too, electronic and print-based communication can produce different perceptions. The important difference is the flexibility of electronic handling. In consequence, definitions and working habits that have evolved in a print-based environment may not be applicable to one dominated by electronic communication. For example, two main forms of communication—formal and informal—have been discussed in this chapter. A researcher sitting at a networked computer terminal may be involved, more or less simultaneously, in sending electronic mail, participating in a computer conference, and dispatching an article to an electronic journal. Indeed, the same information may be involved in all three activities. In these circumstances, the distinction between formal and informal channels is much less useful for computer-based communication. In a sense, we are returning to prejournal days, when research information was sent by "personal" letter, but with the intention that it should be disseminated more widely.

The now well-established system of making high-energy physics preprints available electronically provides another example. These can be accessed and retrieved by anyone with the appropriate network connections. With print-on-paper preprints, the communication initiative lies with the author: with electronic preprints, it lies with the reader. Except for the lack of quality control (an invisible characteristic), this preprint file could well be a full-fledged electronic journal. In fact, one physics researcher commented:

> It has completely changed how people in the field exchange information. The only time I look at the published journals is for articles that predate the Los Alamos physics databases.[34]

When the success of the electronic preprints became apparent, Elsevier set up *Nuclear Physics Electronic*, an online compilation of articles that had already been refereed and were waiting to be printed in the journal *Nuclear Physics*, to speed up their presentation. The distinction between preprint and journal starts to become very hazy here: not least because some of the unreffered abstracts on the Los Almos database are virtually identical with some of the Elsevier refereed abstracts.

If electronic handling can change traditional categories of communication, how will this affect the groups who have been central participants in the traditional channels for printed material, more especially the publishers and libraries? At first sight, publishers seem to be well-placed for the changeover, since much in-house handling is already of electronic material. Authors are increasingly expected to provide their work in electronic form, and it is interchanged in this form with printers. It is only at the final stage that the information is converted from the electronic to the printed version. In practice, the process is not quite so straightforward. In particular, it is a complicated matter to send research material containing tables and graphics on-line to referees. They are still typically provided with printed versions. But the overall picture, that publishers are already accustomed to handling electronic information, remains true.

One problem for publishers is the limitations of electronic publishing as seen by their customers. Individual readers continue to find it difficult to absorb large amounts of information from the computer screen. They want their information to be portable, so they can read it when traveling. They expect an electronic interface to be as simple as a printed book or journal. Ways of handling these requirements are well advanced, but not yet with us. For example, much work is being put into developing the "electronic book." This is effectively a small portable computer with a high-resolution screen, which can play back material contained on a CD-ROM or downloaded from an on-line source. It should, in principle, fulfill many of the requirements that readers have. Till then, the question remains—do the advantages of electronic handling outweigh the disadvantages? The answer, inevitably, depends on the information to be handled. Thus one of the major virtues of electronic handling derives from its ability to search rapidly through large amounts of information. This is a valuable facility for most types of guides to the research literature, such as abstracts or indexes. When multimedia facilities are added, electronic handling has major advantages for reference works, such as dictionaries or encyclopedias. Consequently, these types of publications are already well-represented both on-line and on CD-ROM and are in increasing use. At the other end of the scale come monographs, which are meant to be read continuously. The advantages of electronic handling are less significant for these, and the disadvantages correspondingly greater. They, therefore, do not figure largely among current electronic publications.

Electronic journals lie somewhere between these two extremes. The text of a journal article is not too long to be read on-screen, and rapid access and searching can be helpful for readers. The number of electronic journals available is therefore rising, but their viability is still a matter for conjecture. Electronic publishing, like any other publishing, is basically a question of identifying appropriate niches. The rise of electronic journals depends on the identification of which niches best fit their characteristics at any given time. Currently, two niches are being occupied. The first involves the production of electronic versions of journals that are already available in print. Such parallel production is particularly popular with major journal publishers, who can plan to make all their journals available electronically as one operation. The other niche is for small-scale operations. Small specialisms have always had problems with journal publication, since their number of members corresponds to short print runs of marginal financial viability. For such groups, electronic publishing offers several advantages, not least that most of the publishing operations can be done by unpaid volunteers. In consequence, there has been a rapid growth of the electronic journals aimed at specialist audiences. There is often no explicit charge for access to these small-scale journals, whereas the electronic versions of printed journals may cost as much, or more, than the price of the print version.

Journals of the small-scale sort bypass traditional publishers. One current debate concerns the extent to which this will grow in the future. Clearly, a large journal, handling many articles sent in from all round the world, will always require professional input. Small journals will not. But will the boundaries change with time? In discussing the future, learned and professional societies are likely to have a particular significance. In the first place, unlike commercial publishers, they are concerned with informal communication between their members, as well as formal publications. Electronic communication can allow them to bring these two threads together. In addition, and again unlike commercial publishers, they have their members" subscriptions as a cushion that allows them to experiment.

Librarians have a major interest in electronic journals for two reasons. The first relates to their own role. If journals are made available free of subscription, readers may well access them directly rather than going via the library. Costly electronic journals, on the contrary, will always need to be purchased centrally. Secondly, librarians fondly hope that electronic access will help control the growing cost of journal subscriptions. Unfortunately, for both librarians and individual readers, interface standards for on-line journals are still in a state of flux. Both, therefore, face additional requirements in terms of implementation and training, implying more effort and cost rather than less.

A related problem concerns archiving. Where shall electronic journals be held? If in the library, the storage problems for the host institution are considerable. The major difficulty is that hardware and software will continue to develop rapidly in the future. Consequently, stored electronic material will need to be transferred every few years to new configurations at considerable expense. Storage at the publishers raises similar questions. Will publishers really be able to store and provide free access to their electronic journals into the foreseeable future, regardless of takeovers and other changes in the industry? The same question can be asked of other electronic publications, such as the reference material mentioned previously. For journals, subscription agents may have a role. Such agents have a well-established role as an intermediary between publishers and libraries in the acquisition of printed journals. They are naturally seeking to find a related role in the handling of electronic journals. Perhaps specialist book wholesalers could play a similar role for other types of electronic publication. The most obvious solution is to establish national or regional depositories for electronic publications. Discussions about these are under way in a number of countries, but it will take time to reach agreement on a form of organization that can respond to international, as well as national, needs.

One difficulty with any arrangement for depositing electronic information, whether at a central depot or at any purchasing institution, relates to copyright. In recent years, publishers have become increasingly vigorous in trying to protect the material they publish from unauthorized copying. In terms of photocopying printed material, most feel the situation is now under reasonable control. The major advantage of electronic information—that its handling can be very flexible—has the corresponding disadvantage that electrocopying is harder to control than photocopying. Scholarly publishers are currently making a considerable effort to find ways to supervise copying of electronic material, and a number of countries are revising and updating their copyright laws to cope with electronic publishing. Since copyright is a matter that ties authors and publishers together, it is discussed further in the next chapter.

It may seem that the foregoing problems are particularly acute for on-line publications. Can they not be resolved more easily for CD-ROM? After all, a CD-ROM represents a physical chunk of information that can be handled in much the same way as a journal issue, or a book, by both publishers and librarians. In fact, much reference material is already published in this form; but it does not necessarily resolve all the problems. Readers want the convenience of remote access, so institutions typically network their CD-ROMs. This puts the information on-line, though handling large piles of CD-ROMs does not necessarily lead to speedy retrieval. Since the material is on-line, the possibility of electrocopying occurs again. One difficulty for journals is that a CD-ROM has far more storage space available than individual journal issues require. In fact, CD-ROM really becomes competitive for the storage of a large number of journal issues simultaneously. For these, it obviously takes up much less space in a library than the equivalent printed material. Consequently, it can provide a convenient way of storing journal back runs. There remains, however, a query over the future of CD-ROMs. For example, three issues are: their long-term stability is still somewhat unclear; they may not remain the standard for disk storage in the future; the equipment needed to handle disks may well develop further. Any changes will mean extra costs, especially for libraries.

Electronic Networks and Readers

Forecasting usage of electronic information depends on estimating the access potential readers will have to networks (more especially, nowadays, to the Internet). Table 29 records access by British biological researchers in 1994.[35] Usage has increased since then, but the figures broadly reflect the position in Western countries. A majority of researchers now have access to

Table 29
Availability of Computers to Biological Researchers in the UK

Type of access	University agricultural faculty (%)	University biology department (%)	Research establishment (%)	Pharmaceutical laboratory (%)
Computer on desk at work	66	84	70	98
Networked computer at work	33	73	48	98
Computer at home	55	53	48	42

computers, though not all have satisfactory networked links. There is a financial difference here between Western Europe and the United States. Network usage is considerably more expensive in the former countries. One consequence is that the use of network connections from home is considerably greater in the United States. This apart, it is reasonable to suppose that access to networked computers will be the norm for all researchers in these countries soon.

Presuming that researchers are in a position to access electronic documentation, what characteristics do they expect it to have? Table 30 lists the results of one study that investigated expectations regarding electronic text (other surveys suggest similar results).[36] Paradoxically, the most important requirement is that it should be easy to produce good-quality printed copies. This reflects the fact that many readers find electronic text more difficult to manipulate than printed text.[37] In part, this is because printed matter is essentially a three-dimensional creation, whereas electronic text is two dimensional. In addition, a computer screen can only contain a limited amount of information, as compared with the printed page. Browsing therefore entails rapid scrolling backward and forward. This is a less efficient process than flipping through printed pages. Hypertext does allow for jumping about in an electronic text, but it can lead to navigational problems. Readers of electronic text need more assistance in deciding where they have been, and where they are going, than is necessary for printed text. Similarly, portability and annotation of contents are much more straightforward for printed than for electronic text.

Readers are not indifferent to the potential for design and layout dif-

Table 30
Importance of Different Electronic Text Characteristics

Characteristic	Percentage saying very important
Creation of a print copy	80
Ability to browse graphics	73
Ability to browse text	66
Portability of the text	53
Flipping pages and scanning	45
Ability to underline and annotate	41
Physical comfort	37
Adequate text design and layout	30
Physical contact with material	14

ferences between printed and electronic text, but most expect that electronic publications, at least initially, will resemble their printed equivalents. There are problems here. The computer screen is a different size and shape from a printed page. Though the same rules regarding layout and legibility apply as for printed material, the outcome may be different. For example, there is still disagreement about the optimum numbers of words per screen. Reading from the screen does not seem to be intrinsically more difficult than reading from the page, so long as a high-resolution, good contrast screen is being used. (By no means do all screen displays satisfy this requirement.) However, ergonomic considerations tend to limit the conditions necessary for comfortable reading from the screen, more than for reading from the printed page. As all this indicates, reading electronic text is still, overall, a less satisfactory process than reading print. Given sufficient motivation—for example, speedy access to a wide range of information—readers will accept the limitations. It is really low-level problems that provide the major deterrent. For example, the (not uncommon) long delays in accessing and viewing materials via the Internet is a significant demotivating factor.

As noted earlier, networked information blurs the traditional dividing line between formal and informal communication. Informal networked interaction between groups of researchers comes in various forms, such as bulletin boards, discussion lists, or newsletters (with *electronic* implied in each case). All are basically ways of sharing and discussing information and posing queries. Most of them are open to all researchers, though some are restricted to closed groups. Restricted information is more likely to circulate via electronic mail, which is an increasingly common supplement to traditional types of informal communication. It is particularly convenient, having few of the delays associated with sending ordinary mail or contacting colleagues by telephone. Consequently, electronic mail has become a major link between researchers and research groups.

Such electronic communication introduces some differences as compared with traditional modes of informal communication. For example, because it is easy to send the same information to many people, an individual can maintain more regular contacts than hitherto. Electronic "cliques" (a name sometimes used in this context) can therefore include more people than the traditional "invisible college." Moreover, members of the group are involved in a different way. Electronic mail is a more anonymous way of communicating than traditional letters, with their headed notepaper, or conversation. It does not necessarily indicate the status of the people involved. Junior researchers can have their say along with senior researchers (indeed, since the juniors often have more time available and a greater knowledge of the system, they may communicate more electronically than their seniors). The consequence is that the research hierarchy is less pronounced with electronic communication. In turn, this enhances the value of such communication for junior researchers.

This difference should obviously prove helpful to female researchers, in view of what has been said before. There is little evidence of any gender difference in terms of ability to use information technology for communication purposes. What has happened in the past is that female students have tended to make less use of computers in their preuniversity days than male students. The reasons suggested for this range from school computer usage being concentrated in the sciences to the importance of male-dominated computer games in the early years. At university, female students cope with networked information as readily as their male counterparts. In terms of access to and use of networked computers, female researchers seem to be on a par with male researchers of a similar status and in the same discipline.

Researchers in developing countries adapt equally readily to networked communication. The main problem is obviously to finance and construct the necessary communications infrastructure to allow access to international networks. The way forward that many developing countries are following is to ensure that at least their most important institutions gain access as soon as possible. In most countries, these institutions include the leading universities and research centers. The result is, to some extent, a revision of the existing map of the "information rich" and the "information poor." With traditional forms of communication this tends to coincide with the division beteen developed and developing countries. In the immediate future, there may be an equally important division within developing countries between researchers in institutions that have good access to the Internet and those that do not.

Amateurs face one problem in the growth of networking: unlike professionals, most do not have institutional access to the Internet. However, the growing use of networked computers from home should reduce this disadvantage (and some amateurs already have electronic links to nearby institutions). In practice, electronic communication should offer considerable advantages to amateurs. They can communicate more readily with each other, and international contacts become as easy as national ones. In addition, amateurs can participate in some of the same informal electronic links as scientists, and they can access data sources that have not previously been available to them. Thus a large amount of data derived from space research can be looked at and manipulated without charge. Some institutions—for example, in meteorology—are providing data over the network specifically for amateurs. Valuable data are also being provided on CD-ROM. Home computers can now handle these along with on-line sources; so amateur involvement in research should improve in the new communication regime.

At another level, on-line and CD-ROM reference information sources of interest to the general public are becoming increasingly common. Leading newspapers can be accessed on-line, and often supply additional information in this form. The same is true of a number of specialist magazines. Other growth areas include museum displays, catalogs, and an enormous amount of educational material. The key difference from printed material lies in the potential for interaction and exploration. The advent of information technology here, too, is blurring distinctions that have previously been drawn— for example, between mass communication and personal communication. Thus the same computer can be used for receiving television or for sending a fax. As this reflects, networked computers are both receivers and transmitters. There is no reason why individuals should not prepare personal multimedia programs and disseminate them to a mass public, as readily as they receive programs prepared commercially. Old ideas of what information can be appropriately disseminated via which channels are breaking down at this general level, as well as at the specialist research level.

5

Making Research Public

Carrying out research and communicating it are inseparable companions. During the early stages of a research project, most of the communication is informal, beginning with face-to-face discussions. As the work progresses, preliminary oral reports may be given to small audiences, typically via research seminars. As the project nears completion, oral reports may begin to be given at conferences. The timescale for this widening dissemination depends on the discipline. Preliminary reporting in the sciences may start after the project has been going for a few months, and reporting at conferences by the end of a year. For the social sciences and humanities, oral presentation is likely to extend over a longer period than in the sciences because the projects, themselves, take longer. Despite their more limited time, scientists appear to undertake more oral presentations than researchers in the social sciences and humanities.

After completion of the project, the results are written up and submitted for publication. Whether, or not, the activities of research and writing up are separated in time, depends on the subject. They often are distinct for a short scientific article, but an author writing a humanities monograph will often collect additional data during the writing-up period. Even if no further investigation is necessary, there is usually a short gap between the end of a project and the beginning of writing up. This can be due to the launch of the next research project, but it also allows time, for example, to check whether any more relevant information has appeared since the previous project started. The amount of time required for writing-up is usually shortest for the sciences. One study found that the average time between starting on an article and submitting it to a journal was four months in the physical sciences and seven months in the social sciences.[1] The delays between receipt of the article by a journal and its subsequent appearance in that journal were also systematically different—seven months and 11 months, respectively.

159

Adding the two delay times together, it is clear that formal reporting of research is quicker in the sciences than in the social sciences and humanities.

Though authors often initially report their work orally, this does not necessarily mean that there is no written record. A seminar is typically illustrated with data displayed on (say) an overhead projector. Members of the audience can note the information or ask the presenter for copies of the transparencies. At the conference level, contributors are often asked to provide abstracts. These are circulated to conference attenders and may be printed in journals. Many authors, in any case, prefer to write notes, or a preliminary version of the article, when making oral presentations. Attenders at conferences may request copies: indeed, it is not uncommon for people who have seen the conference schedule, but are not attending, to write for further information. An appreciable proportion of authors in all subjects distribute some kind of report on their work to selected colleagues beforehand. Such preprints are particularly common in the sciences. These various forms of prepublication dissemination often lead to feedback, and this, in turn, to modification of the material that is eventually submitted for formal publication. Rewriting as a result of feedback seems to be less common in the sciences than in the social sciences or humanities.

Types of Publication

Since the mid-1980s, data on research publication have been collected every 3–4 years for staff in British universities. Table 31 lists per capita staff performance for a sample set of universities from information gathered in 1992.[2] The results tend to fall into two groups—science, technology,

Table 31
Per Capita Performance in British Universities

Subject	Authored books	Refereed conference proceedings	Journal articles	Research students	Relative research council income
Science	0.18	1.34	5.52	1.65	0.99
Technology	0.17	3.57	3.45	1.90	1.00
Medicine	0.15	1.99	6.12	0.82	0.44
Social science	0.64	0.76	2.30	0.60	0.15
Humanities	0.68	0.74	2.73	0.56	0.06

Table 32

Publication Pattern of Humanities Faculty in the United States

Type of publication	Percentage who have published at least one
Article in refereed journal	78
Scholarly book review	69
Contribution to conference proceedings	63
Chapter in scholarly book	55
Scholarly book (author)	47
Scholarly book (editor)	29

and medicine (STM), on the one hand, and social science and humanities, on the other. The expected emphasis on journal articles for the former group and books for the latter group is evident, as is the engineers' liking for refereed conference proceedings. The last column reflects not only the higher cost of STM research, but also expenditure on research assistance. Taking this in conjunction with the research student figures underlines the significance of group research and collaboration on the science side.

Table 31 compares the forms of publication that are common to all fields of research. By way of comparison, Table 32 presents the common forms of publication of humanities staff in U.S. universities.[3] It underlines the diverse importance of books in humanities research. It is not only that there are different ways of contributing to books, but also that book reviewing is seen as a significant activity.

Writing takes up less time on average than other aspects of communication, as is indicated by the data in Table 33 from a survey of chemists.[4] Averages, however, conceal the fact that writing activity tends to occur at particular times. Scientists in British universities see writing up research as being almost as time consuming as teaching.[5] (Writing up is seen as most

Table 33

Time Spent on Research Communication by U.S. Chemists

Type of communication	Percentage of total work time
Group discussion	10.3
Individual discussion	9.2
Reading	8.8
Writing	5.0

time consuming by scientists at research institutes, much less so by scientists in industry.) Data on U.S. scholarly authors suggest that the time taken in preparing a journal article depends to some extent on the subject.[6] Mathematicians take over 120 hours, as compared with researchers in the life sciences and social sciences who average about 80 hours, and physical scientists who take less than 70 hours. Most of the time is spent on the actual writing, though making a final search through the literature can also be time consuming. The remaining time is spent mainly on editing the manuscript, preparing graphics, etc.

Research may be reported orally more than once, but it may also appear in more than one type of publication. Many bodies that fund research require a specially written report on the work they have sponsored. Such reports are expected to provide a thorough survey of the project, and typically contain an extensive description of data and methodology, often backed by further details in appendixes. Project reports may be written before any other publication: the latter—for example, a journal article—can then be prepared as a précis. In industry or some research institutes, the reports may be confidential, and access to the research information restricted. Even where the information can be made freely available, not all project reports are published in another form. Self-standing reports seem to be commoner in the social sciences and technology than in the sciences. Many reports are "one-off" publications, but research centers and institutes sometimes produce a research series. In this case, there is an increased likelihood that additional forms of publication will not be used. It is not only the contents that change in the transmutation of a report into a journal article. One survey found that almost a quarter of the subsequent articles had different authors from the report, and a similar proportion had entirely different titles.[7]

Perhaps a fifth of journal articles in the sciences and social sciences may be preceded by reports. A similar proportion are based on research student theses. Research reported in theses may give rise to more than one journal article. In the sciences, less often in the social sciences, the work is written up for publication as it proceeds. In the humanities, and sometimes in the social sciences, a good thesis may be developed into a book subsequent to the completion of the research. Condensing thesis material into journal articles is harder than the same operation for reports, since theses are usually even more verbose. Their intention, after all, is to demonstrate the authors' grasp of the subject: they must assume little and go into considerable detail. Theses are often book length in terms of volume of content, but they are rarely accepted for publication as books without major changes.

Style, organization, and emphasis need alteration, and this usually entails rewriting the entire thesis.

The main problem with the further publication of material in theses is that research students move on to other positions after obtaining their degrees. There is a parallel problem for writing up reports, where research staff, who often know most about the project, have changed jobs because grants have run out. As with reports, the title of the article is often different from that of the original thesis, and the authors, too, may differ. A thesis must, of course, be solely written by the candidate for the research degree, whereas a resultant article may well bear other names, especially that of the supervisor. Indeed, where the student does not have time or opportunity to prepare results for publication, the supervisor may take over the task. A majority of science and social science doctoral theses are subsequently digested into a publication (one British survey put the figure at four in every five theses within eight years of their completion[8]). Engineering theses are somewhat less likely to be published, and humanities theses less still.

Contributions to conference proceedings occupy an intermediate position between reports and theses, on the one hand, and books and journals, on the other. Reports and theses—at least, those publicly available—have effectively been published. However, many researchers see them as intermediate forms—not a proper part of the formal communication network—so the contents need to be made known more widely. The material in proceedings, though based on oral presentations, typically looks like a series of journal articles and is accepted as a formal publication. In fact, some conferences appear as special issues of regular journals. Most researchers would rate a contribution to a conference proceedings as having less prestige than a publication in a well-regarded journal. In consequence, where the authors regard it as worthwhile, research reported at conferences may also appear in journals, often without a great deal of change.

A distinction is often drawn between conferences where contributions are carefully refereed beforehand and only a limited number selected for presentation and those where relevant offerings are accepted with only a minimum of review. Contributions to the former type of conference are naturally regarded as carrying a higher weight. However, neither the conferences, nor the proceedings that stem from them, all follow the same pattern. For example, some conferences are open to any contributions that relate to the interests of the specialism concerned, whereas others are organized round a specific theme. Again, there may be a general call for papers, to which anyone can respond, or, at the other extreme, only invited speakers may be involved, and they may speak to an invited audience. Many conferences lie in between, with a mix of some invited and some proffered presentations. Invited contributions often provide an overview of a field, rather than reporting on a specific piece of research, and are usually specially written for the occasion. It follows that not all contributions to conference proceedings have an identical status. In addition, some proceedings try to take into account their origin in informal communication. The most popular way is by printing a record of the discussion of each presentation. Less commonly, official discussants may be appointed to provide comments on the contributions. These additions underline the intermediate position of conference proceedings in publishing terms.

Different Publication Outlets

There is thus a number of methods by in which the research community may find out about research. A method's relative importance can change with time. For example, the emphasis on applicable research during the 1980s and 1990s has led to a growth in the "gray literature" (mainly reports of various kinds) that is appearing. Nevertheless, refereed journal articles and scholarly monographs are still regarded as the definitive statements of the results of research projects. They are, correspondingly, the items that are preferentially read and cited by colleagues. It follows that, at the end of a project, authors usually have to decide to which journal they will submit an article or to which publisher they will send a book. What factors are involved in making this choice? So far as journal articles are concerned, two factors are clearly basic for authors in all disciplines. The first is the regard in which a journal is held by its research community; the second is the audience reached by the journal. For example, one survey of academic researchers found that 70% regarded the prestige of the journal as important, and 67% thought its readership highly important, when they were deciding where to publish an article.[9] (Only 1% and 3%, respectively, considered these factors to be unimportant.)

A prestigious journal can be simply defined as one that publishes the best research by the best researchers. Even as bland a definition as this suggests that such a journal must have certain characteristics. For example, it must have a well-established reputation throughout the relevant research community. This implies, in turn, that the journal must have existed and been well run for some time past. How long depends on the subject matter. A new journal that is first in the field in a rapidly growing specialism may establish a good reputation within a decade.

Most researchers are able to assess the relative prestige of the various journals in their field. Their estimates differ in detail, but the overall ordering is usually similar. The more highly regarded a journal, the more likely it is that researchers will want to make use of its contents. This suggests there should be a link between prestige and citations to the journal. Looking for such a link is not entirely straightforward. For one thing, different journals publish differing numbers of articles per year. A straight count of citations per journal can, therefore, be biased by the relative numbers of articles they have provided for citing. (In a similar way, a long-established journal will have a greater accumulated number of citable articles than one that has been started recently.) Another factor is that articles in journals often tend preferentially to cite other articles in the same journal. Such self-citation can be of the order of 20% or more. In fact, whether citation measures are corrected for these biases or not, they correlate moderately well with subjective estimates of prestige.[10] Increasing journal self-citation seems to be linked to increasing prestige of the journal. Similarly, because there is considerable pressure from authors to publish in high-prestige journals, these often contain more articles than other titles in the field in any case. More generally, there is a fair correlation, especially in the STM field, between the number of journals produced by leading publishers and the share of the overall citations that they receive. This suggests that the "prestige" distribution of their journals is rather similar.

Prestige and audience are linked. Readers, like authors, are attracted to the leading journals, so, by publishing in these, authors are most likely to reach the audience they want. Nor is this larger audience necessarily within the specialism alone. Some of the most prestigious journals, such as *Science*, cover a broad range of topics and will be scanned by researchers in other specialisms. The target audience in a small specialism may actually be quite limited. Hence, journals with relatively low circulations may still be highly regarded within their specialisms. The key factor for authors is market penetration, and they will define this according to their material. For example, some journals are primarily concerned with presenting research results to practitioners. They may be highly regarded, with many readers among practitioners, but they are seen as "professional" rather than "research" publications. In such cases, researchers may contribute to the journals, but not rate them highly in terms of prestige. The division between professional and research journals is far from clear-cut. For example, the *British Medical Journal* functions as both, yet is highly regarded by researchers. Niceties of this sort are a part of experienced authors' know-how as they work out where to send their research results.

Alongside questions of prestige and readership, there are other factors that come into play to a lesser extent or under particular circumstances. One is a matter of habit. Researchers who find a satisfactory journal in which to publish are likely to send further contributions there in the future. Another is language. Authors obviously prefer to write in their own language, but this may conflict with their other priorities. In disciplines where research activity is international, as in the sciences, most of the high-prestige journals are in English. In subjects with a national orientation (e.g., French history), at least some of the key journals will be in the national language, though they may be internationally read. Depending on the research field, an author may therefore feel compelled to write in a foreign language in order to reach the desired audience. This obviously makes for harder work, even where assistance from translators—as in Japan—is readily available.

One other factor of interest is speed of publication. How long does it take from dispatching an article to a journal before it appears in print? It might be expected that authors would want the delay to be as little as possible. Though no doubt this is true, rapid publication is usually regarded as less important than prestige and readership. Interest in speed of publication is discipline dependent. In recent decades, a number of "letters" journals have appeared. Their purpose is to publish brief accounts of research appreciably more quickly than is possible via the average standard journal. It was initially supposed that these brief announcements would be followed up later with a longer article in an ordinary journal. Today, many "letters" are ends in themselves, and letters journals are used for the speedy transmission of results in areas of research that are developing rapidly. Such journals have mainly proved necessary in the sciences: research in the social sciences and humanities is normally communicated at a more leisurely pace. Even in the sciences, however, most researchers, most of the time, do not regard very rapid publication as essential. The problem seems to be that what researchers regard as a reasonable delay time can differ appreciably from what publishers' manage to provide. Table 34 compares authors' views on the maximum time it should take from submission of an article to its appearance with the actual delay times they had encountered.[11] Though scientists may expect speedier publication, with social scientists and humanities researchers willing to accept a slower pace, it seems that a significant number of authors in all groups are encountering longer publication delays than they regard as reasonable.

Table 34

Scholars' Expectations and Experience of Journal Delays
(by Percentage of Respondents)

Period	Expected maximum publication delay	Average publication delay experienced
0–3 months	22.9	3.6
3–6 months	48.8	21.1
6–9 months	6.4	11.3
9–12 months	14.2	29.7
1–1.5 years	1.4	12.5
1.5–2 years	0.7	6.0

Scholars who wish to publish their work in book form have similar concerns to those publishing journal articles, but the process of deciding on an outlet has significant differences. Questions about prestige now refer primarily to the publisher. A large university press, for example, will be considered by most researchers as a more prestigious outlet than a small commercial publisher. However, this can depend considerably on the field concerned. Small publishers, who may not be much known in the research world as a whole, can concentrate on a particular subject area—philosophy, say—and build up an excellent reputation in the specialism. Such specialization means that they can market the book efficiently—perhaps better than a large general publisher—to the audience that its author wishes to reach. When authors look at publishers, they have in mind, like writers of journal articles, a satisfactory trade-off between prestige and readership.

Speed of publication is normally less important for scholarly books than for journal articles. The whole timescale for books is longer. They not only take more time to write than articles, but it is also expected that they will continue to have value to researchers for longer. Having said that, scholarship in any field can become outdated as new research appears. A delay of more than a couple of years in the production of a book may begin to raise questions about the currency of the contents whatever the subject matter. Language, too, is less of a problem for books than for journal articles. Authors tend much more to write in their own language (at least, so long as it is one of the recognized languages of scholarship). If there seems to be a market elsewhere, the book may then be translated.

The major difference between books and journals lies, however, in the differing author–publisher relationships. Authors of journal articles rarely make contact with the editors or publishers before submitting their offerings.

Only inexperienced, or ill-advised authors of scholarly books fail to make prior contacts. (Since the world is full of first-time authors, there remain numerous researchers who embark on writing before considering to which publisher they will send their books.) Experienced authors first select a possible publisher, get in touch, and submit an outline of the intended contents. If the publisher is interested, the next step may be for the author and editor together to consider the readership and potential sales of the proposed book. Unlike publication in journals, finance is an explicit factor in deciding whether scholarly books will be published; though a limited number of highly considered manuscripts may be published, even if their sales are expected to be small. At the other end of the scale, a few scholarly authors can command a sufficiently large readership for them to employ the services of literary agents in their negotiations with publishers.

The result is that, for many scholarly books, the author and the publisher have concluded a contract while the writing is still in its early stages. This does not guarantee publication, but makes it much more likely. It, therefore, encourages the author to put in the much greater effort required for producing a book as compared with a journal article. It also means that there can be editorial input during the writing process itself. Indeed, the original initiative can come from the publisher rather than the author. For example, if the publisher produces a series of books on a particular topic, it is quite possible that an author will be sought to contribute a title on a specific topic. (There is a parallel in journals devoted to reviews of research, where authors are often invited.) More generally, scholarly publishers have their contacts, mainly in universities, who can direct their attention to potential new authors, or the publishers may send their own commissioning editors round university campuses. Such involvement means that book publishers play a much more active role than journal publishers in determining what research is published.

Experienced researchers thus have a number of points in mind when they think of publishing their work. Initially, and usually before the research gets under way, they will have decided whether to publish it as a book or as journal articles. As the research progresses, ideas may crystallize further. Research for a book may generate supplementary material that can be used for a journal article. Experimental results may prove sufficiently interesting for it to be decided that they should be written up quickly for rapid publication in a letters journal. One question, particularly for journal publication, is whether the results should all appear as a single unit or whether they should be separated into more than one publication. It has been asserted for years past that authors sometimes choose to divide their material when it would best have been published together. (The alleged rationale, of course, is that the process adds a greater number of publications to the author's curriculum vitae.) This habit of "salami" publishing, as it has been called, is cordially detested by editors and generally disliked by readers. Nevertheless, there are occasions when it is valid to divide up material: for example, when the research falls into two distinct sections or when the results are too long to include readily in a single article.

Final decisions on publication depend on a consideration of specific journals (or publishers) and the extent to which their publishing policies fit the wishes of the author. For example, different journals have differing preferred lengths for articles: some have no explicit limits stated (though most editors have a gut-feeling as to the lower and upper limits they regard as reasonable). Very short articles may be accepted for publication in a separate section of the journal, or even in a different journal, as a "letter" or a "short contribution." Very long articles may similarly be published in a distinctive "memoirs" publication. Another length-related factor is whether the journal demands page charges. Although page charges are not compulsory, those articles for which payment is made receive fast-track treatment. The system is disliked by many authors, especially by those who do not receive research grant funding to assist publication.

Alongside policy on such material points, selection of a journal can depend on editorial policy regarding the type of research that is acceptable for publication. Sometimes this relates to the journal's definition of the specialism concerned. A geophysics journal may reject an article dealing with a planet other than the earth, or a medieval history journal may not accept an article that deals with happenings outside a specified set of dates. Sometimes the policy may relate to methodology. There were, for example, a number of social science journals that expected analysis to have a Marxist base. Journals typically contain statements of their publishing policy, usually on the front or back inside covers; but authors quite often blithely ignore what is said. Indeed, some authors may go by the title of the journal only. Similarly, investigation of which publisher is appropriate for a particular book can be very superficial.

Authors, then, are concerned with matching their thoughts on prestige and audience with their assessments of journals or publishers. They are aware that the higher the prestige of the outlet, the more competition there is to publish via it. The likelihood of their work being accepted for publication is therefore less for high-prestige outlets. They plan accordingly. It can make good sense to choose a lower prestige outlet, if it reaches the desired audience. Experienced authors, consciously or unconsciously, assess their own work. Research assessed as important goes to top-rank journals. Good, but more routine, work goes to lower ranking journals. Items that will interest other specialists, but represent relatively minor advances in knowledge, may go to other journals still. Journals develop their own niches to cater for these differing author requirements (though some may change with time and move into new niches). The author now decides on a specific journal, or perhaps a limited number of similar standing. The article is written for that journal, which entails taking into account its requirements. Are there guidelines regarding length; how should references by included; should the manuscript be submitted on disk? Questions of this sort need to be obtained from authors' instructions, for both articles and books, before the writing starts. (The emphasis here is on researchers who are acquainted with the trade of writing. Any editor can retail stories of authors whose submissions ignore their carefully laid-down instructions.)

Writing for Publication

The way an article or book is actually written depends on the background to the research. For example, writing up on the basis of a preexisting thesis or report is obviously different from starting from scratch. It will also depend on who has been involved in the research. If it is a research student and a supervisor, the student may write the first draft, as part of the research training, and the supervisor add a final polish. Alternatively, where the supervisor is a co-author, all the writing may be done by the supervisor. If authors of equal status are involved, one may write a first draft of the entire manuscript for comment by the others, or they may each write a particular section. (The former is more popular for journal articles, and the latter for books.) Many permutations are possible, though there is nearly always one person who takes the lead throughout. For example, a study of a team of scientists came up with the following description of how they put a journal article together.[12]

- The figures (charts, graphs) are roughed out by those who have collected the data.
- The materials/methods and results sections are written by one or more of those who have collected the data.

- The title and introduction are written by the main writer (a team member who usually is not the laboratory director).
- The discussion section (whether independent or incorporated into the results) is written by the main writer.
- The abstract is prepared by the main writer.

The prime aim of most researchers is to do research rather than to write about it. Many feel that their writing skills are deficient and that writing up their research takes more time and energy than it should. Correspondingly, many find writing up research to be a tedious occupation. These feelings are particularly common in the sciences and some social sciences, but can exist in any discipline. Most researchers see their writing as a process that allows them to present new ideas or knowledge to their peers. Though it certainly has that aim, it has other roles as well. For example, the researcher's reputation is tied up with the acceptability of the final manuscript. The writing must therefore not only present the research, but also convince readers that it is research they can accept. Moreover, putting research into concrete terms and organizing it into a logical pattern can reveal gaps in the argument or unnoticed assumptions. The process of writing can thus help researchers make better sense of their own work and its relationship to other work in the field.

As might be expected, experienced authors are better able to cope with these various strands than novices. The former try to judge how a reader will consider what they are saying and so try to write in a "reader-oriented" way. The latter not only write from their own viewpoint ("author-oriented") but also have greater difficulty with the more mechanical problems of producing correct prose and organizing text. The differences show up especially in what happens when the first draft is being revised.[13] Experts revise their manuscripts more than novices do, and they do so in a more global way (i.e., reorganizing text rather than just altering words). In part, this is because they are better able to detect problems in a text and are more skillful in devising appropriate remedies. However, both experts and novices find it harder to detect problems in their own text than in other people's. Articles written collaboratively gain from the interchange of opinion, leading to an improved final version of the text.

The conventions of the academic style of writing have evolved to suit the requirements both of the discipline and of the individual reader. Impersonal accounts are partly intended to defuse ad hominem arguments, but they also lend an air of authority. For rapid absorption of information, text should contain no surprises in terms of its vocabulary and organization. This helps any surprise in terms of content to register fully. One virtue of the standard academic style is that it allows a reader to move between different articles and books with well-founded expectations of how the text can be approached. In general terms, the more widely accepted the framework within which a researcher writes, the more readily other researchers can absorb the information conveyed. *Framework* can have two connotations here. One refers to the overall structure of the article or book, which puts the contents into a clear and logical sequence for the prospective reader (for example—introduction, methodology, results, and discussion). The other relates back to the discussion in an earlier chapter of the theoretical framework within which researchers do their work and how widely it is accepted by all researchers within the discipline. The two meanings are linked to the extent that agreement on presentation is easier when there is a widely agreed way of doing research. As might be expected, this means that writing conventions are most evident in the sciences, less so in the social sciences, and still less in the humanities. However, writing conventions are not static: the degree of impersonality, for example, has increased markedly over the last two or three hundred years.

During the twentieth century, one of the main pressures has been the increasing problems that readers encounter in trying to find relevant items among the flood of information that surrounds them. The most-used attribute of an article or book for retrieval purposes is the title. Correspondingly, titles have tended to become more specific with time, something that is particularly obvious for journal articles.[14] Titles are now more informative, mainly by including a greater number of keywords that indicate the contents of the article. This means that they have grown in length. The information explosion has affected science journals most, and it is articles in these that have developed longer and more complex titles, much more than articles in humanities journals.

After the title, most researchers regard the abstract as the best way of identifying relevant articles. Having abstracts actually attached to articles (as distinct from letting them appear in separate abstracts journals) has been standard practice for journals founded during the past half-century. Journals established prior to that often did not carry abstracts, though most now conform to the pattern. Letters and brief communications were originally considered not to need abstracts, but, in the interests of being more informative, have often acquired them, too. Abstracts, like titles, have been growing longer and more informative in recent decades.[15] Again, these developments have affected science journals a good deal more than those in the humanities. Indeed, it has been a matter of debate how well research in the humanities can be described via an abstract. In addition, the introductory sections of scientific articles have become increasingly likely to mention the results, a development that is less evident in other disciplines.

Parts of articles that contain routine matters are now played down. This is most evident for the methods section, which may be printed in smaller type, or even placed as an addendum at the end of the article. Brief communications may, indeed, omit almost all reference to methods. To some extent, background of information of this type may be transferred to the captions of figures included in the articles. Data can be presented either via tables or graphics. The two forms are meant to be complementary, with tables providing the precise results, whereas the graphics help readers understand the relationship and trends involved. In practice, graphics have become increasingly popular, often at the expense of tables. This helps readers absorb the information more quickly and may take up less space in the journal. Not least, computing developments have made it much easier to produce high-quality graphics. The overall effect in recent decades has been to emphasize the results and enhance their impact on the reader. Correspondingly, the older idea that a research publication should contain enough information to allow the work it reports to be repeated has become increasingly diluted.

Being recognized as the author of a publication is obviously an important reward for a researcher. Moreover, names of authors, along with titles and abstracts, are one of the commonest ways of identifying relevant information. When publishing an article or book, one key decision is therefore who shall be listed as an author. For research entirely carried out and written up by one person, this presents no problems. The only need is for the author's name to be supplied in the form required by the journal or publisher. Otherwise, it is necessary to make a decision on who should count as an author. Editors tend to suppose two things. The first is that anyone listed as an author will have contributed significantly to the research (and, conversely, that everyone who contributed substantially has been considered for possible inclusion in the list of authors). Secondly, all authors should know enough about the research to accept responsibility for the overall accuracy of the report.

In practice, these presuppositions may hold for many jointly authored books, but are by no means true of all journal articles. In terms of "significant contribution," a number of studies have found that people not directly involved in the research project may have their names attached to reports of it. Thus one biomedical survey found that half the respondents were prepared to accept the head of the laboratory as a co-author, and nearly as many would accept the person who obtained research funding for the project.[16] (Presumably, in both cases, this was in recognition of their contributions to the general well-being of the research.) Conversely, a fifth of the respondents said they had been excluded as an author from an article when they should have been included. Two-fifths said they had been involved in authoring articles where one of the other authors should not have been included. If senior authors have not been actively involved in the research, they contribute their personal prestige to the publication without being able to vouch for the accuracy of the results. A number of the scandals about manufactured data in recent years have involved eminent researchers who co-authored publications without a full knowledge of the research background. Equally, in large research projects, researchers who contribute a particular kind of expertise (e.g., computing skills) may be in no position to guarantee the overall integrity of the research. Being an "author" can therefore have a number of different connotations today.

Having decided who shall be counted an author, it is next necessary to decide, for multiauthor publications, the order in which authors shall be listed. This can be a matter of considerable sensitivity, since the first-named author, in particular, is likely to be more visible to the research community. For example, if the publication is subsequently cited, the citations will appear against the name of the first author. Likewise, if there are several authors, references to the publication may simply mention the first-named author and summarize the remainder as *"et al."* The implicit assumption here is that authors are being listed in the order of their contribution to the reported research. This is, indeed, the commonest way of putting the names in order, but, where the various authors contributed to different aspects of the research, the relative importance of their work can be hard to assess. Consider the following description of an important development in molecular biology:

> Making the discovery was one thing; making it known was another. The first problem was the authorship of the paper . . . . Matsuo felt that his name should be first. Baba, who had worked for a year longer on the structure and done all the groundwork, considered that if he weren't the first author, then Schally, not Matsuo, should be.
>
> Schally took a detached view of the dispute. "What did it matter to me? It's my lab—I got the glory anyway", he observes.[17]

One way of avoiding this kind of debate is to list the authors in alphabetical order (though, if there are only two or three authors, readers may not realize that this is the intention). The most famous example of this approach is to be found in an article on cosmology. The basic work for this was done by an eminent physicist, George Gamow, who then involved an even more eminent colleague—the Nobel prizewinner Hans Bethe—and a research student, Ralph Alpher. The article was published with the authors in alphabetical sequence, thus allowing the concepts contained in the article to be labeled the "$\alpha\beta\gamma$" theory.

The growth of teamwork has increased the difficulties of listing authors' names. This is especially a problem of "big science": it was encountered first in high-energy physics. Some brief contributions in this field today seem to require as much space for the authors' names as for the contents. Occasional articles have even done away with specific authors and simply listed the participating institutions. This has not proved popular with the researchers. Recognition is still seen as linked to appearance as an author. Another example of the same preference can be found in biomedical research—also an area of increasing teamwork. The most important guide to biomedical publications is *Index Medicus*. This previously listed the first six authors, but has now been pressurized to include the first 24 plus the last author.

Both books and articles may contain acknowledgment of assistance from colleagues. Traditionally, this has been considered appropriate when the person acknowledged has made a clear contribution to the research, but one not large enough to justify coauthorship. For articles based on teamwork, there can be a fine dividing line between being added to the list of authors, or appearing in the acknowledgments section. The line can be drawn in different places by different groups. There is, similarly, a hazy borderline between acknowledged and unacknowledged assistance. A considerable proportion of researchers feel they have experienced times when the assistance they have given should have been acknowledged and was not.[18] Assistance is nearly always informal—much of it advice and comment given in conversation—so there is plenty of room for confusion. It is very easy for researchers to absorb ideas and then believe they have thought of the innovation for themselves, a habit that greatly annoys the original progenitors of the ideas.

Acknowledgments are one way of thanking people who have helped, but who would not normally figure as an author. Laboratory technicians who have given special help with a project are one obvious group. The emphasis here, as with research colleagues, is on "special help." Assistance that is given as part of the normal activities of the employee is not usually acknowledged. A few authors, carried away by their democratic instincts, may try to mention almost anyone who has been associated with the project. For example, the acknowledgment section of a report on a series of clinical trials listed 63 institutions, 55 physicians, 51 committee members and the secretaries involved.[19] These acknowledgments, hardly surprisingly, took up a substantial part of the entire article. Some journals now limit the length of the acknowledgments section. Thus the *New England Journal of Medicine* has specified the maximum space it can occupy in any article they publish. An unanswered question is whether those who are to be acknowledged should be told beforehand. The argument in favor is that some may feel that to be mentioned is equivalent to giving some approval to the contents. In practice, most researchers do not bother to make contact except for a major item, such as the dedication of a book. If they take action, it is more likely to be by sending the person acknowledged a copy of the publication after it appears.

Before sending their manuscripts to the publisher, there is one more question that authors need to consider—who will own the copyright? It is customary for authors to retain the copyright in scholarly books, though not necessarily in multiauthor or multiedition works of the type often found in medical or legal publishing. In journal publishing, on the contrary, authors today are typically asked to assign the copyright in their articles to the publishers. It is claimed that this makes life easier for everyone in terms of enforcing copyright claims or in giving permission for copying. A consideration of the number and mix of authors contributing to major journals gives some backing to this claim. At the same time, it is a little odd that scholarly authors retain copyright in books, where they often do object to extensive copying, but not in journal articles, which they are usually happy to have widely copied. In any case, transfer of copyright does not apply to all authors of journal articles. Articles by government employees, for example, virtually always have the copyright retained by their employer.

In recent years, academic institutions have begun to query whether their employees should assign copyright to publishers. They argue that they have provided the support that allowed the article to be written. If an employee relinquishes the copyright, it ought therefore to be in favor of the parent institution, not the publisher. A high-prestige journal can reply simply enough: if people do not like the rule, they can send their contributions elsewhere. This is potentially a clinching response to researchers and institutions concerned with their reputations. However, the many journals that are not of the highest prestige may find this type of response less useful. In addition, a considerable proportion of high-prestige journals are the products of learned societies or professional associations. These cannot take too cavalier an attitude to authors, since these include their own members. The growth of electronic publishing has been a major stimulus of this debate. Institutions are becoming increasingly concerned with intellectual property rights. This is exacerbated by their belief that authors and their institutions are contributing even more effort to electronic publications than they have done to printed publications. Publishers claims to copyright are therefore regarded with increasing suspicion.

For book publication, it is not only copyright that has to be negotiated. The publisher's contract—a fearsome-looking document for the inexperienced author—also has to be scrutinized and signed. Its complexity is partly related to the additional factors that arise when publishing a book. For example, there is the question of payment of royalties and, perhaps, of an advance on royalties to the author. (In scholarly publishing, the royalties are typically low, and advances may be nonexistent.) Again, a book contract includes the date when it is expected that the manuscript will be submitted, though it rarely specifies the date when the publisher will produce the book. Virtually all contractual arrangements in the field of scholarship leave the balance of power with the publisher. As has been remarked:

> Every standard contract contains a clause specifying that the publisher will accept for publication a manuscript only when the publisher finds it satisfactory. No contract ever specifies that an author can terminate a publishing contract if he or she finds the publishing house's services to be unsatisfactory.[20]

Editors and Referees

The crunch point for both books and journal articles is the acceptability of the material submitted for publication. For scholarly publication, this means acceptability by the appropriate research community. On the one hand, publication is a major aim of researchers, especially, though not solely, those in the academic world. It is, after all, tied in with the system of rewards, both material and immaterial. On the other, the research community must scrutinize new contributions with some care before accepting them as a part of communal thinking (the norm of "organized skepticism"). It follows there must be some form of quality control, approved by the community, that is applied to new material. This control is exerted, in the first instance, by editors, who act as gatekeepers. They take the lead in deciding whether a contribution shall achieve publication and, if so, how it shall be presented. The acceptance process is more complex, and also more revealing, for journal articles, since they normally arrive out of the blue, without prior consultation with the editor.

Major journals have editors with backgrounds relevant to the subject matter of the journal who work full time at the publishers. They cooperate with scholarly editors in the fields concerned, who do editorial work part time, usually from their own institutions. Such scholarly editors are chosen because they are well-known in their community, though not necessarily the most productive researchers. They also often come from institutions with a well-established reputation in the field. Many continue as editors for an extended period of time, picking up editorial skills as they go along. Major journals provide them with honoraria and secretarial assistance. Further down the scale, minor journals may rely almost entirely on unpaid editorial work by researchers. For both major and minor journals, there are basic tasks that editors must fulfill. From the publisher's viewpoint, one of the most important is getting out issues on time. For authors, the importance of editors is that they have both the first and the last word on manuscripts submitted for publication.

When a manuscript arrives, it is first vetted by the editor, who decides how it shall be handled. One option is to reject it out of hand. A high-prestige journal, receiving many more articles than it can publish, turns away a significant proportion of the submissions at this initial stage. (One study of a major medical journal found that over half the incoming articles never progressed beyond the editorial office.[21]) For such journals, the editor can actually influence the development of research in the subject: for example, by favoring articles that deal with specified topics or that treat the subject in a particular way. For most journals, the editor's role as a gatekeeper is more circumscribed. Editors are at the mercy of what arrives. Apart from commissioned articles, they are effectively left with the job of sifting through the material that authors are prepared to write.

In times past, editors carried out much of the quality assessment themselves. Growth, both in the degree of specialization and in the volume of submitted material, has made this more difficult. Specialization means that few editors are likely to understand fully all the incoming articles, whereas the volume factor means they may be submerged if they try to read it all in detail. A few journals still rely on a limited amount of checking. For example, members of the National Academy of Sciences can publish their work in the Academy's *Proceedings* after only a fairly informal review. (It is presumably supposed that members, being all experienced authors, know what constitutes an acceptable article.) But, over the past half century, most journals have moved to a system that involves external referees. Their job is to evaluate the manuscripts that pass the editor's initial trawl. The process has become so common that publication in a "properly refereed" journal is now often seen as synonymous with acceptable research. Referees thus form a supplementary gatekeeping group linked to the editors.

The use of referees is not new: they have been around for more than two centuries. It is simply that their deployment has become increasingly common. Referees are traditionally chosen by the editor of the journal. There are certain obvious criteria for selection, though there are also some disciplinary differences.[22] The obvious criteria are that referees should be competent researchers who are up to date in the subject of the submitted article. In the sciences, this is usually considered sufficient, although major journals will also expect referees to be aware of the interests and requirements of the specific journal. Some areas within the general scientific field look for additional points. Thus medical editors are happiest if their referees are recognized authorities in the specialism concerned. The social sciences and humanities, as a group, have requirements that differ somewhat from those of the sciences. Editors in such fields are typically concerned that their referees should be able to make "balanced" judgments. (This means, for example, that they should be sympathetic to different types of methodology.) They should also be able to assess whether the article will interest readers of the journal other than those concerned with the specific subject matter.

These varying requirements are reflections of disciplinary differences. For example, the additional requirements for referees in the social sciences and humanities reflect both the range of theoretical frameworks within which researchers may work in these disciplines and the greater range of interdisciplinary research as compared with the sciences. The variations can also lead to the selection of referees with somewhat differing characteristics. Thus the emphasis on choosing "authorities" in medicine means that the average medical referee is likely to be more senior than those in science as a whole. Equally, the emphasis on detailed technical criticism in mathematics leads to referees in this field being more junior on average than in other sciences. The latter point reflects a basic problem of refereeing. As it is an unpaid activity, often not of immediate relevance to their own work, researchers can only devote a limited amount of time to it. For junior researchers, selection as a referee may imply a welcome recognition of their expertise. For senior researchers, refereeing is an activity they often undertake primarily from a sense of duty (the norm of "communality"). Correspondingly, junior researchers are apt to spend more time on refereeing an article than senior researchers do. The latter may take only a few hours to assess an article and to comment on its good and bad points. An invitation to referee is often seen as a request for negative criticism. It takes a confident (which usually means experienced) referee to be even handed in providing both positive and negative comments.

Most journals provide instructions to referees on what they should have in mind when assessing manuscripts. Some relate to style and presentation. For example, do the title and abstract properly reflect what the article is about? Some are specific to the discipline. The appropriateness of the experimental setup may need to be assessed in the sciences, whereas the nature of the statistical analysis may be an important issue to examine in the social sciences. However, most refereeing instructions ask for comments on three basic points—the originality, the soundness, and the significance of the reported research. To do justice to these requires an extensive knowledge of the field together with considerable experience as a researcher. Hence, referees tend to be among the better-established people in their speciality. Such people have developed their own ideas of what constitutes publishable research. Table 35 indicates what a group of referees in the social sciences said they looked for in a manuscript.[23] They were asked to grade the different factors on a scale running from 1 (= low importance) to 7 (= high importance).

Table 35
Referees' Views on the Relative Importance of Different Assessment Criteria

Criterion	Mean score
Value of the findings for advancing the field	5.8
Acceptability of the research design	5.6
Theoretical relevance of the work	5.4
Level of scholarship demonstrated	5.4
Presence of creative ideas	5.2
New empirical evidence	5.0
Sophistication of methodology and analysis	4.3
Relevance of the article to the journal's focus	4.3
Display of ethical sensitivity	4.1
Value of findings for everyday life	2.9
Entertainment value	1.5
Background and reputation of the author	1.3

Most editors believe they can select referees for the majority of the submissions they receive on the basis of their own knowledge of the research community. They are usually in informal contact with a considerable number of researchers in the field and can turn to colleagues if they need further suggestions. Where the scope of the journal is broad, there may be an editorial board, or a group of editorial advisers, to provide more formal assistance in choosing referees. Files of referees' names are increasingly being kept on computer. This allows quick identification of appropriate referees when the editor receives a new article. It also provides a check on referees' activities. Most editors try not to overburden referees, so it is useful to keep a record of when each referee has been approached in the past. Equally, editors are concerned with the speed with which a referee responds. For rapid-publication journals, in particular, it is essential that referees comment quickly (within, say, 2–3 weeks). However, there are limits on how far editors can press referees. The number of suitable referees in a particular specialism may be small, and they may have material sent to them from more than one journal. For example, a study of the referees recruited by a public health journal found that they were, on average, evaluating articles for three to four different journals each year.[24] An editor's latitude for selection can, therefore, be limited by the pressures on the publication system as a whole.

Table 35 lays out the factors that referees thought were important for an acceptable research article. Table 36 lists the main problems actually found in a sample of articles submitted to two management studies journals.[25] Clearly, the defects are particularly related to the marrying of theory with practice. This is a widespread problem in the social sciences. A study of manuscripts in journalism and communications found that people who had acted

Table 36
Problems Found in Management Studies Manuscripts

	Percentage of total problems found	Percentage of manuscripts with this problem
Lack of theory	22	51
Theory and practical investigation not aligned	14	32
Ill-defined theory	11	24
Ill-defined research design	11	24
Poorly structured argument	10	23
Poorly written article	9	21

as referees considered theoretical interest as much more important than did nonreferees.[26] The latter, conversely, valued practical implications much more highly than referees did. This is also often an author–reader divide.

It is not altogether surprising if experienced researchers—which is what referees are—differ from others in their assessment of what must be emphasized in research articles. But referees can also differ between themselves in their assessment of articles. For example, referees of articles submitted to a journal of radiology were habitually asked to grade all the manuscripts they scrutinized on a scale running from 1 (= outstanding) to 9 (= unacceptable).[27] The mean score averaged over all referees came out at 4.8. The referees whose averages lay more than 1.5 standard deviations from this mean value were examined. It appeared that 5–10% were consistently high in their gradings, and a similar proportion consistently low. In other words, among the main bulk of referees it was possible to distinguish small groups of "strict" and "lenient" referees.

It might be supposed that editors would cease to use referees whose views on submitted articles consistently differed from those of their peers. This does happen, but by no means always. Editors get to know the foibles of referees whom they use regularly and so can make allowances when assessing their comments. Indeed, the individual differences can sometimes be exploited by an editor to help determine the progress of an article. An article that an editor particularly wants to publish can be sent to a lenient referee, whereas one regarded with suspicion can go to a strict referee. In practice, this oversimplifies the situation. Most of the major journals have manuscripts read by more than one referee. The obvious rationale is that, by combining opinions, the idiosyncrasies of individual referees can be ironed out. This does not necessarily happen, because editors often choose referees with differing backgrounds, so that they review different aspects of the manuscript. One comparison of referees' comments on social science manuscripts concluded that: "While there were few contradictions and numerous matches (especially among criticisms), most comments were neither contradicted nor matched. Instead, the referees simply observed and commented on different aspects of the manuscript."[28] Under these circumstances, there is no contradiction in the referees reaching different conclusions. For example, if two referees assessed an article in psychology, one looking for originality and the other for statistical validity, they might well differ in their views as to the acceptability of the manuscript.

A referee can make three basic recommendations (though journals often ask for finer gradings than this). An article can be accepted, or returned for revision, or rejected. Most major journals only accept a relatively small proportion of the incoming manuscripts for publication without change. A majority of the articles published undergo modification, ranging from the minor to the very extensive. For example, a study of articles published in the *British Medical Journal* found that over 80% had been revised.[29] As Table 36 indicates, referees' criticisms fall into two main groups—those aimed at the research content and those concerning presentation. Among the medical articles published, over half had alterations made to their contents—for example, by the addition of more data or by the provision of more information on the methodology or analysis. Correspondingly, almost half the articles required alterations to the presentation, in many cases involving a shortening of their length. Upholders of the value of refereeing often point to this ability to improve the quality of published articles as being more important than its role in proposing acceptance or rejection of articles.

Referees and Authors

From the authors' viewpoint, peer assessment looks rather different. They hope to have their work accepted for immediate publication as it stands. The need to make changes implies that the authors have been deficient in some way, and they may find this hard to concede. Apart from emotional attachment to their creation, authors can find the interpretation and fulfillment of referees' suggestions difficult. Referees may differ from authors in their views of how the research should be done, and they may misinterpret or misunderstand authors' arguments. One estimate in biomedicine was that a fifth of all referees' reports contained factual errors.[30] Where there is more than one referee, their comments may not always be reconcilable. Nevertheless, referees' criticisms are conveyed to authors by editors, who presumably support them. However annoyed authors may be, they must still take account of the criticism, if they wish to publish in the journal. Effectively, revision of an article represents a process of negotiation between the author and the referees via the (not always neutral) editor.

If authors are not always happy at having to revise their work, they are still less happy at having it rejected altogether. The likelihood of rejection increases for major journals: competition for publication in such journals as *Science* or *Nature* is high. But hopes of avoiding rejection also depend significantly on the subject field of the submitted article. Table 37 examines the rejection rates of the leading journals in a number of different subjects.[31]

Table 37
Rejection Rates for Leading Journals in Different Subjects

Subject of journal	Mean rejection rate (%)
Physics	24
Biological sciences	29
Chemistry	31
Mathematics	50
Economics	69
Sociology	78
Philosophy	85
History	90

Rejection rates are clearly lowest in the sciences and highest in the humanities, with social sciences in between. In fact, this can be pushed further in terms of a "hard–soft" differentiation. Subjects that have both "hard" and "soft" components, such as psychology or geography, tend to have lower rejection rates for journals dealing with the hard aspects, as compared with those catering for the soft aspects.

An obvious interpretation of these results relates to the nature of the disciplines: How widely do the researchers in a subject agree on the same conceptual framework? The greater the uncertainty concerning how research should be presented and evaluated, the more difficult it is to produce an acceptable account. In the sciences, because the evaluation criteria are fairly clear, articles are accepted when no reason can be adduced for rejecting them. In the humanities, the argument tends to work the other way: a manuscript can be rejected unless there are strong reasons for publishing it.

This differentiation in terms of the nature of the subject only tells part of the tale. Any journal has a physical limitation on the number of articles it can publish each year (usually set by financial considerations). The average science journal can afford to publish many more articles than the average humanities journal; it can, therefore, allow a lower rate of rejection. From this viewpoint, the peer review system is a way of matching the flow of manuscripts from authors with the capacity of the journal. In practice, both conceptual and practical factors are at work, and they interact in the determination of input and output. Indeed, this applies to publication in general. Many scholars in the humanities feel that their arguments are better deployed via book-length rather than article-length publications. The difficulty of having articles accepted by leading humanities journals makes books a still more attractive option. In publishing terms, books are handled differently from journals, so their financial limitations are also of a different kind. Again, this offers scholars an alternative way forward; so the choice between publishing in books and journals is influenced by both conceptual and practical factors.

Authors usually have a considerable amount of intellectual capital tied up in the research article they are trying to publish. In addition, the amount of time, money, and effort that goes into an article can be considerable. One estimate puts authorship costs per article at the equivalent of about a quarter of the average researcher's annual salary.[32] Hardly surprisingly, therefore, the peer review system is often fiercely criticized when it delays or rejects work. Complaints fall into two categories. The first is that the system is inefficient. It is, "unreliable, invalid and harmful to the best type of research—that which is innovative."[33] The second is that the system is biased. "Sizable majorities of scholars in seven broad disciplines think the peer-review system for deciding what gets published in scholarly journals is biased in favor of established researchers, scholars from prestigious institutions, and those who use currently fashionable approaches to their subjects."[34] Refereeing also takes time and effort. A study of biologists found that some 15% of the more experienced researchers in universities were involved in refereeing each year (along with about half that proportion in research establishments and industry).[35] If each refereeing exercise costs a few hundred dollars, this represents a considerable amount of donated effort. Another complaint is that refereeing slows down the publication process, perhaps by several months and leads to further costs as authors are required to revise their manuscripts. In the light of all this criticism, how effective is peer review in practice?

The key question concerning the effectiveness of the system is—do referees assess manuscripts consistently and correctly? The simplest way of testing this is to look at the level of agreement when two or more referees are sent the same article for their independent assessment. One study of psychology journals measured this degree of agreement on a scale running from −1 (completely contradictory recommendations) to +1 (complete agreement).[36] The average score for the journals came out at +0.27. In other words, there was moderate, but far from perfect agreement. This seems typical of the social sciences in general. Agreement in the physical sciences is usually appreciably better, but the results of biomedical refereeing are closer to those of the social sciences. An examination of decisions on whether to accept or reject articles found that there was 97% agreement among referees for a leading physics journal.[37] For two biomedical journals, this fell to 75%; as compared with 73% for a sociology journal.

A typical editorial policy is to send an article out to two referees. If they disagree in their assessment, a copy of the article is then dispatched to a third referee (or more) for further consideration. Attempts have been made to improve the certainty of the process by using several referees (into double figures) simultaneously. This has not been overwhelmingly successful. In some cases, it simply widens the spread of opinion while decreasing the feedback from individual referees. Given the problems of finding a large number of competent referees and of communicating with them, use of several referees has not proved to be a popular option. In any case, the statistics on agreement have to be interpreted with care. As has been noted earlier, referees may be assessing different aspects of a manuscript, and this can lead to differing opinions. Disagreements of this kind can usually be resolved by the editor.

Agreement between referees is generally best on which articles are definitely not up to the standard required by the journal. Most difficulties, inevitably, are raised by borderline articles. Rather more surprisingly, it seems that overall assessment does not depend critically on particular expertise in the topic of the article, though special expertise may lead to more suggestions regarding modifications to the contents. Some journals allow authors to suggest the names of potential referees. This helps satisfy them that appropriate experts are being consulted (and also provides new names for the editor's file of referees). The editor must obviously monitor the responses of such referees with care: their comments may be particularly important where there is disagreement on what constitutes acceptable research. Perhaps this is best illustrated by an experiment in an area of psychology, where the researchers did not hold such a single view. The referees of a U.S. psychology journal were sent articles that had basically similar content but some introduced variations.[38] More especially, the data sections were adjusted to give results that were thought likely either to agree with, or to contradict, the presumed theoretical standpoint of the referee. Manuscripts that agreed with the referee's conceptual framework received higher gradings than those that contradicted it.

This leads to a wider question: how important is such unwitting bias in refereeing? There are several ways in which it might occur. One would be if manuscripts from eminent researchers were to be treated more gently than those from unknowns. Anecdotal evidence suggests that this can happen, but, in practice, it is very difficult to demonstrate. Eminent researchers gain that status because they produce more significant research. If peer reviewing is doing its job, the work of eminent researchers should therefore be more likely to receive a positive evaluation. Investigations that have allowed for this have found little evidence for a bias in favor of "big names." One survey of a major physics journal found only two differences in the way articles from high-status and low-status physicists tended to be refereed.[39] Those from high-status physicists were handled more quickly than those from low-status physicists. The other difference actually worked the opposite way: young low-status authors had a higher proportion of their manuscripts accepted than elderly high-status authors. Investigation of refereeing bias in terms of contributing authors can, in any case, be affected by other trends in refereeing. For example, there is evidence that the rejection rate for manuscripts with several authors is less than that for single-authored manuscripts in the sciences.[40] The reason may lie in the contents. Multiauthored articles are more likely to reflect well-funded experimental or observational projects, which referees find it less easy to criticize. However, collaborative writing is also likely to iron out some of the deficiencies in the original manuscript so that referees see less need for major revisions.[41]

Questions about bias in refereeing can be asked of institutions, as well as individuals. Do articles submitted from high-prestige institutions have an easier passage than those from less well-known institutions? Once more, there is anecdotal evidence for such differentiation. For example, a researcher in psychology has reported finding it easier to publish in leading journals after he moved from North Dakota to Harvard.[42] Yet survey evidence for such a bias is limited. Perhaps the best comes from a study of refereeing for two physical science journals in the UK.[43] Referees were divided into two groups—from "major" and "minor" universities—and their assessment of manuscripts from each other's groups was examined. Table 38 indicates the proportions in each category that were classified as "good." Clearly, referees from minor universities graded manuscripts at much the same level regardless of source. Referees from major universities were significantly more likely to grade manuscripts from other major universities more highly than those from minor universities.

Another small-scale study is worth citing.[44] Recent issues of a group of leading psychology journals were scanned, and an article with an author from

Table 38
Proportion of Manuscripts Rated "Good" by Referees

	Minor university authors (%)	Major university authors (%)
Minor university referees	65	68
Major university referees	50	83

a high-prestige institution selected from each. Slight alterations were made to the articles, including new authors' names and new (fictitious) authors' institutions. The revised articles were then resubmitted to the journal that had originally published them. Of the 12 articles involved, three were detected to be resubmissions. One of the remaining nine was accepted for publication; the others were rejected. Does this imply an institution-related bias? The study has been criticized from a number of viewpoints. For example, the rejection rates of the group of journals was high (around 80%). Given the variety of viewpoints that different referees can have, it is possible that even unchanged articles might have been rejected on resubmission. Nevertheless, the authors of the original study argue that the implication of institutional bias should not be ignored.

One way of trying to avoid such bias is obviously to delete the author's name and affiliation before sending copies of the manuscript to referees. Some journals do this, either habitually or on request. It is not always sufficient to guard against identification. Apart from referees' knowledge of other people working in the field, there are clues within the article, such as references to previous work. Though referees actually often guess wrong, authorship can be determined in these ways for an appreciable number of allegedly anonymous articles.[45] More importantly, studies of such blind refereeing suggest that it does not greatly affect the outcome of the refereeing process.[46] Another frequently voiced suggestion is that referees should cease to be anonymous. In earlier times, it was often common knowledge who had assessed whose work, but anonymity has grown along with other ways of depersonalizing research communication. The rationale for having named referees is primarily that authors can more readily discern bias, conflict of interest, or incomprehension, when they know who is involved (and the referees will be under greater pressure to justify any criticism). Most referees do not like the idea. They believe it could lead to tedious arguments with irritated authors. As their activities are voluntary, referees can refuse to assess articles from a journal whose requirements seem to them to be too demanding. Without the referees' cooperation, editors, even if they want to, can do little, so open refereeing remains limited in extent.

There are, then, some hints of systematic bias in refereeing, though nothing on the scale often postulated by authors. Indeed, most such apparent bias can readily be submerged by the random variations of judgment that occur. The evidence seems to suggest that the basic factor at work is one that would be difficult to eliminate. Referees look for views that are congruent with their own. If the research framework, values, or beliefs that are adopted by the author differ from the referees' own, they are more likely to reject the article. The more uniform the research background, the fewer the problems of agreement between referees.

Particular Problems

A major breakthrough in any field is potentially at variance with accepted beliefs and practices. Important innovations may therefore encounter difficulties in passing through the peer-review system. Anecdotal evidence to this effect is much commoner than survey data, not least because major developments are necessarily somewhat limited in number. An anecdotal example is provided by the journal *Nature*, a major outlet for reports on significant recent activities in the sciences. Between the two world wars, the journal rejected, on the advice of referees, three of the really important scientific advances of the time. It is said that the editors, partly as a result of this, attached rather less importance to the refereeing process after the Second World War. One survey has looked at the publication process for some two hundred of the most highly cited scientific articles.[47] It found that about 10% had experienced problems in being accepted for publication.

The question of bias relating to gender is more difficult to resolve. For example, female researchers have certainly been involved less as journal editors pro rata than their male counterparts. However, this may simply reflect their differences in status, since editors are usually senior people in the field. In more recent years, the balance has begun to adjust. For example, the number of women serving on the main editorial committees of the Modern Language Association of America rose from two (out of 18) in 1973 to 17 (out of 33) in 1985.

In terms of publishing in journals, name ordering seems to depend similarly on contribution and position for all authors regardless of gender. If there is a problem here, it probably lies at a deeper level. For example, a multiauthor article has more chance of smooth passage through the peer-review system than an article with a single author. Hence, differing male/female levels of research collaboration could affect rates of acceptance. Some journals have had the policy of differentiating between male and female authors in the article heading, typically by assigning initials to the former and spelling out first names for the latter. Where the policy is to use first names for all authors—more typical of the social sciences than the sciences—gender differences are obvious in any case. This indication of authors' gender does not seem to have much effect on acceptance, judging by experiments with blind refereeing.

Women do tend to feel, more than men, that there are biases in the refereeing system. Table 39 gives the proportions of male and female researchers in social sciences and the humanities who were found in one survey to believe that refereeing bias occurred frequently.[48] The interesting point is that the responses from women indicated a greater belief than men in bias across the board, not just in a bias that favors male authors. This may reflect lesser female experience of refereeing: if so, it can be expected to decrease with time. There is, in fact, no firm evidence that editors or referees are significantly biased against female authors.[49] Even in the humanities, where existence of such a link has been specifically alleged, it has not been supported by the evidence.[50]

It is similarly difficult to determine whether there are systematic biases between referees from different countries. Many leading journals try to use a geographical spread of referees to guard against this. However, employing referees who are close at hand is often quicker and easier, so they tend to be overrepresented. The question is whether this imbalance leads to a bias against foreign authors. For articles sent from developing countries to Western journals, there can be good reasons why rejection rates are higher than for other authors. Communication difficulties and lack of support in the country can mean that the research submitted is already dated in Western eyes. The problem of writing in a foreign language may lead to ambiguities in the text, or even to incomprehension on the part of the editor or referee. Indigenous publications in developing countries experience their own difficulties in terms of peer review. For example, expert referees are often in short supply, and delays can be considerable.

The best way of looking for national bias in refereeing is therefore to examine mutual peer review between two countries that are generally similar in their journal-publishing habits. The most detailed survey of this kind has compared U.S. refereeing of British manuscripts and vice versa in the physical sciences.[51] The results suggest there may be a hint of bias in favor of

Table 39

The Existence of Bias in Refereeing Judgments

Favored group	Bias frequently occurs (%)	
	Female	Male
Established researchers	63	47
Scholars using "currently fashionable approaches"	59	49
Scholars in prestigious institutions	51	38
Males	32	7

manuscripts from one's own country, but the difference is slight. Any differences here, as for gender, are probably best explained by referees preferring manuscripts that are most congruent with their own research approach.

Whether or not refereeing biases occur, a large number of would-be authors can be left at the end with rejected manuscripts. The question is what they do next. To some extent the answer depends on their background. A researcher in a field where rejection rates are low may feel more inclined to give up than one in a field where rejection is common. Again, would-be authors working in industry may be less motivated to pursue publication than academic authors, since publication is less vital to their careers. However, most researchers, having put considerable effort both into the original project and into writing it up, try again. A study of articles rejected by the *British Medical Journal* found that three-quarters of those whose subsequent history could be tracked were published in other journals.[52] It might be supposed that their chance of acceptance had been enhanced by the referees' comments from the first journal. In fact, only about a fifth of these articles had been revised prior to resubmission elsewhere. These figures are quite typical. Another survey across a number of subjects in science, technology, and the social sciences found that some 60% of authors whose manuscripts were not accepted by their journal of choice later resubmitted them to another journal.[53] Only about half carried out any revision, but about 90% of the submissions were accepted by the second journals.

Most studies have looked at manuscripts submitted to major journals. Targeting such journals indicates that their authors, at least, thought they were presenting significant research. Consequently, if balked at their first attempt, they turn to another where they calculate their chances of publication to be better. These second-choice journals are usually ones judged by the authors to be further down the pecking order, where publishing pressures are less. (They are joined there by first-time articles submitted by authors with more modest initial aims.) Authors' judgments of journals appear to be reasonably well founded. Studies of resubmitted articles typically show that they go to journals with lower impact factors, and there they receive fewer citations than articles published in the first-choice journal.[54] Resubmission means that a new group of editors and referees have added their comments: after consequent revision, it is fairly good odds in most subjects that the resultant article will prove acceptable. All this involves extra time and effort. Each resubmission can add weeks or months to prepublication delays, as well as requiring more peer-review input and more authoring activity. Still it reinforces the common belief that any reasonable article can find a home somewhere.

It is commonly found that a small, but not insignificant, proportion of rejected manuscripts are subsequently submitted to, and accepted by, journals whose standing is equal to, or better than, that of the first-choice journal. This suggests that authors' strategy on resubmission depends on their assessment of the importance of their work. It also underlines the element of subjectivity in refereeing. This is as likely to work in favor of authors as against them. For example, whatever the status of the journal, referees sometimes overlook errors in the contents. Incorrect handling of statistics occurs quite frequently and is especially liable to be missed by referees. Another area where there are problems for referees is recognizing that authors have failed to refer to all relevant research that has appeared. These oversights can be attributed partly to simple lack of knowledge on the part of the referee and partly to the limited time devoted to refereeing.

In most cases, authors' errors and omissions do not entirely invalidate the conclusions reached in their publications. The same is often true of more deliberate omissions that a referee can hardly be expected to spot. For example, an author may leave out data points that deviate greatly from the mean. Such changes, if pushed too far, can begin to verge on fraud—a term generally reserved for research where data have been deliberately falsified. There have been a number of cases of such fraud identified in recent years.[55] The most publicized have mainly been in biomedical research in the United States. There has been considerable debate as to whether these instances can be generalized to other subjects and countries. Pressure to publish is particularly strong in biomedicine, so there is more temptation to commit fraud there than in most other subjects. At the same time, the U.S. biomedical community has been especially active in tracking down fraud, not least because erroneous results can be dangerous. Looking at other countries, fraud in biomedical research certainly occurs outside the United States. Whether it is found depends, apparently, on whether it is looked for. The odds are that fraudulent research has always existed. There has, for example, been a bitter debate for several years past over the observations of the astronomer, Ptolemy, in the second century A.D., and whether they represent a piece of creative accounting. In view of the pressures, the surprising thing is that fraudulent publications do not appear more often. As it is, genuine errors are as likely to bamboozle readers as deliberate fraud.

Authors' lack of acknowledgment of earlier research may be because they never read about it or read about it and forgot. There is a fine line here between unknowingly repeating research and copying work without due acknowledgment. Again, a distinction must be made between taking ideas without acknowledgment and actually reproducing another researchers' words. Plagiarism of the latter type is easier to demonstrate. In extreme cases, it can mean that researchers take previously published articles, make cosmetic changes (new author and institutional affiliation, perhaps new title, etc.), then publish them as their own in other journals. Such plagiarism may go unchallenged by editors, referees, or readers for a long time. A French mathematician republished a number of mathematical articles in this way between the two world wars,[56] and during the 1970s an Iraqi biomedical researcher in the United States published some 60 articles that mostly plagiarized other people's work.[57] In general, if fairly obscure work is republished in minor or specialist journals, referees are quite likely not to spot what is happening. Plagiarism tends to go astray if it becomes too ambitious. For example, the French mathematician was unmasked when he tried to republish an article by a well-known researcher in the field. Though such plagiarism is a form of fraud, the contents of the reprinted articles are at least likely to contain reliable research.

Plagiarism is not necessarily restricted to authors. One of the recurring complaints about the peer-review system is that referees can take ideas from the manuscripts they assess. It is very difficult to prove that this is occurring. Referees are often working on topics similar to the authors' topics: that, after all, is why they have been chosen as referees. This difficulty was at the heart of a biomedical dispute in the 1980s.[58] An adjudicating panel finally had to be formed, which decided that the referee had been guilty of: "patterning his experiments after those detected in a manuscript sent to him for review, using the information to publish his own work and falsifying his records to claim credit." It is probably fair to guess that actual theft of this sort is, nevertheless, less common than authors tend to suspect.

Some learned and professional societies already have codes of ethics that they expect authors to follow when carrying out research and reporting the results. The Commission of Research Integrity in the United States has recently proposed a definition of research misconduct that can be applied, at least across all the sciences and social sciences, as a basis for deciding when a researcher has been guilty of unacceptable conduct.

> Research misconduct is significant misbehavior that improperly appropriates the intellectual property or contributions of others, that intentionally impedes the progress of research, or that risks corrupting the scientific record or compromising the integrity of scientific practices. Such behaviors are unethical and unacceptable in proposing, conducting, or reporting research, or in reviewing the proposals or research reports of others. [59]

Such strictures are aimed, in the first instance, at authors. Referees have to begin with the assumption that authors are telling the truth. They can only question this if there is evidence, more especially in the manuscript itself, that arouses suspicion. Editors bear more responsibility for what is published, but, even so, much of their work involves trusting in the integrity of their colleagues. The question is—what can be done about articles that are later found to contain errors? The usual response is for a notice of correction to be published in a subsequent issue of the journal concerned. Most such corrections come because the authors, themselves, spot errors. They are usually minor, in the sense that they do not fundamentally change the conclusions reached. Thus an analysis of the corrections published in a medical journal found that about a third dealt with errors of fact, somewhat less than a third added information missing from the original, and the remainder covered typographical errors, mistakes in authors' affiliations, etc.[60] The drawback to this system is that such insertions may pass unnoticed by the reader. More importantly, people who read the original article at a later date may have no way of knowing that a correction exists.

Much more rarely, a notice may contain a retraction of what was published rather than a correction. The impetus for such a retraction can come from the author, but, in recent years, it has often come from elsewhere—for example, from the author's home institution. The most difficult cases of this sort have been where the researchers suspected of misconduct have been co-authors rather than sole authors of the questioned articles. The other authors then come under pressure to explain what their roles were: almost inevitably, there is an implication that they have been negligent. Journal editors have to tread a cautious path through such disputes. If the authors are in contention with each other or with their institutions, publishing a retraction can become a legal minefield. Most editors will, at best, restrict themselves to a note that a particular article needs treating with care until, and unless, the legal position becomes clear. Under these circumstances, researchers are most likely to hear about the problems via informal channels, which may be of little use to researchers who read the articles in later years.

Quality Control of Books

Peer assessment of publications other than journals follows a similar overall pattern, but often differs in the way it is organized. For example, conferences may begin with a request for prospective contributors to send in abstracts of their proposed talks. These may be assessed by members of a program committee, who will decide on which abstracts to accept. If conference proceedings are to be published, the full texts of the presentations are usually required at, or before, the conference. They may undergo further assessment prior to inclusion in the published volume. This is the ideal. In practice, the initial assessment of abstracts may be limited in scope; the actual presentations may differ considerably from the abstracts initially submitted; speakers may fail to deliver the full text of their talks. Consequently, the quality of conference proceedings and of individual contributions in the same proceedings can vary greatly, without this necessarily being obvious to the unwary reader.

Scholarly books often have a rather similar sequence of vetting to conference proceedings. As with journals, editors make the first decisions about publishing. There may be more than one type of editor involved. For example, a monograph series may have an in-house editor and an advisory editor from the academic world. Equally, manuscripts arrive in diverse ways, which can affect the likelihood of their being accepted. Table 40 outlines the position for a scholarly press in the United States that concentrated mainly on the social sciences.[61]

The first row in the table provides the best parallel to the way articles are submitted. Acceptance rates vary with the publisher—some are appreciably less stringent than the figures quoted—but the relative rates of acceptance in the three categories are characteristic of much scholarly publishing. Overall, it is clear that trying to publish a book can be an even more chancy activity than trying to publish a journal article. One survey found that the typical book published in the social sciences or humanities had been to two or more presses before it was finally accepted.[62] Though the questions of

Table 40

Acceptance Rate for Books Published by a Scholarly Press

Acquisition category	Estimated number of submissions	Number published	Percentage of submissions published
Author had no previous contact with press	3,640	21	0.6
Author had previous contact with press	940	79[a]	8.4
Acquired on editor's personal initiative	100	35	35.0

[a]This includes a number of revised editions, paperback editions, etc.

prestige (in this case, of the publisher) and audience outreach is as much in the minds of book authors as of authors of articles, the former are more concerned than the latter with identifying any reasonable outlet that will allow their work to appear in print.

The importance of prior contact with the publisher is evident from Table 40. This is underlined by the fact that book editors reject more submissions on their own initiative than journal editors do. Such reliance on in-house judgment can lead to a greater possibility of bias in the selection of book manuscripts than for journal articles. This is most evident in terms of institutional background. One editor-in-chief has been quoted as saying: "People at good schools write good books and people at poor schools write bad books or no books at all. It's that simple. You can't go wrong publishing the books of people at the élite schools."[63] This actually glosses over the main factor at work. Editors at scholarly publishers usually establish strong links with a limited number of major institutions rather than weaker links with a large number of minor institutions. The former are, after all, more likely to house the high-quality, highly productive researchers. Hence, submissions from the former are more likely to be heard of via the editorial grapevine. This enhances the probability that such manuscripts will be scrutinized with care. The likelihood of immediate acceptance remains low, but such authors have a greater chance of clearing the publication hurdle. Similarly, if senior authors seem to have an easier life than junior authors, one reason often lies in their better contacts with the world of publishing. Perhaps because there are many more female editors in book publishing than in journal publishing, female authors do not seem to have more problems than their male peers in making contact and in having their work published.

If editors decide that a submission should be taken seriously, it is usually sent out to be reviewed by experts in the field. Submissions come in various forms. They may be complete manuscripts, but, especially for experienced authors, an extended outline or an outline plus a sample chapter can be deemed adequate. This material will be dispatched to one or two external experts for assessment. In the case of an outline, the same or other reviewers may also comment on the final manuscript. (The word *reviewer* is used more often than *referee* when talking of book assessment: the connotation in terms of peer-review activities is similar.) Editors often select reviewers from their informal network of contacts in the scholarly world. More particularly, they are likely to turn to authors whom the press has previously published successfully in the same field. Book publishers, like journal publishers, usually provide standard forms to guide reviewers' comments. In contrast with journal refereeing, book reviewers are offered a small fee for their opinions (though the emphasis is on "small").

Editors obviously wish to be satisfied that the book they are publishing will be a contribution to knowledge, but they must have more than that in mind when selecting manuscripts for publication. Above all, the question of finance is of much more immediate consequence for a book than for a journal article. A scholarly publisher cannot afford too many titles that do not break even in financial terms. Reviewers are therefore often asked not only for their ideas on the target audience, but also for possible estimates of individual and institutional sales. The editor must then juggle estimated sales against the cost of producing the volume (including any available subsidy) to see whether it is a financially feasible proposition. The final decision will depend on the current situation at the publisher. If there is an unexpected shortfall of material, a borderline case may go forward in order to keep staff occupied and make some contribution to the overheads. In consequence, whereas assessment of a journal article relates primarily to its quality, the assessment of a scholarly book is concerned with both its quality and its commercial viability.

The significant difference between peer review of books and journal articles comes after publication. Articles, unless they are among the limited number subsequently discussed in review surveys, are rarely subject to a further critique. Scholarly books, on the contrary, are commonly reviewed after they appear. The reviews can be found in some general publications, such as newspapers and magazines, and in specialist publications, such as journals. Both authors and publishers regard this retrospective peer review as of major importance. For authors, the reviews are where most of their colleagues will gain an impression of the book; for publishers, good reviews are often linked to sales (more especially, to library purchases). Reviewers in specialist publications are usually researchers in the same general field as the author. Their reviews may provide an extended commentary—often called an "essay review"—which can become a research publication in its own right. Writing book reviews is a very common activity in the humanities and social sciences. Some two-thirds of researchers in these fields contribute a book review at some time in their career.[64] There is the usual skew distribution, with a small number of reviewers being called on frequently. These overlap with the group who review scholarly books in newspapers and magazines, though the latter includes generalists who may not be researchers at all.

The commonest number of reviews per book lies in the range 6–10 (with history and geography at the top end of the range), but approaching

5% are reviewed across more than 20 publications.[65] The latter titles may also be reviewed in general outlets, though the selection for these is governed by a range of factors, such as the prestige of the publishing house. For example, major providers of reviews, such as the *New York Times Book Review*, tend to give greater emphasis to titles published by the larger university presses in the United States and the UK. Newspapers and magazines naturally review more rapidly. Half the reviews appear in the same year as the book and almost all the remainder in the following year. Specialist journals (which may have only a few issues per year) average much longer. Less than 10% of the reviews appear in the same year as the book, whereas about 80% have appeared by two years after publication. The remaining 20% are spread out over succeeding years: it is quite possible for a review to appear after the book reviewed has gone out of print. Books in the social sciences are reviewed somewhat more quickly than those in the humanities, partly, perhaps, because scholars in the humanities tend to write more books. It is also the case that humanities journals are considerably more likely to review books on the social sciences than vice versa, which may reflect the greater emphasis on interdisciplinarity in the humanities.

Unlike journal articles, books are brought to the attention of scholars in more than one way. Potential readers can encounter scholarly books, both at one remove via book reviews and at first hand in academic bookshops. From the publisher's viewpoint, the important thing is that this audience should purchase as many copies of the book as possible. The financial pressure on the book publishing process means that some titles can appear that purport to be scholarly but would be rejected by the relevant research community. The controversy over Velikovsky's writings on links between supposed happenings in the solar system and the course of human history is a case in point. The first book in the series appeared under the imprint of a publisher with a considerable reputation in the scholarly world. Researchers saw this as a debasement of the standards expected from such a publisher and complained so vociferously that the book was transferred to another imprint. There was subsequent debate whether this did not verge on censorship. In fact, it was mainly brought about by a desire that material properly reviewed and accepted by scholars should not be confused with other types of publication. There have been similar complaints when, as occasionally happens, a journal editor individually decides to accept a questionable article. In both cases, the scholarly audience is insisting on the need to abide by the appropriate ground rules. Indeed, editors and referees often identify pseudo-scholarly material via its adherence to ground rules of its own. For example, many writings in this category often have a casual and highly selective approach to evidence, a characteristic that becomes immediately apparent to a professional researcher in the field concerned. As one researcher remarked: "by now, having been at it for many years, I feel that I can spot a crank paper in physics after reading a few lines."[66] In physics, with a well-defined conceptual framework this is quite easy: for subjects with less clearly defined frameworks, the division between the scholarly and the spurious can be a good deal hazier.

Research and the Media

Reports of research in the media extend this problem a stage further. The selection principles that apply to the media are not only different from those used by researchers, they can actually contradict them. For example, the media are particularly interested when things go wrong or in highly speculative ideas. Neither of these ranks high with researchers. Despite this, researchers are usually keen to have their work reported by the media. Funding agencies, university administrators, and colleagues in other fields may all spot media reports of research. When rapid release of information is considered vital, media reporting can easily beat all the usual forms of publication. The announcement of cold fusion in 1989 provides a good example. The possibility of producing cheap nuclear energy at room temperatures was seen by the researchers and their institution as a major step forward that needed immediate publicity. The results were, therefore, first announced at a press conference. The U.S. scientific community first heard of the research via either the CBS evening news or the *Wall Street Journal*. This was actually all they did hear of it for some time, since the note that the authors sent to *Nature* for publication in the usual tradition of research was rejected by the referees.

Announcing results to the media prior to a proper peer review is an anathema to the research community. Some journal editors go a stage further and object to media exposure before the results appear in their journal, which may be some time after the refereeing process has been completed. A number may refuse to publish material that has had prior media exposure. This is often referred to as the Ingelfinger rule, since it was notably applied by Franz Ingelfinger when editor of the *New England Journal of Medicine* in the late 1960s. It obviously has to be applied with discretion: few would deny, for example, that urgent medical information should be circulated as soon as possible.

Research reported by the media falls into two categories—that which is presented as news and that contained in specially written articles for newspapers and magazines or radio and television documentaries. The first category is almost always prepared by media professionals. They also generate much of the second category, but are joined there by some researchers as providers or advisers. Researchers are also involved, at one remove, in the first category. Many journalists set up their own network of reliable contacts among researchers, to whom they turn when they need authoritative advice.

There is a problem for a researcher in being a media contact. Colleagues are likely to see this as a claim for instant authority across a range of specialities and to react accordingly. Their suspicion is part of the general love–hate relationship between researchers and the media. One problem is the form of the presentation. There is little room in the media for the qualifications and the hedgings that decorate a typical scholarly publication. Even if the researcher accepts the original description of his or her work as outlined by the journalist, it is quite likely to have been transmuted by the time it reaches the public. In a newspaper, for example, limitations of space can lead to ruthless cutting of the original. Perhaps most contentious of all is the headline. Headlines are not usually written by the journalist who provides the text, but by a subeditor, who typically has little knowledge of the subject and is working under considerable time pressure. Hardly surprisingly, misinformation in headlines provides one of the commonest causes of complaint by researchers. More generally, editorial gatekeeping in the media can be a major problem in providing information to the general public. There is some reason for supposing that journalists who specialize in writing about a particular field of research are a good deal more in tune with researchers than the editors who finally decide what is to be published.[67]

Electronic Publishing

Researchers increasingly expect that future work will be published primarily via electronic channels. In principle, they accept this: in practice, they have reservations. In terms of input to publishers, a growing number of authors are providing their material in electronic form. Collaborative writing has certainly been made easier by networked communication, especially where the authors are geographically separated. Any author can add or change the text or graphics at any time while indicating to co-authors what has been done. Such highly interactive writing can change the final product, as compared with a publication composed entirely in a paper-based environment. Indeed, use of a computer by an individual author writing alone may also do this. It has been claimed, for example, that writing style can be affected even by such minor changes as use or nonuse of a mouse.[68]

One query about electronic publishing relates to the structuring of text. Material in printed articles and books is currently structured as a linear sequence, which basically supposes that a reader starts at the beginning of the text and follows it through to the end. An electronic text can introduce hypertext links, allowing jumps backward and forward through the text, so is it appropriate to present text as a linear sequence when it is in electronic form? One answer is that, as we have seen, readers skip backward and forward through the printed text as well. The sequence provided by the author is less important than readers' ability to follow their own paths through the material: it is this that must be supported electronically. It is less obvious that some other features of printed publications need to be retained in exactly the same form in electronic publications. For example, sectionalization of text may need reconsideration. It could be argued that smaller, more numerous sections, dividing the information into finer categories, might fit the electronic format better. One particular problem is that different readers may be using differing software to access electronic publications. This means that the appearance and handling qualities of the publications may change from reader to reader.

The indications are that most authors would prefer electronic publications to bear some resemblance to their printed counterparts, at least for an initial period. They also see it as important to maintain the integrity of the presentation so that different readers do not perceive different things. Table 41 gives the responses of academics from a range of disciplines when they were asked what the printout from an electronic journal should

Table 41
Whether the Form of Presentation Imposed by the
Author Should Be Maintained in Printouts

Retain original form of presentation	Percentage of authors
Unnecessary	23
Desirable	56
Necessary	17
Donut know	4

look like.[69] Clearly, only a minority are in favor of experimentation at this stage.

Change of whatever kind requires acceptance by a majority of the research community involved. At present, the status of electronic publications is still not fully established. Some universities have yet to accept that electronic publications can be equivalent to paper-based ones for such purposes as deciding on the promotion of a staff member. Some journal editors regard publishing on the Internet as being similar to media reporting. They will not subsequently accept the material for publication in their own printed journals, nor will they regard it as an acceptable source to cite. Indeed, there is a basic problem in citing electronic publications. No standard scheme can yet be imposed, and constantly changing ways of providing electronic information may make it difficult to establish one. As a simple example, what is the best way of citing "page" references for material in electronic form? More fundamentally, one worry for authors of electronic publications is how long their material will be extant, since publishers have yet to come to terms with the problems of long-term storage. Given all these difficulties, it is hardly surprising if the authors of electronic journal articles are currently restricted in number. They fall mainly into three groups—enthusiasts; groups needing rapid publication; groups with few available paper-based outlets.

The obvious solution to these various drawbacks so far as authors are concerned is for their material to be produced in parallel as both paper-based and electronic publications. The current rapid growth in the number of electronic journal titles available is, indeed, a consequence of this approach. It also allows publishers to experiment with the capabilities of electronic communication while retaining the established financial base provided by the printed publication. Given the reassurance of a traditional outlet, authors can see some obvious potential advantages of electronic publications. Space limitations are much more relaxed for electronic handling. Not only can authors spread themselves in describing their work, they can also supply original data and images in a form that readers can manipulate for themselves. Multimedia publications can represent some important aspects of research—for example, how variables change with time—in a way that is impossible with print-on-paper. Networked publications can be linked to a wide range of external sources of information. For example, the references at the end of an article can be linked to the full text of the sources cited; images can be linked to databanks containing other images of the same objects; textual analyses can have links to the manuscripts and their variants that are being discussed. Electronic publishing can also remedy some of the defects of paper-based communication. The obvious one is speed of distribution: once the electronic publication is ready, it can reach networked recipients almost immediately. Another relates to corrections. In an electronic journal, these can be attached to the original articles, so that subsequent readers cannot miss them.

Some of these possible developments will require expenditure of greater effort on electronic publications than on their printed equivalents. Publishers will naturally try to transfer to authors as much of the effort of preparing material for electronic handling as possible. As electronic systems continue to change, this will impose a continuing learning requirement on authors. The purpose of networked publishing is to improve information handling by the human links. Overloading, both of the networks and of the individual's information burden, can reduce some of the advantages of electronic handling.

A major final question relates to quality control and peer review. An electronic journal can be more flexible in how this is carried out than is feasible with a printed journal. For example, any number of referees can be involved with little additional editorial effort. Indeed, the whole readership of a journal can be asked to look at submitted material and return their opinion. Though researchers generally acknowledge the benefits of peer review, there is a growing feeling that it might be handled in a more relaxed way electronically. The electronic preprints service in physics has shown that many readers are prepared to read and assess for themselves unrefereed material. This point has been followed to its logical conclusion by the American Physical Society.

> We will be installing an APS e-print server, which will make available unrefereed and unedited articles in all fields of physics . . . . While it will be linked to potential submissions to and refereeing for APS' journals, authors may submit their articles for publication to any other journal, or not at all.[70]

As this suggests, the fairly clear dividing line for printed journals between published and unpublished articles is becoming blurred in electronic publishing. This is having both good and bad consequences. The good result is that new research is being reported more quickly and read more widely than hitherto. The bad result is that informal/formal channels and refereed/unrefereed information are becoming more difficult to disentangle. Speculative ideas and dubious data can more readily intermingle than has been customary with paper-based communication. There are already anecdotal instances of dubious material gaining some currency. A further problem is that, with the mass media becoming increasingly concerned with information from electronic sources, such dubious material may be called to the attention of a much wider audience who are in no position to judge its acceptability.

6

Finding Out about Research

Seeking Research Information

Two stages in the communication process have been looked at so far. In the first, researchers generate information; in the second, they input it to one or more of the communication channels available to them. They encounter various obstacles relating to the generation process (e.g., an intended journal article can be rejected by the referees). The information handled by each channel is similarly subject to the restrictions that the channel imposes (e.g., printed media do not permit easy feedback from readers to authors). These limitations affect the concluding act, when those who wish to know about the research try to retrieve relevant information from a channel. This chapter deals with the activities and problems that arise at this final stage.

In general terms, the research community and its intermediaries try to structure the information passing through the channels so that it best suits the way recipients structure their knowledge. Thus for several centuries past, it has been customary among European languages to list items in alphabetical order. Authors and readers now automatically assume that a list of (say) authors' names will be searchable in alphabetical sequence. The index of a book is a more complex example of alphabetical listing: more complex, because, unlike authors' names, there are no clear requirements for what should be included or excluded, and in what form. The person who indexes a book may not see its contents in the same terms as the reader seeking information from it. Some expected entries may not appear in the index at all, whereas others may be listed under headings different from those supposed by the reader. A variety of factors can influence this mismatch. An obvious one is when the knowledge base of the information seeker is too limited. (Perhaps the reader knows the common name of a plant, but it is listed under its proper botanical name.) Again, concepts change with time. Abstracts journals are typically subject based and subdivide the material they contain into different specialities. As the subject develops, so the specialities change: old ones merge, and new ones appear. So, correspondingly, do the headings under which a subject is listed. Searching for information on a particular topic from some years back can become a guessing game.

Indexes and abstracts are specific examples of generally available aids that are intended to help searchers find relevant information. They may be constructed by the researchers, themselves, or they may be produced by professional intermediaries (such as indexers or information scientists). The intention, in either case, is to provide the information with a standard structure. Information providers and seekers alike are required to accommodate the way they personally structure knowledge to within the bounds of flexibility permitted by the information aid concerned. For example, the community has expectations, sometimes made explicit in journal instructions, regarding the structure and contents of abstracts. Authors, intermediaries, and readers have to be prepared to understand and follow those conventions. This standardization is an important factor in allowing intermediaries to play a useful role. Researchers presumably understand the information they generate, whereas those seeking the information certainly hope to understand it. Intermediaries do not necessarily operate at the same level. They may have a general understanding of the field, but only a limited knowledge of specifics. Because they comprehend the way messages are structured, they should, nevertheless, be able to reconstruct them so as to aid potential readers.

An example of this in practice can be found in the use of "keywords." These are the words in a text that provide particular insight into its contents. As noted earlier, when words are ranked in the order of the frequency with which they occur, the frequency decreases regularly and moderately quickly with rank order. Words that occur very frequently—such as *the*, or *to*—are useless for identifying relevant material, since they appear in all texts regardless of their subject matter. Equally, rare words are not very helpful for retrieval purposes, since they may appear in only a few of the textual items that are actually relevant. Identification of text relating to a particular topic is therefore best done by using words that occur with a moderate frequency—which is a fair description of keywords. Selecting words on the basis of their frequency, and so retrieving text, can be done without a great knowledge of the subject matter of the text. An intermediary can discuss possible keywords with an information seeker and so help to pin down relevant material. Indeed, computers have, for a long time, been used for keyword searching and the retrieval of appropriate items. On the one hand, automated handling can lead to a more flexible use of keywords: a simple example is the computer-produced KWIC (keyword-in-context) indexes. On the other, computer manipulation can be extended from individual words to groups of words, sentences, or more. For example, automated production of abstracts from digital text is already well advanced.

Information of one sort or another impinges on a researcher all the time. Most of it flows past unabsorbed: what is required is "relevant" information. The adjective here is placed in quotation marks because one of the fundamental problems of information retrieval is actually deciding what "relevant" means in a particular context. It can, in the first instance, be time dependent. Information is often required at a specific point in the development of a research project. If it is identified and retrieved at that point, it may be highly relevant; if not, it may become totally irrelevant. Again, the information must be available in an appropriate form for it to be relevant. For example, when seeking to learn about previous work immediately relevant to their projects, researchers may turn to journals. When seeking information from other research fields, they may rather turn to books; and for "know-how" on techniques to be used, they may turn to colleagues for advice. What constitutes an appropriate form can also depend on the seniority of the researcher. For example, research students are the main users of other students' dissertations in most subjects. The general requirement is that information must be supplied at a time, and in a form, that makes it most likely that the researcher will absorb it. Even so, the absorption is typically selective. One of the findings of mass-media research is that members of the audience tend to restructure what they see or hear to fit in with their own preconceptions. Researchers are not exempt from this tendency. When different researchers consult the same sources of information, they may see quite different things in them. "Relevant" information becomes, in effect, whatever researchers are prepared to take aboard in the belief that it may be useful for their work.

In selecting appropriate information, researchers can either play a relatively passive role, choosing from the information streams they encounter in their work, or they can actively seek what they want, searching information sources they would not normally encounter. In practice, this distinction can be blurred. Researchers often configure their environment so as to increase the likelihood of receiving information that will help their work. For example, the colleagues with whom a researcher chats over coffee may prove to be the ones whose comments are particularly valuable. Nevertheless, the distinction between passive acceptance and active searching is worth making because the motivation and activities of the researcher can differ between the two. When researchers actively look for information, they must know that there is a gap in their knowledge that they are trying to fill. The same is not necessarily true of information gained by passive exposure. Their actual recognition of an information gap may not be very well defined. This often comes to light when researchers approach intermediaries for help. The reference interview (as librarians and information scientists call it) nearly always requires some clarification of what the researcher wants. At this point, words must be used with care. *Wants* and *needs* are often mentioned when talking of information that researchers desire to have, but the two words have slightly different connotations. The information that researchers want may not be what they actually need. To quote from one librarian's reference interview: "He already had in his mind what he wanted me to produce and I had a lot of trouble getting from him enough information even to look."[1] The more uncertain the nature of the gap in a researcher's knowledge, the more likely it is that the perceived *want* may not be the real *need*.

Formulating the information need comes first. It is followed by identification of possible sources containing the required information. Then comes the process of extracting and absorbing the information from these sources. Finally, the information must be evaluated and, if it seems satisfactory, incorporated into the research activity. Most researchers in the academic world carry out all these four steps either by themselves or with their colleagues and students. (In industry, the second stage and some of the third stage is often undertaken by intermediaries.) The initial action, after deciding what information is required, is therefore to seek appropriate sources. The typical method is to find starter material that can get the retrieval process under way. This can come from a variety of places—the researcher's prior knowledge, suggestions from colleagues, or from the primary and secondary literature. For example, a researcher may know of a journal article on a topic related to the point at issue. A study of the references attached to the article may lead to additional relevant articles. The references in these may indicate still more relevant material, and so on. In parallel with this, the researcher will be scanning secondary sources—reviews, abstracts services, etc.—for appropriate items.

These initial steps are common across the disciplines. All groups tend to differentiate between information sources in terms of such factors as qual-

Table 42
Ranking Orders for Different Methods of Acquiring Information

Method of acquiring information	Ranking order	
	Physicists	Chemists
Following up citations in relevant articles	1	1
Keeping up by reading current publications	2	2
References from conversations with colleagues	3	5
Unpublished material obtained from colleagues	4	10
Use of abstracts journals and indexes	5	3

ity, level, types, and language.[2] Emphases can vary. Scientists often make more use of secondary services (including computer-based services) than social scientists do. They are also more concerned about possible errors in the information they find. Social scientists and humanities researchers are more likely than scientists to carry out large-scale reviews of the literature before they start. Even between closely related subjects, there can be some differences in emphasis, as Table 42 indicates for physics and chemistry.[3] The sample groups were asked to rank 12 different methods of acquiring information in terms of their perceived value. The table lists the top five favorites. These are very similar, though there appears to be some disagreement about the fourth entry.

Differences can occur within disciplines because of the variety of types of research carried out. For example, in the humanities, some research requires the study of large amounts of published and archival material and so involves considerable traveling. Other research entails the comparative study of material that may be most available locally. Still others may require intensive consideration of a limited range of documentation, which may all be in the possession of the researcher. In the sciences, there is a parallel range of research activities. Some researchers must travel extensively in order to obtain the data they need. Others can obtain what they require from work carried out entirely at their own institutions. Theoreticians may not have to look much beyond their own desks for their basic data. In terms of information management, the approaches of researchers in quite different disciplines may show similarities.

Information Requirements

What researchers are seeking is information: what the formal communication system provides is documents. At the input end, research information is packaged in a variety of ways. At the output end, researchers can choose between these packages, selecting preferentially those that best serve their own research needs. The resultant choice can vary with subject. Thus U.S. researchers in linguistics use dissertations as a source of information more than other groups in the humanities,[4] whereas their colleagues in psychology have a particular penchant for multiauthor volumes.[5] Not all modes of packaging are equally easy to access (i.e., some channels of research information are less well organized by intermediaries than others). For example, reports are an important information source in the social sciences; yet they are often difficult to track down, especially if there has been a lapse of time and the producing group has dispersed. The following plaint on behalf of political science is typical:

> Virtually every public policy field has its coterie of groups that produce materials relevant to the public policy debate. In the area of defense alone, there are dozens of them, each producing monthly or occasional reports. In the areas of social, environmental, and budget policy, the situation is similar. These reports, not collected by libraries and not indexed in major indexes, are invaluable, but hard to get.[6]

Information requirements can change with time, as the research emphasis within a given specialism varies. Sufficiently large changes can affect the nature of the demand for documentation within the specialism. In recent decades, humanities research has increasingly favored an interdisciplinary approach, encouraged by an ever-widening definition of what constitutes an acceptable research topic. The consequence is that humanities scholars now require access to a considerably wider range of sources than hitherto. In the past, researchers in the humanities have typically given more weight to their personal research materials than to institutional resources. The cost of acquiring a much wider range of material can, however, move beyond the individual pocket so that a growing reliance on the institution becomes unavoidable. In a similar way, scientific research in recent decades has seen a shift from the curiosity oriented to the mission oriented, in part due to the pressure from funding agencies for applicable research. Mission-oriented research demands a wide range of information sources. One study of the essential information required for a project in engineering found that it required some 70 separate documentary items.[7] Of these, the majority had been generated by universities in Germany, Japan, Rumania, Sweden, the UK and the United States, whereas the remainder came from industry and research establishments in the UK, the United States, and the then Soviet Union. This wide spread of sources demands good institutional resources for the acquisition of information. Consequently, a shift to mission-oriented research has implications for the nature and scale of the information backing that needs to be provided.

Engineering provides a good example of an applied discipline concerned primarily with mission-oriented research. Comparing engineering research with curiosity-oriented scientific research, the most obvious contrast lies in the end-product. For science, the output is usually new knowledge published via journals, whereas, for engineering, it is more likely to relate to a product or a process (though publishable new knowledge may arise from this). The difference in aim leads to a difference in the information-seeking habits of engineers, as compared with scientists.[8] Thus engineers consume a good deal more from formal sources than they contribute to them. Though they and scientists use a similar range of sources, the engineers give a good deal more emphasis to reports, often produced within their own organizations. Similarly, trade literature is much more important for engineers than for the average scientist. Engineers often accumulate reports, trade literature, and reference books, along with their own notebooks, to form a personal information resource. Oral communication is even more important for them than it is for scientists. If their personal files do not yield an answer to a question, their next port of call is likely to be colleagues. These differences underline a point made earlier: researchers ultimately need information rather than documents. Traditional publications are less well tailored to provide the type of information required by engineers than they are to satisfy the information needs of scientists; so the former group turn more to other sources.

Researchers must also cope with the rapid growth in the amount of research literature appearing. Though they try to limit their information burden (by specializing, by collaborating, etc.), the number of items inviting their attention has inevitably risen. For example, a survey of the information gathering habits of research scientists first carried out in the 1960s was repeated in the 1980s.[9] Table 43 records how the intensity of information searching rose over this period. This is paralleled by Table 44 which indicates how many documents were subsequently required for working on a project. Despite the growth these tables record, many researchers still feel they are not reading all that they should. A survey of scientists in universities, industry, and government establishments found that they believed they were only reading some 40% of the relevant literature.[10]

Table 42 listed the methods that researchers regard as important for gathering information. This can be extended by asking how frequently specific information sources are tapped. Table 45 indicates the number of

Table 43
A Comparison of Information-Seeking Activities over Time

Activity	Researchers' estimates involved (%)	
	1960s	1980s
Following up citations in relevant articles	80	96
Keeping up by reading current publications	77	95
Searching abstracts journals	58	68
Using a personal index	47	54
Using a library catalog	10	31
Asking an information officer to make a search	8	24

times per week samples of scientists from three different subject fields made use of various sources.[11] The results for computer science differ from the other two. Computer science is, in fact, often as closely related to engineering as to science; the differences recorded here are like those noted earlier for engineers. Some two-thirds of the information obtained via this usage of information sources was deliberately sought. The remaining third of the information was gained unexpectedly. The latter type of information acquisition can be related back to the type of activity mentioned in row 2 of Table 42—"keeping up by reading current publications." Browsing printed material, along with informal discussion, are major sources of information that has not been specifically sought.

Browsing is rarely a totally undirected activity. It is mostly a process of sampling sources that the researcher believes may contain useful information. Serendipitous discovery—where the information recovered comes from a quite unexpected source—occurs, but is much less common. The obvious example of "directed" browsing is the regular scanning of journals to see if they contain anything of interest. This is done automatically for those jour-

Table 44
Number of Documents Used by Researchers

Approximate number of documents	Researchers' estimates (%)	
	1960s	1980s
About 6	40	28
About 12	39	38
About 20	10	22
More than 20	11	12

Table 45

Average Number of Times Particular Information Sources Have Been
Used in One Week

Information source	Chemistry	Genetics	Computer science
Refereed articles	8.5	8.7	3.8
Colleagues	6.0	6.0	7.5
Books	4.4	3.0	5.9
On-line databases	2.2	2.6	3.1
Abstracts	3.4	2.5	1.4

nals to which the researcher subscribes personally and that are presumably closely related to his or her research interests. Many researchers also arrange regular visits to the library to check on recent issues of other potentially relevant titles. Nor is their browsing confined to the primary journal literature. Researchers often also browse through some of the secondary literature in their field. Thus some researchers scan *Current Contents* to see what is appearing in journals that they do not regularly access. Similarly, chemists may browse through *Chemical Abstracts*, as a guide to or as a substitute for the original chemical publications.

Books, too, can be browsed in various ways. Many researchers, especially in the humanities, look around bookshops, read publishers' catalogs, and look at book reviews to pick up information about the contents of relevant new titles. In using a library, they typically scan the shelves round the book they are actually seeking to see whether there is anything else of interest. Indeed, now that library catalogs have been automated, they can be used as an easy aid to browsing. Relevant keywords can be fed into the system to produce a series of potentially useful titles. The shelves where these titles are situated can then be visited and scanned for additional items of interest. Most researchers employ a mixture of such approaches to establish their own preferred pattern of gathering information. Which they choose depends partly on the nature of their research and their information environment, but the selection is also partly a result of personal taste.

Whatever methods of approaching the literature are preferred, most researchers spend considerable time reading. One estimate for research and development personnel in the United States was that they spent some 375 hours a year on work-related reading.[12] Most studies similarly suggest figures of a few hundred hours. For example, one British survey found a median value for reading time of about four hours per week for biologists.[13] Perhaps a quarter of this will be general reading (for current awareness, professional development, etc.). These averages can conceal different patterns of reading. Some readers, especially in the social sciences and humanities, prefer major reading sessions at longer intervals rather than shorter sessions more frequently. One study of scientists found that two-thirds of their reading sessions were for an hour or less.[14] The contrast is reflected in the following comments from a sociologist and a chemist.

> I think there are long lags when I don't keep up with it and I'm just too busy to do the reading. Every year I sort of catch up. [Sociologist]

> My estimate is there must be 200 new journals coming in every week .... I look at 100 at least. [Chemist][15]

The personal element cannot be ignored in information retrieval. It may be a major factor in reducing the efficiency with which human intermediaries or computers can assist researchers in their work. Various attempts have been made to define the personal characteristics that affect attitudes to information handling. The basic question is whether it is possible to categorize the differing information "styles" that researchers have. For example, in one study, the scientists at a research establishment were interviewed and the resultant data subjected to a cluster analysis.[16] This led to the identification of two basic groups—characterized as active information seekers and passive information receivers. When the data were examined in more detail, it became apparent that some of the interviewees made only limited attempts to keep up with new research. Another group, mainly people new to the field, were involved primarily in routine information gathering and made extensive use of the library. All the other researchers accessed information from a range of channels, but mostly in a fairly disorganized way. The main exception was a group who were working in a very rapidly expanding field. They found themselves flooded with information and were therefore forced to formulate some kind of program in advance. Browsing formed an important element in this strategy. As one of them reported: "I tend to journal browse. I try to get up there [to the library] at least half an hour each day. If I leave it to once a week it's just too large a task."

Organizing Personal Information

Personal knowledge, backed by personal collections of documents, form the natural starting point for any researcher seeking information. Researchers differ in the way they organize retrieval from their personal information files. Their filing systems range from the neat to the messy. As might be expected, those with tidy offices and well-organized files are better able to lay their hands on required documents than their less well-organized colleagues. However, this is only part of the story. Neatness and tidiness depend, in part, on how easy the documents are to classify. The problem is that a document often contains a range of information, different bits of which might be classified under different headings. Unless several copies of each document are made, the original document can only be physically situated under one of these classifications. The crucial question then is whether the researcher can readily remember which of the categories was finally assigned to the document. Someone concerned with a restricted range of information, all of a similar type, has a relatively easy classificatory task and can hope for easily manageable files. This is not usually true of researchers, who may be involved simultaneously in a number of projects, each of which requires a wide range of information. They apparently alleviate some of their difficulties by introducing a certain degree of untidiness, which allows them to blur differences in classification.[17] A researcher may, for example, group documents into a number of different piles distributed round the office. This system allows documents to be assigned temporarily to one group, but to remain visually identifiable so that they can be regrouped elsewhere if necessary. The very fact that a document is lying about is a constant reminder of its existence. If it lies near the top of a pile, this may be a further reminder that it has arrived relatively recently. Documents piled close to where the researcher sits can be those relevant to the work immediately in hand: piles further away may relate to less urgent work. The office effectively becomes a method of spatially organizing information in a way that fits in with the individual researcher's requirements.

From the viewpoint of information retrieval, a reliance on individually evolved methods has both a negative and a positive side. The negative aspect is that relying on one's own methods can solidify into information-seeking habits that are less than optimally efficient. A survey of British scientists found that the commonest reason for not using particular types of information sources was lack of awareness of their existence.[18] The second commonest reason was reliance on habit—sticking to tried sources, even if a new method might potentially be helpful. The same reliance on habit is found in the United States.[19] Researchers tend to work outward from what they know personally when looking for information. Since they buy books and journals for themselves, they are correspondingly happy to use these items in a library. Most do not have their own access to print-based secondary services, and, hence, may be less likely to know about, or use, the corresponding library services. There is consequently a gap between the information channels available and researchers' use of them.

> the historians' own user patterns . . . would horrify the average librarian . . . . Most historians distrust the academic credentials of librarians and are themselves illiterate in the jargon of librarianship. Such concepts as user education, current awareness, or even the difference between a series and a serial are strange to the historian, and over-busy university libraries often fail to clear up misconceptions.[20]

As this implies, librarians are more likely to respond to enquiries than to initiate discussions with researchers. Researchers, in turn, tend to seek assistance only when they encounter major obstacles in their search for information. One virtue of the new electronic information sources is that both researchers and librarians accept the need to publicize their existence and provide training in their use. However, the researcher is always assessing—perhaps subconsciously—the trade-off between information gained and the time and effort expended in gaining it. A researcher who uses printed abstracts may decide it is worth spending half an hour learning how to use the CD-ROM equivalent, because it will save time in the future. Another, who does not use printed abstracts, may find the trade-off offered by electronic abstracts still unattractive.

This question of trade-off between effort and return applies across all information-seeking activities. A book provided on microfilm may not be read, whereas a printed copy of the same book is. The query in the researcher's mind is whether the information return to be expected from the book is worth the effort and time required to go to the library and use the microfilm reader. A different example relates to browsing through the titles of books on library shelves. Books on shelves high up, or low down, tend to be looked at less because they require more effort. More generally, the frequency with which an information channel is accessed depends both on its usefulness and on its accessibility. For example, one study found that researchers rated their personal files and the library of their institution as equally useful sources.[21] Yet the former were accessed much more frequently than the latter—a reflection of their greater accessibility. Again, the same researchers saw electronic mail as less useful than face-to-face discussions, but used the former more often. This, too, reflects the relative ease of setting up the contacts.

The positive aspect of a diffuse, personalized approach to identifying relevant information is that, though not optimally efficient, it is sufficient to satisfy most of a researcher's requirements. Unless they are specifically compiling reviews of a topic, researchers rarely need a comprehensive view of the relevant literature. They want to identify key works along with a representative sample of others. Indeed, researchers would often be happy if they could simply assume that no previous relevant work existed. As one historian commented:

> it is rather fear of some learned reviewer's "the author appears to be ignorant of the important conclusions drawn by Dr Stumpfnadel" than a desire to know these conclusions for their own sake which, at the latter end of my own researches, drives me to consult the later authorities.[22]

All researchers gather information via a variety of formal and informal channels. Some of the information obtained from these is unique, whereas the remaining items overlap to a greater or lesser extent. The overlap helps the channels to reinforce each other and so shapes the researcher's view of what is, and is not, important. Continued interaction between researchers and information sources is vital in establishing viable patterns of information handling. The choices that researchers make may prove to be wrong, but it is difficult for an automated process, or even a human intermediary, to match an individual researcher's experience of sources and their value for him or her. Consider, for example, the following account by a psychologist of personal reactions to relevant sources:

> The main source of information is *Current Contents*, which we get, the *Social Sciences Current Contents* and the *Life Sciences*. The *Life Sciences* has some stuff, but it's usually not relevant; the *Social Sciences* is much more relevant to me . . . . Things like *Psychological Review*, it depends very much who the editor is for the period of three years or whatever; the previous editor had quite a lot of stuff I was interested in. *Psychological Review* covers a broad area, and if it's in my area, then I look at it a lot, whereas at the moment it's not so I don't have to look at it carefully.[23]

The Scatter of Information

Researchers concentrate their attention on the particular information sources that they have found most helpful in the past. Relevant information is scattered across a wide range of sources, and the researcher knows from experience which are likely to be "core" sources for the type of information required. For example, when using journals, researchers effectively ask the following question. I am interested in a specific topic: how are articles relating to that topic distributed across the various journal titles available to me? A statistical answer to this question was found over half a century ago. Suppose the specific topic is within a broad subject field such as chemistry or history. The range of journals in the field can often be roughly divided into three groups, each of which generates approximately a third of all the articles relevant to the specific topic in the journals. The first group of journals is relatively small in number, but contributes a large number of relevant articles. The next group consists of a larger number of journals that are moderately productive, so far as relevant articles are concerned. The final group covers a large number of journals, each of which contains the occasional relevant article. This distribution is usually called "Bradford's law of scattering," after Samuel Bradford, a British information scientist, who first noted it. The point about Bradford's law is that there is typically a fairly simple numerical link between the number of journals in each of the three zones. In Bradford's original work, for example, the number of relevant articles found in one journal in the core zone was matched by five journals in the intermediate zone and 25 (= 5^2) in the outer zone.

The scattering of articles comes about because each journal covers a spread of topics. The more specialized the journal, the less the spread. Some dispersion is unavoidable, not least because the individual articles themselves may cover more than one topic. For example, an article on Charles Dickens in a literary journal may contain information on the Victorian world that is useful to a historian. The core journals are those where the editorial policy emphasizes the centrality of the topic interesting the researcher. Journals in the second zone tend to be in adjacent fields. Though their editorial thrust centers on other topics, the spread of contents provides some overlap with the researcher's interests. Journals in the third zone are, in terms of editorial intentions, more distant. Their spread of contents therefore only occasionally takes in matters of concern to the researcher. As a description, this is an oversimplification. For example, since the concern is with the number of articles retrieved, the usefulness of a journal depends on the number of articles it publishes, as well as its editorial objectives. From this viewpoint, a specialist journal concerned solely with the topic at issue may be no more "core" than a general journal that publishes many articles a year only a small proportion of which are on the topic.

The degree of scatter is, to some extent, subject related. In fields with a well-defined subject structure and journal provision (such as physics), the core journals may provide a relatively high proportion of the relevant articles. In other fields, such as botany and zoology, where both the subject and the journal provision is more fragmented, the scatter may be greater. Research of an interdisciplinary nature, such as is common in technology, normally leads to a wider dispersion of relevant material than is found in the sciences. The same is usually true of research in the social sciences and humanities. Even within a particular subject, different specialisms may exhibit differing degrees of dispersion. This is illustrated in Table 46 for two specialisms in chemistry.[24] Again, the dispersion may change with time. For example, when a new specialism appears, articles about it may be scattered across a range of journals to which the research is partly relevant. As the subject develops further, new journals targeted at the specialism are set up and begin to form a core group which researchers can consult. (The word *core* here needs treating with some caution. In terms of dispersion, it simply refers to a journal with a high number of relevant articles; but, to a researcher, it usually also carries a connotation of high quality.)

Bradford's law proclaims a moral similar to the law of diminishing returns in economics. It tells us that obtaining some relevant information is not too difficult, but that providing anything like complete coverage requires a considerable expenditure of effort. This applies to other information sources (e.g., retrieval from databases), as well as journals. In this, it is akin to the 80:20 rule beloved of librarians (that 80% of readers' usage is aimed at 20% of their library stock), which also applies across a variety of information sources. Both are further instances of the skewed distribution of information generation and use that crops up so frequently in the communication of research. Indeed, Bradford's law can be rewritten in a mathematical form that is similar to other distributions (e.g., Lotka's) that have appeared in previous chapters. Like them, it represents a simplification of what actually occurs, but it provides a useful guide to the way in which relevant information is distributed across a range of potential information sources.

Table 46
The Relative Scatter of Articles in Two Chemical Specialisms

Proportion of articles articles covered (%)	Number of journals required	
	Terpenes and steroids	Electrochemistry
25	3	3
50	9	11
75	20	32
100	99	146

The Age Distribution of Information

Bradford's law describes how relevant items are distributed across a set of information sources at a particular time. A related question is how relevant information is distributed in terms of time, going from the present backward. Journal literature—to take this again as an example—has been growing rapidly in volume for many years past. This means that far more journal articles have appeared recently than in the dim and distant past. If relevant items are scattered at random over the published journal literature, current retrieval should therefore identify many more recent items as being relevant. This is, indeed, the case, but it only forms part of the story. When actual usage of research is examined, it becomes apparent that researchers in some fields are even more interested in recent journals and even less interested in the older literature than its quasi-exponential growth would suggest. In part, this partiality for recent information simply reflects the attempts by researchers to keep up with the developing research front in their subject. Much browsing, for example, concentrates on journals and books that have just become available. Directed reading provides a fairer assessment of the extent to which researchers wish to investigate older literature. As Table 47 indicates, journal reading in the sciences and social sciences is overwhelmingly concerned with recent literature.[25]

Perhaps a better way of considering the value of past literature is to look at the material researchers choose to cite when they write up their work for publication. This provides some guide to the kind of timespan their readers are expected to cover. The starting point for this type of study is usually by making a list of the references attached to all the articles in a journal or a group of journals. Since references are usually only dated by year, this is the customary time unit used for the counts. These data can be used to plot

Table 47
Distribution of Article Readings by Year of Publication

Year of publication	Proportion of readings (%)
Current year	65
Previous year	17
2–8 years ago	15
More than 8 years ago	4

a graph of the number of references cited each year against the corresponding year. The resultant graph (or some development of it) is often referred to as a "citation decay curve." It is then possible to define a "half-life" for such a curve. The analogy is with the decay of radioactive material, where the half-life is the length of time required for half of the original amount of material to decay into something else. A "half-life" for citations is obviously different, since journal literature does not disappear: it is simply not cited. Nevertheless, it is feasible to define a "citation decay half-life" as the period of time during which half the currently cited literature (as defined by the journal, or journals, examined) was published. The value of such a parameter is that it allows easy comparison between journals, specialisms, and subjects. Unlike radioactive material, which has an invariant half-life, a citation decay half-life can vary according to the circumstances.

The analysis of journal references is an easy and helpful way of looking at the usage of past literature, but it has various limitations. For one thing, it supposes that the inclusion of references constitutes a standard and unchanging procedure. In practice, this is not entirely true. Thus the average number of references attached to an article can vary systematically with subject. Moreover, the average number of references has changed with time in some subjects. Again, identifying usage via citations tends to underrate the importance of very recent research, since it takes time to acquire and absorb information from the literature as it appears. In addition, there is a lag between research results being known (e.g., via preprints) and their publication in a journal. Consequently, journal references, unlike reading, do not necessarily peak with the most recent work. Not least, there is more than one way of determining how past literature becomes obsolescent. Instead of taking a current journal and working backward, it is possible to take a set of articles published some years ago and find how often they have been cited every year since up to the present (using the relevant citation index). The two methods do not necessarily give the same result.

However, these sorts of problems are of relatively minor significance. The variations in the half-lives recorded in Table 48 are sufficiently large to make it certain that researchers in different subjects do refer to past literature differently.[26] The figures basically reflect the nature of the subject and the way it is changing with time, two factors that interact with each other. Thus physics is a quantitative, cumulative subject. New information is quickly absorbed (so that it soon ceases to be necessary to refer to the original article), and this helps maintain rapid change in the state of the subject. Correspondingly, physics literature shows a short half-life. Biblical criticism

Table 48
Variation in Citation Half-Life with Subject

Subject	Median citation age in years
Physics	4.6
Computer science	5.0
Archaeology	9.5
Mathematics	10.5
Biblical criticism	21.6

is a considerably less quantitative and cumulative subject, and change is relatively slow. This encourages use of older material and so leads to a longer half-life.

It has been suggested that journal articles can be categorized as either "ephemeral," or "classical."[27] The former are of interest for a limited amount of time, whereas the latter retain their interest over a longer period. The underlying citation decay curve then relates to the classical articles: it is added to in recent years by the admixture of ephemeral articles. Though an oversimplification, this picture receives some support from the observation that the older references are often more international in their coverage than recent references. (It should be added that references to the author's own work do not necessarily age in the same way as references to other people's work.) The division into recent and older references is, in any case, a useful way of distinguishing between literature habits in different subjects.

Half-lives for entire subjects are calculated from journals that cover most of the specialisms in the subject. Different journals, apparently dealing with the same subject, can have appreciably differing half-lives. For example, Table 49 lists half-lives for journals in information science.[28] Some of the differences may relate to editorial policy, but the commonest reason is that the journals contain different mixes of articles from the various constituent specialisms. Thus journals in information science that concentrate mainly on developments in computing and networking tend to have shorter half-lives than the average for the subject as a whole. More generally, journals that deal with traditional, well-established research topics are likely to record a longer half-life than those that concentrate on newer areas of growth. For example, geological journals dealing with newer, quantitative specialisms, such as geophysics or geochemistry, typically have shorter half-lives than those dealing with older, more descriptive specialisms, such as stratigraphy or paleontology.[29] This analysis can be pushed further to look at articles from different

Table 49
Half-Lives of Information Science Journals

Title of journal	Half-life in years
Scientometrics	3.6
Journal of Information Science	4.1
Journal of the American Society for Information Science	6.9
Aslib Proceedings	7.1

specialisms in the same journal. The overall half-life for each, within the journal, can differ. For example, journals that cover the whole of astronomy include articles on both classical astronomy, which refers a good deal to older literature, and space-based astronomy, where most of the references are recent.

References to books tend to include a higher proportion of older material than journal references. The main reason is that researchers, especially those in the sciences, look to books and journals for rather different kinds of information. Information on more distant fields is often gathered preferentially from books or review articles. Correspondingly, references to material in other disciplines often average out as older than references relating to the researcher's own discipline. In terms of half-lives, however, subjects with short half-lives for journal citations also typically have short half-lives for book citations. A study of physics, for example, found a half-life for book citations of 5.8 years, only slightly longer than the half-life derived from journal articles in physics.[30] At the other end of the scale, citation decay curves for journal and book citations in the humanities are often similar in appearance, with both recording long half-lives.

It is harder to generalize about the decay time for report literature, since it depends on the nature of the report and its use. Reports generated for in-house use in industrial and government establishments mostly relate to recent or current projects. They are, therefore, mainly consulted in the first year or two after their appearance. By way of contrast, major surveys that are made publicly available as reports (e.g., in geology, social work, local history) may well be referred to for many decades after their publication. Again, short-lived reports cluster in fields where the half-life recorded for much of the information is short.

Patents are not a major source of information in the academic world, though of considerable importance to those who do use them. Some

10–20% of academic scientists and engineers use patents frequently, as compared with some 80% in industry.[31] Patents are generally similar, in information-handling terms, to other types of research literature.[32] For example, productivity in applying for patents follows the same kind of skewed distribution described by Lotka's law. More significantly for the present discussion, the way in which patents cite other patents falls off with time in a fashion similar to that found for journal references. For a fast-moving topic, such as electronics, the patent half-life may be only a quarter or a third of that for a slow-moving topic, such as shipbuilding. In a rapidly developing, research-based specialism, such as biotechnology, journal articles and patents are often closely linked and show parallel aging effects. In terms of overall usage, patents have much in common with journal articles.

Implications of Literature Usage

Both the scatter of relevant information and the decay in the use of literature with age have significant implications for the work of librarians. For example, the existence of scatter means that, even when researchers seem to have well-defined interests, their literature requirements will spread more widely. The decay of usage means that researchers, at least in some subjects, may demand the acquisition of new literature, but have little interest in it once it ages. Special librarians, working within industrial research groups, may find ways of alleviating these problems. For example, they typically purchase only core journals and books, obtaining any other literature that is required via interlibrary loan or document delivery services. Equally, they can be ruthless in discarding any material that is not being used. In universities, where researchers from different disciplines have differing demands, often on the same literature, librarians have traditionally preferred to collect and retain as much of the literature as possible. It is widely believed that there is a link between the size and quality of a university's library collection and the strength and breadth of its research programs. To quote one comment:

> It is hardly a coincidence that universities with large numbers of active doctoral programs are the same universities that have large—and growing—collections. The strong interaction between graduate education and faculty scholarship and research makes this relationship an even tighter one. Research collections designed to serve expanding graduate programs and faculty who are themselves deeply committed to scholarly and research agendas face unremitting pressures to keep growing.[33]

Table 50

Increases in the Prices of Academic Books

Field	Average price ($) (1980)	Average price ($) (1990)
Technology	33.64	76.61
Science	37.45	75.20
Business	22.45	45.17
Education	17.01	37.80
History	22.78	35.48

In fact, universities in most developed countries have had their budgets squeezed in recent decades. At the same time, both journal and book prices have continued to rise, as is indicated by the representative examples in Tables 50 and 51.[34] (The figures quoted do not allow for inflation, but the increases remain substantial even when it is included.) Inevitably, the rate at which additions are made to library stock has slowed down. As the tables suggest, the main problem is finding funds for the acquisition of science-related journals, but science-related books have also increased rapidly in price. Indeed, the increase in the prices of such books during the 1980s was more than the total cost of some books and journals in the humanities and social sciences. Although scientists have complained vigorously about limitations on the purchase of the literature they want, researchers in the humanities and social sciences may have even more cause to feel aggrieved by the knock-on effects of diverting increasing amounts of acquisitions funding to science.

In the United States, researchers, regardless of their discipline, typically subscribe personally to a number of journals (perhaps four to five titles per head). Many of these are linked with membership of societies. Until the lat-

Table 51

Increases in the Prices of Academic Journals

Field	Average price ($) (1982)	Average price ($) (1990)
Chemistry/physics	177.94	412.66
Engineering	61.54	138.84
Business/economics	32.67	63.25
Education	28.18	56.33
History	20.37	35.51

ter half of the twentieth century, journals usually came automatically as a part of the membership subscription. In many societies their purchase is now optional, though the personal subscription prices are kept well below those charged to institutions or nonmembers. The level of personal subscription to journals varies from country to country. It is, for example, appreciably higher in the United States than in the UK. In the academic world, personal subscriptions are almost always paid by the individual researcher, but the employer may subsidize the cost in industry. The library (central or departmental) is the main source for the remaining journals that a researcher reads—which is why so much attention has been paid to it here—but it is not the only one. Borrowing from colleagues is common, and a department may also subscribe to, and circulate, particularly popular titles.

Most surveys in developed countries suggest that library users are reasonably satisfied with the materials available and the services provided. As might be expected, users of the leading research libraries are appreciably happier than those using smaller college libraries.[35] To offset this, there seems to be a general feeling among users of small libraries that interlibrary loan and photocopying work quite well to fill the gaps. However, such surveys have to be interpreted with some caution. Library users in general, and researchers in particular, say they are satisfied with a library when it fulfills their expectations. If their expectations are low, the library may provide for their "wants" while falling well short of satisfying their "needs." This point becomes obvious when looking at libraries in developing countries.

Researchers from developing countries often seem to be surprisingly satisfied with the library resources available to them, even though they would be regarded as unsatisfactory by a researcher from a developed country. It seems that low expectation of success in obtaining publications, coupled with a lack of awareness of what is available, means that many researchers do not really recognize that there is a problem. For example, one survey examined the access that researchers from developing countries had to English-language publications. In many cases, this proved to be quite restricted. A significant fraction of the researchers made little effort to follow up material that was not immediately available. Those who did, tried a number of channels, often unsuccessfully (see Table 52).[36] Yet the overall response was one of moderate satisfaction with the situation.

Along with lack of material, libraries in developing countries often suffer because the information they do have is out of date. For example, readers often have to use research monographs that have been superseded in developed countries. Their problems are exacerbated by the fact that much

Table 52
Methods Used by Researchers in Developing Countries to
Obtain Publications Not Immediately Available

Method of access	Percentage claiming "usually successful"
Interlibrary loan	35
Direct ordering from publishers	27
Ordering from bookseller	32
Requesting from contacts abroad	44
Requesting through foreign cultural representatives	21

material is in a foreign language (usually English), which they may find it difficult to follow. Hardly surprisingly, browsing is a less common activity in developing countries. Researchers who have worked for some time in developed countries are more likely to be critical of both library resources and services than their colleagues. The problems are, however, subject dependent, being a good deal more acute in science-based disciplines.

Electronic Retrieval of Information

Over the past few decades, use of research literature in developed countries has been increasingly affected by the introduction of electronic methods of handling information. They are now beginning to influence activities in developing countries. Two main aspects affect researchers directly—automated means of finding out that information exists and actual provision of the information in electronic form. The former activity has been commonplace for some decades among intermediaries, though its manifestation to researchers, as by OPACs (Online Public Access Catalogues), is more recent. Such catalogs are one kind of electronic bibliographical database. Other databases in this category are increasingly replacing traditional printed guides to the literature. For example, numerous electronic databases now exist to provide information on publications in a given discipline, including title, author(s), abstract, etc. (Indeed, many disciplines are covered by more than one electronic database, though they usually differ somewhat in the range of publications they include.) Their increasing use by researchers raises a question—how information retrieval by electronic means can best be made to fit the needs of the research community.

The most basic requirement is that, whatever methods are used, they should function efficiently. One long-standing method of examining how well automated systems perform depends on a comparison of two standard ratios. The first—labeled "recall"—is the ratio of the number of relevant documents retrieved to the total number of relevant documents in the database. The second—labeled "precision"—is the ratio of the number of relevant documents retrieved to the total number of documents retrieved. For a perfect retrieval system, both these ratios should be unity: all relevant documents should be retrieved and no irrelevant documents. Most retrieval is done by keywords (including with that short phrases), which have to be matched to words (or phrases) in the various documents. Many studies have shown that this approach creates an immediate problem. It is possible to achieve a high precision ratio by choosing very specific keywords, but this then usually leads to a poor recall ratio. In other words, too narrow a selection of keywords means that a lot of potentially relevant documents may be missed. The obvious response—to use less specific keywords—certainly increases the number of potentially relevant documents that are found. Unfortunately, it also typically reduces the precision ratio (i.e., it produces even bigger increases in the number of irrelevant documents retrieved).

A variety of strategies have been tried to improve the situation. For example, the drawback of retrieving a large number of irrelevant entries is that the researcher finds the useful return too small and gives up in disgust. One method of alleviating this is for the system to calculate how well each retrieved document actually fits all the criteria originally specified by the researcher.[37] The calculations are then used to put the items in order according to how well they fit. With any luck, the reader will find a sufficient number of relevant entries at the top end of the list so that it will not be necessary to look further. Of course, the automated process makes no allowance for prior knowledge of the literature on the part of the researcher. So even this prioritized list may not provide much new information. Again, researchers do not always select the best keywords or phrases for the search they want to implement. This is an especial problem where the automated system does not work directly on the raw material, but on some index to it that has been compiled. The keywords selected by the researcher may then not coincide with those chosen by the system. Strategies on how searches should proceed under these circumstances have been explored for some time, and there are undoubtedly ways of overcoming the problems.[38] However, they tend to be used more by intermediaries than by the researchers themselves.

The word *relevant* has been used a number of times. As we have seen, it is one of those words that are hard to pin down. Whether or not a document is "relevant" depends on the judgment of the individual researcher. This can vary with the situation. It is often not sufficient for the retrieved document simply to be dealing with the target topic. The basic problem is that, in terms of literature selection, each researcher is idiosyncratic. When researchers are deciding which documents to pursue, their personal backgrounds and experience are brought to bear, often in a fairly hazy and individualistic way. As one researcher explained: "I'm looking for phrases or terms that alert me to something relevant to me . . . for me, these concepts aren't very precisely defined but they orient you to looking for that kind of thing."[39]

The best external judge of a useful reference is likely to be a fellow-researcher in the same field. Even such a colleague is likely to differ in detail on such matters as what constitutes an acceptable document, who are the interesting authors, or which journals (other than core ones) are worth consulting. Consider the following comments by researchers:

> It has to be readable; it can't be too technical. If it sounds too technical I'm not going to read—and all these [retrieved documents] sound very technical.

> I got this because he [the author of the retrieved document] is a very distinguished scholar and a very thoughtful man. This is not an empirical study [the object of the search] at all, but I was sure it would be interesting.

> I'm not going to consult this one [retrieved reference]. The reason is that this is a psychology journal and psychologists have a different kind of approach to doing research that is not helpful to me . . . . They are more interested in individuals . . . . I'm more interested in patterns and institutions.

> Again, this word "correlates" is a key word for me. Studies that have "correlates" in the title are often atheoretical, that is, exploratory studies which are often very limited. This is not helpful for me.[40]

It is unlikely that even close colleagues would take exactly the same decisions, nor, equally, would sophisticated keyword searching. Automated techniques can, of course, be extended to improve the element of personalization. For example, an automated profile of a researcher's interests can be drawn up over time by recording which proffered documents are accepted and which rejected. This provides feedback to the system on such matters as more or less preferred authors and journals. Indeed, such profiling can be done at a variety of levels, according to the nature of the researcher's requirements.[41] At one level, the target may be the research group (e.g., economic historians interested in the nineteenth-century United States). At the next, the profile may deal with the personal characteristics of the researcher. At a more detailed level still, it may deal with the specific requirements of each search session. In practice, there is probably a limit to how far refinements can improve retrieval. Thus studies of how well two human judges agree on the relevance of a document indicate levels of 40–75%.[42] Automated retrieval methods produce precision ratios in much the same range. Human characteristics (including their changes with time) prevent perfect retrieval. Equally, they make it feasible to operate with less than perfect retrieval. Given a sufficient amount of relevant initial material, researchers can usually find all the other information they need, one way or another.

Electronic searching, unlike manual searching, was almost always carried out by library and information staff on behalf of the researchers until the advent of the desktop computer. In recent years, researchers have increasingly begun to access on-line databases directly. For example, a survey of university chemists found that 90% used on-line searches, with some three-quarters of them doing their own searching.[43] It appears that this level of end-user searching is now common in academic research, but that a considerable number of researchers in industry and government research still delegate their searching to trained information staff.[44] The difference is mainly a reflection of work priorities in university libraries, as compared with the other types of institution. Researchers are prepared to delegate searching if there is someone with good subject knowledge, who can carry out the task quickly. This is less likely to be the case in universities, so academic researchers often do the work themselves. In general, researchers are reasonably satisfied with the results of on-line searches, whether they delegate them or carry them out personally; but it is evident that they can sometimes find the process, or their knowledge of it, too unsophisticated to be of great help. The problem is often that automated systems can produce information overload. Indeed, it is already apparent that simply increasing the information available often results in the researcher feeling increasingly pressurized. As one disillusioned researcher commented:

> Computer searches I have not found to be helpful. I certainly have had students try it many times. It has not been helpful in terms of finding things we didn't already know about, or narrowing down the information that I needed. Usually we get so many citations that it's just impossible to sort out what's there.[45]

In part, these problems are caused by lack of knowledge regarding both procedures and what information sources are available. This shows up clearly when newer retrieval systems, more complex than the standard on-line data-base, appear. Of the group of chemists previously noted who carried out their own information retrieval, fewer—about half—went on to access more advanced systems. At the other end of the scale, use of simple systems is growing rapidly. Thus an increasing number of researchers in all disciplines are setting up their own personal electronic bibliographies/databases. The overall reaction to electronic retrieval is probably mirrored in the comments of one faculty member on all such aids:

> We have . . . taken much of the drudgery out of the process and made it easier to find sources, but we still have to read carefully—probably more carefully than ever—and we still have to think. The difference is that searching no longer takes much time and energy from the scholarship of thought.[46]

The use of electronic guides to the literature can have knock-on effects for libraries. For example, electronic library catalogs—now often available from the researcher's desktop—are leading to better exploitation of a library's collection, as more stock is sampled. At the same time, researchers can unearth more potentially relevant references from electronic databases, some of them from lesser known sources, than is usually possible with manual searching. Their requests for the material they have identified put greater pressure on the library's acquisitions budget and personnel. The assumption is that the research is correspondingly enhanced, either by an improvement in quality or by avoiding duplication of research. The evidence for this is, perhaps, more obvious in a large-scale compilation, such as a biography, than in the average short article.

At the end of the day, electronic retrieval still means that researchers must go and seek the printed documents. It would obviously be more convenient to have the identified items already in electronic form. Retrieval is then not only speeded up, but, like the original searching, it can be done directly by the researcher. Moreover, the items can be looked at quickly on the screen and, if desired, rejected without going through a lengthy acquisitions process. It is obviously essential, if researchers are to be encouraged to follow this route, that a wide spread of current literature should be available in electronic form. With journals, for example, the original appearance of only a small number of on-line journals was insufficient to generate much interest. The number of readers has grown in step with increases in the number of journals in electronic form. In the first instance, researchers wish to browse through current issues. If the browsing has to be done partly on-line and partly in the library, the perceived advantage of on-line journals is lost. This lies in the ability to consult them, both at home and work and at any time of the day or night, from one's own chair. Browsing is usually done soon after a journal issue appears. This means that electronic journal issues should not lag behind the printed versions in terms of publication. In fact, most researchers automatically assume that electronic distribution will be more rapid.

Electronic Communication

Browsing is, of course, only one reason for accessing material. Literature in electronic form must equally satisfy the researcher's need to track down, for more systematic reading, information published in the past. This does not present much difficulty for journals available only electronically, so long as their files have been maintained. After all, none of these journals are more than a few years old, so there is only a relatively small amount of material to be handled. The situation is less straightforward for electronic versions of existing printed journals. Many of these have lengthy back-runs: a decision has to be taken about the availability of this material in electronic form. The amount of earlier literature that must be available to satisfy the needs of researchers is subject dependent, but, on average, something like 20–30 years of past issues are required to cover most of the likely demand.[47] This means that a great deal of retrospective conversion of print to electronic material is necessary, if researchers are not to require library access to the print versions alongside electronic access. Though such conversion is under way, there is still some way to go, so directed reading of the electronic versions of journals is not yet as convenient as for print literature. For reading purposes, the electronic version of an article is, in any case, often printed out; the important difference is that this can be done locally, whereas consulting the printed copy entails a visit to the library.

The position for books is different. In the humanities, reference material, including edited and annotated texts, is increasingly appearing in digital form, usually via special projects that concentrate on particular topics and/or periods. However, monographs presenting major research in the humanities are much less well covered electronically. It seems to be true, regardless of discipline, that the availability of documents on-line stimulates more use of their printed equivalents. This is equivalent to saying that electronic and print access can often supplement rather than replace the other.[48]

Searching techniques concentrate on the identification of discrete documents (journal articles, books, etc.) that can then be retrieved. In other words, this type of electronic retrieval is still structured in terms of print. Full-text retrieval can be done at a much finer level of detail—for example, paragraphs—so that the whole document may no longer be necessary. At this stage, therefore, retrieval becomes less concerned with printed surrogates for information and more with the actual information, itself. Retrieval can occur from a variety of sources, and the information that is collected can be combined and manipulated as desired. This is much closer to the way that a researcher thinks. Hence, electronic access to research information, once handling based on printed documents ceases to be customary, may well fit in better with researchers' work styles.

One thing that is changing as a result of these developments is the researchers' view of the role of libraries. An all-electronic library is necessarily concerned with providing information of all sorts to readers wherever they are situated rather than requiring them to seek physical access to a geographically fixed store of documents. Researchers see such a "virtual library" as becoming increasingly a part of their future environment. A survey of British scientists in 1993, found that more agreed than disagreed with the statement: "In my view the library of the future will be an access point for information rather than a place of information storage."[49] Their main doubt was whether they would receive sufficient support and training to ensure that they could use a virtual library efficiently. Most thought that current user training in how to access electronic searching facilities was inadequate. Correspondingly, a considerable proportion felt they were not entirely confident in their use of such facilities. This lack of confidence increased with the researcher's age. From this and other surveys, it seems clear that, if libraries do shift toward the "virtual library" model, they will need to provide much more training and assistance than they do at present.

The assumption that all researchers will want to move to a totally electronic environment is actually questionable. Most surveys suggest that researchers envisage a future in which they will use a mix of printed and electronic sources; so they expect libraries to function in both modes. For example, a survey of U.S. chemists found that less than half believed that electronic journals could be used for all their scholarly journal reading.[50] (All-electronic book reading is seen as even less likely.) Unfortunately, electronic handling is not a cheap option for the library. Hardware and software have to be changed at intervals (and there are other extra commitments, as with training). As a consequence, the total cost of storage and retrieval in an all-electronic library can be higher than for a traditional library.[51] Depending on how it operates, a mixed print/electronic library could be even more costly.

The "virtual library" concept is, in principle, more advantageous for researchers in developing countries than for those in developed countries. One of the problems of doing research in such countries is that it may lag behind what is being done elsewhere because of difficulties in keeping up with the research front. Restrictions on the printed literature available and delays in acquiring it mean that browsing cannot have the same value in developing countries as in developed countries and that attempts at directed reading are often frustrated. Electronic provision can overcome these deficiencies and put researchers in all countries on a similar footing. The proviso, of course, is that the researchers have access to equivalent electronic infrastructures. Funding limitations make it difficult to keep up with the ever-changing level of technological complexity. Facilities that are adequate for international electronic mail may well not be sufficient for the acquisition of sophisticated electronic journals. Similarly, electronic versions of such journals normally cost at least as much as the print versions (though access to contents page and, sometimes, abstracts may be free of charge). This puts most of them beyond the reach of researchers and their libraries in developing countries. An example of these problems can be found in the states of the former Soviet Union, where scientists make extensive use of electronic mail with foreign countries, but have only limited opportunity for more sophisticated on-line information retrieval.[52]

The ready availability of on-line access has brought some change to the information retrieval habits of researchers. For example, Table 42 in this chapter recorded the various traditional ways in which chemists have acquired information. A more recent survey found that browsing and following up citations continued to be the top priorities, but on-line searching now came third.[53] Categories of information needs are imposed by the research structure of the subject. Researchers move quickly to exploit networked resources that are more helpful than traditional channels in satisfying these needs. Thus chemists have always been more concerned with thorough literature searches than the average scientist. Consequently, networking attracts chemists because it allows more comprehensive coverage. As one chemist explained:

> The networks make it possible to do more thorough literature searches when doing proposals and papers. There's no excuse now for not knowing what's been done. Also, *Chemical Abstracts* lists all papers, including those in

foreign languages, but the abstracts are in English, so you can know what people in other countries are doing. And speed. There's a quicker pace in research.[54]

Chemists give less emphasis to electronic mail as a means of acquiring information. Various factors are at work in this. One of them relates to technology. Chemists wish to transmit graphics—more especially, diagrams—as well as text. As yet, electronic mail has not been an easy way of doing this, so they have found it easier to use fax. Since improvements in software are now allowing transmission of much better molecular structures than can be managed on paper, this limitation may soon vanish. There is also a communal factor that acts to diminish the value of electronic mail for chemists. A large proportion of chemists work in industry, where the use of electronic mail is often constricted by the requirements of confidentiality.

For mathematicians and physicists, unlike chemists, electronic mail typically figures as more important than on-line searching. The interest in these two subjects is more on information exchange via collaboration, so their use of networks emphasizes this need. The actual form of such collaboration differs between the two. In mathematics, collaboration is frequently between individuals. Since there are many specialisms, researchers may find themselves isolated, with no close colleagues locally. Electronic mail is becoming an indispensable way of circumventing this. By way of contrast, collaboration in physics is often between groups. Electronic mail, in this case, is often important not only for the exchange of research information, but also for the planning and coordination of research activity. A nuclear physicist commented:

> We have a collaborators' meeting every two months. We have 100 people there from all over the world. E-mail is essential. The success of the meeting depends on the organization and the effective use of the net. The two experiments I'm on use different techniques. For the collision experiment they have set up [an electronic bulletin board]. All collaborators (except the Russians, Chinese and Indians) are on. News goes on that. Then all can access it and find out. The agenda is sent around this way.
>
> The other experiment I'm in doesn't use [e]mail as effectively. It's a personal trait of the organizer. As a consequence, the collaboration is less effective. People aren't organized. They don't know what they are supposed to do.[55]

This quotation suggests how developing countries can miss out if their researchers cannot access the appropriate electronic networks. Researchers in developed countries outside the academic world may also have rather greater problems in accessing the network, but it has to be remembered that their information needs are different. For example, a study of information flow in the construction industry found that three categories predominated—information generated by the specific project, information generated by the organization, and general information.[56] Only the last of these required much by way of input from the external world. Much the same can be said of informal communication. Practitioners in industry rely even more than university researchers on personal contact when they need information. When engineers are faced with a problem that they cannot solve themselves, for example, their first step is nearly always to contact someone with additional experience, such as a colleague or a supervisor. Again, this is typically internal to their organization. Correspondingly, electronic mail internal to the institution often has a greater popularity than external usage for researchers in industry.

There are exceptions to this—for example, in a rapidly expanding science-based area of technology (such as biotechnology). Here, industrial firms have to call extensively on the knowledge being generated in universities. University–industrial exchanges of information are common and are modeled, in part, on the way university researchers access information. The major difference is the imposition of confidentiality on the process of information dissemination. As political and economic factors lead to increasing university–industrial collaboration, so academic researchers are expressing concern about the sharing of information. Information groups are being set up, with access controlled by institutional affiliation and ability to contribute valuable information. This limitation of information dissemination is similarly reflected by the growing role of patents in academic research. The positive effect of increasing university–industrial cooperation has been to improve the flow of information to the participating university researchers. The negative side is that life has become harder, in information terms, for those who do not participate.

These restricted information groups are sometimes referred to as information *clubs*. However, the term has a wider connotation. It is used to describe the electronic equivalent of a society headquarters. Subject-specific electronic club sites are beginning to appear that fulfill a range of society functions. They provide electronic "meeting rooms," places for individual discussions, job vacancy lists, and, not least, libraries. People can join and use these facilities, just as they do with an actual club. The difference is that such clubs have membership open to anyone who wishes to join. Interestingly, commercial providers have begun to see the opportunities that this offers them for competing in the electronic sphere with traditional societies: something they could not do with traditional modes of communication.

The Mass Media

The promoters of these wide-ranging information clubs see them as providing for everyone with an interest in the subject concerned. Conversely, the mass media, though aimed at the general public, can often act as useful sources of information for researchers. This is hardly surprising, since the researchers, themselves, often contribute directly to the media. An obvious example is in the writing of book reviews. In one survey, over 80% of researchers in the humanities and social sciences read such publications as the *New York Times Book Review*.[57] More surprisingly, over 40% (mainly social scientists) read popular science magazines, such as *Scientific American*. An even higher proportion of scientists and engineers naturally read these magazines. Engineers, in particular, obtain valuable information from magazines and newspapers. For all researchers, the two main uses of mass-media information are to see what is generating interest in one's own discipline and to gain some idea of what is happening in other disciplines.

The importance to researchers of information in the mass media was most clearly demonstrated during a period of 12 weeks when the *New York Times* was on strike. The newspaper frequently reports on medical research, obtaining much of its information from the *New England Journal of Medicine*. During the strike, items continued to be selected, but were not published. A comparison has been made between the number of citations accorded to the *New England Journal of Medicine* articles selected during the strike and those selected outside the strike.[58] Citations in the research literature were significantly more numerous for articles in the latter group than in the former. This seems to provide good evidence that media mentions of research can influence researchers, as well as the general public.

Researchers particularly mention up-market newspapers and specialist magazines as useful information sources. Television has both a greater and a wider impact on the general public than these channels. Unfortunately, the nature of television encourages brief presentations of items expressed in simplistic terms. As noted previously, such presentation can give the wrong impression of the research results to a general audience. A controversy over the effects of ethylene dibromide (EDB) in the 1980s illustrates the point:

If one relied mainly on television for news about EDB, unwarranted fear would have been a predictable reaction. Those who relied on *The New York Times*, on the other hand, had access to a generally sufficient amount of reliable information. Given the media habits of Americans, it seems reasonable to conclude that in this instance there was a great deal more unwarranted fear at large than well-informed opinion.[59]

The problem in such cases is not just that the audience gains a wrong impression. Beyond this, their reactions to that impression can influence further developments: this can include affecting support for the work of the researchers, themselves. At worst, public reaction to mass-media information can distort the pattern of research within the field concerned.

It is possible, however, to show that media coverage of health risks has an impact on public policy. The EPA [Environmental Protection Agency] has found that budgetary and other priorities for regulating environmental hazards often correlate more closely with public opinion than they do with the priorities of professional risk assessors and managers.[60]

Looking to the future, networking allows the convergence of all the different information sources, so that they become available for access both by general and specialist users. Multimedia retrieval means that mass-media channels, such as television and newspapers, can be viewed on-screen along with the more detailed information sources used by researchers. For example, a report on television can be backed by additional information files to whatever depth the user requires. People interested in, or concerned by, a news item can then explore, in whatever detail they wish, what the research was actually about. But behind this pleasing scenario lies a basic difficulty. Members of the public, as well as researchers, are feeling increasingly swamped with information. Unless information retrieval is highly personalized (i.e., the right level and content, and immediately available), users will not explore further. T. S. Eliot's oft-quoted question[61]—"Where is the knowledge we have lost in information?"—may be one of the most important queries to resolve in the twenty-first century for all users of research information.

Postscript

The main theme of this book has been change and diversity. Research communication has always undergone change. When the main media were the printed and spoken word, this happened relatively slowly. The new media created by information technology have accelerated the tempo. Research communication is now experiencing a period of rapid evolution. The basic question remains how the properties of a given medium can best be used to satisfy the communication needs of the research community. The general trends may be obvious, but the details, which are often crucial for developments, are more difficult to discern. For example, electronic networks were established originally to allow the rapid transfer of large data files. It was then found that researchers wanted to use them for electronic mail. Now networks are designed from the start with the needs of electronic mail users in mind.

Though researchers are the ultimate deciders of whether, or how, a medium is used, their collective response is affected by the various pressures at work—from the economic to the ergonomic. Not least, they work, often unconsciously, on the basis of the established practices of the research community, determined by its history and its social norms. Methods of presenting and handling information during the transition to another medium are inevitably influenced by this collective memory.

The basic characteristics of researchers, and of their community, change slowly. Thus the statistical distributions that have been used to summarize communication activities in preceding chapters reflect something more fundamental than the communication medium employed. Hence, they should survive a transition from one medium to another. For example, the skew distribution of productivity—with a few researchers producing many publications, and many producing a few—can be confidently expected to survive a shift of medium. This does not necessarily mean that the distribution will always have exactly the same form in different media.

Financial pressures limit the number of professional researchers in existence, which limits, in turn, the research publications that appear. But there is an assumption here: that productivity, defined in terms of volume of output per researchers, remains constant. Computer-based activities seem destined to enhance productivity in coming years, so allowing the amount of research information in circulation to continue to increase. Nevertheless, the need for comprehension of the results of research by researchers puts some limitation on the extent to which productivity can grow.

Just how electronic communication affects the community depends then on the pressures, especially the economic pressures, at work. A networked computer costs considerably more than a book, but can deliver far more information. A developing country may find the cost of equipping all researchers with their own computers and connecting them to networks too much for national resources to bear. Researchers in such countries who gain network access will find themselves better integrated into the worldwide research community than was ever possible via the medium of print. Those who fail to gain access will become even more cut off than before. Another line may appear between those who can afford the latest hardware and software and those who cannot. The division between the information-rich and the information-poor researchers in an electronic environment will certainly differ both in position and impact from that drawn for a print environment.

The differing properties of electronic and print media have implications for other divisions that have been drawn in the past. The most obvious is the traditional distinction between formal and informal communication. An electronic environment is much more flexible than a print environment, so, in it, the old distinction between formal and informal loses much of its force. This has a down-side and an up-side. An important down-side is that the quality of the information provided becomes harder to judge. One important up-side is that electronic communication is more democratic, in the sense that it tends to deemphasize differences between participants. Another is that it encourages collaboration and interdisciplinary working.

Blurring of the formal and informal may be of value across all disciplines, but the indications are that it will prove especially congenial to researchers in the social sciences and humanities. In a rather similar way, a shift to electronic media may lessen the differentiation between professional and amateur researchers, leading to the more productive involvement of amateurs in research. Multimedia developments are likewise bringing together the way research information and mass-media information is handled. So the boundary line between amateurs and interested members of the general public will also become hazier.

At least authors and readers have the advantage that new communication systems are expected to cater for their requirements. For publishers and librarians the requirement is rather that they adapt their activities to suit the way communication is going. The vital question is whether these existing institutions can adapt quickly enough. Can they remain financially viable during a transition period when they must handle both printed and electronic publications? Societies, because of their involvement in all types of communication, seem better placed to survive the new electronic environment. They can, for example, set up both face-to-face meetings and video conferencing and vary the balance between the two to match the changing wants of their members. However, commercial organizations have already noted the value of such expanded communication coverage and are likely to challenge the societies in this area. So the latter cannot afford to dawdle during the transition period.

The scholarly communication marketplace can best be thought of in ecological terms. An equilibrium existed in the print environment of the past between the groups of participants (in this case, the publishers). They occupied, without excessive competition, the various niches offered by the environment. The introduction of electronic communication is creating new niches and changing old ones. It is not yet clear which institutions will be best fitted to occupy the revised niches offered by the brave new world of communication. Judging by what happens in the natural world when there is rapid environmental change, some existing institutions will survive, whereas others will be replaced by new ones. Again, societies may be better placed to survive this transition because they possess an adaptable and loyal clientele.

Ecological arguments can equally be applied to other players in the world of research communication. Subscription agents, for example, have in the past facilitated the easy passage of printed journals from publishers to libraries. Do they have a niche in electronic publishing? They are certainly evolving rapidly to try and ensure that they do. The leading agents are assuming, surely correctly, that the publisher–library interface for electronic publications will require just as much special assistance in the future as printed publications have in the past. Here, too, the basic question is whether they can maintain their financial viability during the transition period.

In some ways, libraries have the hardest job of all. They, more than other intermediaries, are controlled by the complex requirements of their users. They will be expected to cater for demands for both present and past material whether in printed or electronic form. They must help their customers—who are, in any case, suffering from information overload—both to locate required information and to access it. This is a costly and time-consuming scenario. It becomes well nigh impossible if the library has to preserve into the distant future all the printed and electronic material it accumulates. Clearly, niches are changing in the library world, too. Is the answer a move to virtual libraries? They cannot, at present, provide for all the information needs of researchers in every disciplines. When will they be able to do so?

Throughout this book, it has been supposed that we are at the beginning of a transition period, in the course of which the dominant communication medium will change from print to electronic. The duration of the transition, defined in this way, obviously depends on the particular aspect of communication that is being studied. It is generally expected, for example, that electronic dominance will occur for journals well before it happens for books. Those university librarians foolhardy enough to commit themselves tend to guesstimate that half their journal subscriptions may be for electronic versions only by 2005–2010. Supposing this to be about right, interesting times for research communication are due to continue for several years yet. Who can tell when most researchers will really be able to claim that they work in a post-script world?

References

Chapter 1

1. A. Johnston (ed.) *Francis Bacon*, "In praise of knowledge" (Schocken Books, New York; 1965) p. 13.
2. A. Johnston (ed.) *Francis Bacon*, "The advancement of learning" (Schocken Books, New York; 1965) p. 61.
3. D.A. Kronick, *A history of scientific and technical periodicals* (Scarecrow Press, New York; 1962) p. 60.
4. D.A. Kronick, *A history of scientific and technical periodicals* (Scarecrow Press, New York; 1962) p. 149.
5. M.F. Katzen, "The changing appearance of research journals in science and technology: an analysis and a case study." *In:* A.J. Meadows (ed.) *Development of science publishing in Europe* (Elsevier Science Publishers, Amsterdam; 1980) p. 184.
6. J.E. McClellan III, *Science reorganized: scientific societies in the eighteenth century* (Columbia University Press, New York; 1985) p. 1.
7. J.E. McClellan III, *Science reorganized: scientific societies in the eighteenth century* (Columbia University Press, New York; 1985) p. 9.
8. J.Z. Young, *An introduction to the study of man* (Clarendon Press, Oxford; 1971) pp. 342–348.
9. E.G. Edwards, "The need for a history of higher education." In: History of Education Society, *The changing curriculum* (Methuen, London; 1971) pp. 87–100.
10. A.M. Carter, "Scientific manpower for 1970–1985," *Science, 172*, pp. 132–140 (1971).
11. G. Holton, "On the recent past of physics," *American Journal of Physics, 29*, p. 1 (1961).
12. A.J. Meadows, "Too much of a good thing?: quality versus quantity." In: H. Woodward and S. Pilling (eds.) *The international serials industry* (Gower Publishing, Aldershot, UK; 1993) pp. 23–43.
13. W. Goffman, *Coping with the biomedical literature explosion: a qualitative approach* (Rockefeller Foundation, New York; 1978) pp. 11–19.
14. M.J. Le Bas and J. Durham, "Scientific communication of geochemical data and the use of computer databases," *Journal of Documentation, 45*, pp. 124–138 (1989).
15. C.B. Wooton, *Trends in size, growth and cost of the literature since 1955* (British Library Research and Development Department, London; 1977) p. 71.
16. F. Rider, *The scholar and the future of the research library: a problem and its solution* (Hadham Press, New York; 1944) p. 6.
17. *The L.I.S.T. (Library and Information Statistics Tables for the UK)* (Library and Information Statistics Unit, Loughborough University, Loughborough, UK; 1994) Table 21.
18. E.J. Huth, "The information explosion," *Bulletin of the New York Academy of Medicine, 65*, pp. 647–661 (1989).

19. J.G. Crowther, *British scientists of the nineteenth century*, [Vol. I] (Penguin Books, Harmondsworth, UK; 1940) p. 113.
20. J.B. Priestley (ed.), *The Bodley Head Leacock* (Bodley Head, London; 1957) p. 161.
21. J. Ben-David, *The scientist's role in society* (Prentice-Hall, Englewood Cliffs, New Jersey; 1971).
22. J. Evans, *A history of the Society of Antiquaries* (Society of Antiquaries, London; 1956) p. 374.
23. L. Huxley, *Life and letters of Thomas Henry Huxley*, [Vol. I] (Macmillan, London; 1900) p. 424.
24. *Nature*, *8*, p. 381 (1873).
25. A.G. Bloxham, *Nature*, *50*, p. 104 (1894).
26. *Nature*, *3*, p. 423 (1871).
27. D. Pendlebury, "Science's go-go growth: has it started to slow?" *The Scientist*, *3*, p. 14 (1989).

Chapter 2

1. L.R. Veysey, *The emergence of the American university* (University of Chicago Press, Chicago; 1965) p. 133.
2. F. Machlup, *Knowledge and knowledge production* [Vol. I] (Princeton University Press, Princeton, New Jersey; 1980) p. 69.
3. G.R. Elton, *The practice of history* (Fontana, London; 1969) p. 17.
4. F. Machlup, *Knowledge and knowledge production* [Vol. I] (Princeton University Press, Princeton, New Jersey; 1980) pp. 73–74.
5. F. Machlup, *Knowledge and knowledge production* [Vol. I] (Princeton University Press, Princeton, New Jersey; 1980) pp. 73–74.
6. J. Ziman, *Knowing everything about nothing: specialization and change in scientific careers* (Cambridge University Press, Cambridge; 1987) p. 6.
7. A. Quiller-Couch, *On the art of writing* (Guild Books, Cambridge University Press, Cambridge; 1946) pp. 144–145.
8. M. Hunt, *The story of psychology* (Doubleday, New York; 1993) p. 563.
9. M. Hunt, *The story of psychology* (Doubleday, New York; 1993) p. 310.
10. R.K. Merton, *The sociology of science: theoretical and empirical investigations* (University of Chicago Press, Chicago; 1973) pp. 267–278.
11. T.S. Kuhn, *The structure of scientific revolutions* (University of Chicago Press, Chicago; 2nd Edition 1970).
12. K.R. Popper, *Conjectures and refutations* (Routledge and Kegan Paul, London; 1963).
13. T.S. Kuhn, *The structure of scientific revolutions* (University of Chicago Press, Chicago; 2nd Edition 1970) p. 167.
14. T.S. Kuhn, *The structure of scientific revolutions* (University of Chicago Press, Chicago; 2nd Edition 1970) p. 171.
15. M. Callon, J. Law, and A. Rip, *Mapping the dynamics of science and technology* (Macmillan, London; 1986) p. 4.
16. P. Rainbow (ed.) *Foucault Reader* (Pantheon Books, New York; 1984) pp. 334–335.
17. S.B. Barnes, "On the reception of scientific knowledge beliefs." *In*: B. Barnes (ed.) *Sociology of science* (Penguin Books, Harmondsworth, UK; 1972) p. 278.
18. I. Spiegel-Rösing, "The study of science, technology and society (SSTS): recent trends and future challenges." *In*: I. Spiegel-Rösing and D. de S. Price (eds.) *Science, technology and society: a cross-disciplinary perspective* (Sage Publications, London; 1977) p. 20.
19. P.H. Phenix, *Realms of meaning: a philosophy of the curriculum for general education* (McGraw-Hill, New York; 1964).
20. S. Neill, *The interpretation of the New Testament 1861–1961* (Oxford University Press, London; 1964) p. 338.

21. B. Bergonzi, *Exploding English: criticism, theory, culture* (Clarendon Press, Oxford; 1990) pp. 15–16.

22. B. Bergonzi, *Exploding English: criticism, theory, culture* (Clarendon Press, Oxford; 1990) p. 141.

23. S. Gubar and J. Kamholtz (eds.) *English inside out: the places of literary criticism* (Routledge, New York; 1993) p. 114.

24. R.K. Merton, *Social theory and social structure* (The Free Press, New York; 1968) pp. 50–51.

25. G.R. Elton, *The practice of history* (Fontana, London; 1969) p. 38.

26. L. Wolpert, *The unnatural nature of science* (Faber and Faber, London; 1992) p. 121.

27. A. Biglan, "The characteristics of subject matter in different academic areas." *Journal of Applied Psychology*, *57*, pp. 195–203 (1973).

28. D.J. de S. Price, "Citation measures of hard science, soft science, technology, and non-science." *In*: C.E. Nelson and D.K. Pollack (eds.) *Communication among scientists and engineers* (Heath, Lexington, Massachusetts; 1970) pp. 1–12.

29. S. Baldi and L.L. Hargens, "Reassessing the N-rays reference network: the role of self citations and negative citations," *Scientometrics*, *34*, pp. 239–253 (1995).

30. S.E. Cozzens, "Using the archive: Derek Price's theory of differences among the sciences." *Scientometrics*, *7*, pp. 431–441 (1985).

31. *Nature*, *225*, p. 126 (1970).

32. A. Rip and J.-P. Courtial, "Co-word maps of biotechnology: an example of cognitive scientometrics," *Scientometrics*, *6*, pp. 381–400 (1984).

33. R.J.W. Tijssen, "A scientometric cognitive study of neural network research: expert mental maps versus bibliometric maps," *Scientometrics*, *28*, pp. 111–136 (1993).

34. D. Lindsey, *The scientific publication system in social science* (Jossey-Bass, San Francisco; 1978) p. 81.

35. D. Lindsey, *The scientific publication system in social science* (Jossey-Bass, San Francisco; 1978) p. 83.

36. H. Zuckerman and R.K. Merton, "Patterns of evaluation in science: institutionalisation, structure and functions of the referee system," *Minerva*, *9*, pp. 66–100 (1971).

37. P. Earle and B.C. Vickery, "Subject relations in science/technology literature," *Aslib Proceedings*, *21*, pp. 237–243 (1969).

38. A.J. Nederhof, R.A. Zwaan, R.E. De Bruin, and P.J. Dekker, "Assessing the usefulness of bibliometric indicators for the humanities and the social and behavioural sciences: a comparative study," *Scientometrics*, *15*, pp. 423–435 (1989).

39. A.J. Meadows, "Quantitative study of factors affecting the selection and presentation of scientific material to the general public," *Scientometrics*, *20*, pp. 113–119 (1991).

40. J.S. Kidd, "The popularization of science. Part II. Patterns of topical coverage," *Scientometrics*, *15*, pp. 241–255 (1989).

41. E.W. Said, *The world, the text, and the critic* (Faber and Faber, London; 1984) p. 144.

42. A. Clayton, M. Hancock-Beaulieu, and J. Meadows, "Change and continuity in the reporting of science and technology: a study of *The Times* and the *Guardian*," *Public Understanding of Science*, *2*, pp. 225–234 (1993).

43. The Royal Society, the British Library, and the Association of Learned and Professional Society Publishers, *The scientific, technical and medical information system in the UK* (British Library R and D Report No. 6123, London; 1993).

44. G. Philip, "Use of leading edge information systems by academic chemists in the UK. Part II." *Journal of Information Science*, *22*, pp. 93–106 (1996).

45. H.C. Morton and A.J. Price, *The ACLS survey of scholars* (American Council of Learned Societies, Washington, D.C.; 1989) p. 42.

46. B.V. Lewenstein, "Cold fusion and hot history," *Osiris*, *7*, pp. 135–163 (1992).

Chapter 3

1.   W. Tuckwell, *Reminiscences of Oxford* (Smith, Elder, London; 1907) p. 124.

2.   L. Wilson, *American academics: then and now* (Oxford University Press, New York; 1979) p. 15.

3.   D.C. Pelz and F.M. Andrews, *Scientists in organizations* (John Wiley, New York; 1966) pp. 214–260.

4.   G. Watson, *The literary thesis: a guide to research* (Longman, London; 1970) p. 3.

5.   S. Cotgrove and S. Box, *Science, industry and society* (George Allen and Unwin, London; 1970).

6.   A.J. Berry, *Henry Cavendish* (Hutchinson, London; 1960) p. 21.

7.   E.T. Bell, "Gauss, the prince of mathematicians," *In:* J.R. Newman (ed.) *The world of mathematicians* [Vol. 1] (George Allen and Unwin, London; 1960) pp. 305–306.

8.   L. Huxley (ed.) *Life and letters of Thomas Henry Huxley* [Vol. I] (Macmillan, London; 1900) p. 70.

9.   L. Huxley (ed.) *Life and letters of Thomas Henry* Huxley [Vol. I] (Macmillan, London; 1900) p. 69.

10.   D.K. Simonton, *Scientific genius: a psychology of science* (Cambridge University Press, Cambridge; 1988) p. 124.

11.   D.J. de S. Price, *Little science, big science* (Columbia University Press, New York; 1963) p. 52.

12.   P.E. Vernon, "Historical overview of research on scientific abilities," *In:* D.N. Jackson and J.P. Rushton (eds.) *Scientific excellence: origins and assessment* (Sage, Newbury Park, California; 1987) pp. 40–66.

13.   L. Hudson, *Contrary imaginations* (Methuen, London; 1966) p. 155.

14.   F. Barron, *Creative person and creative process* (Holt, Rinehart and Winston, New York; 1969) p. 68.

15.   W. Gratzer (ed.) *A literary companion to science* (W.W. Norton, New York; 1990) pp. 147–148.

16.   F. Barron, *Creative person and creative process* (Holt, Rinehart and Winston, New York; 1969) pp. 99–101.

17.   A.H. Halsey and M. Trow, *The British academics* (Faber and Faber, London; 1971) p. 297.

18.   S. Kyvik, "Productivity differences, fields of learning, and Lotka's law," *Scientometrics, 15*, pp. 205–214 (1989).

19.   S. Hodges, B. Hodges, A.J. Meadows, M. Beaulieu, and D. Law, "The use of an algorithmic approach for the assessment of research quality," *Scientometrics, 35*, pp. 3–13 (1996).

20.   K. Prpic, "The socio-cognitive frameworks of scientific productivity," *Scientometrics, 31*, pp. 293–311 (1994).

21.   A.J. Lotka, "The frequency distribution of scientific productivity," *Journal of the Washington Academy of Sciences, 16*, pp. 317–323 (1926).

22.   D.J. de S. Price, *Little science, big science* (Columbia University Press, New York; 1963) p. 46.

23.   S. Hodges, B. Hodges, A.J. Meadows, M. Beaulieu, and D. Law, "The use of an algorithmic approach for the assessmentof research quality," *Scientometrics, 35*, pp. 3–13 (1996).

24.   E. Munch-Petersen, "Bibliometrics and fiction," *Libri, 31*, pp. 1–21 (1981).

25.   H. Grupp, "On the supplementary functions of science and technology indicators: the case of West German telecommunications R and D," *Scientometrics, 19*, pp. 447–472 (1990).

26.   L. Liming and L. Lihua, "Scientific publication activities of 32 countries: Zipf-Pareto distribution," *Scientometrics, 26*, pp. 263–273 (1993).

27.   J.P. Rushton and S. Meltzer, "Research productivity, university revenue, and scholarly impact (citations) of 169 British, Canadian and United States universities (1977)," *Scientometrics, 3*, pp. 275–303 (1981).

28.   M. Weinstock, "Citation indexes," *Encyclopaedia of Library and Information Science, 5*, pp. 16–40 (1971).

29. D.E. Chubin and S.D. Moitra, "Content analysis of references: adjunct or alternative to citation counting?" *Social Studies of Science, 5*, pp. 423–441 (1975).

30. C.G. Prabha, "Some aspects of citation behavior: a pilot study in business administration," *Journal of the American Society for Information Science, 34*, pp. 202–206 (1983).

31. J.R. Cole and S. Cole, *Social stratification in science* (University of Chicago Press, Chicago; 1973) p. 22.

32. B. Cronin, "Rates of return to citation," *Journal of Documentation, 52*, pp. 188–197 (1996).

33. D.K. Simonton, *Scientific genius: a psychology of science* (Cambridge University Press, Cambridge; 1988) p. 84.

34. A.H. Halsey and M. Trow, *The British academics* (Faber and Faber, London; 1971) Chapter 12.

35. W. Shockley, "On the statistics of individual variations of productivity in research laboratories," *Proceedings of the Institute of Radio Engineers, 45*, pp. 279–290 (1957).

36. Quoted in: D.K. Simonton, *Scientific genius: a psychology of science* (Cambridge University Press, Cambridge; 1988) pp. 50–51.

37. Quoted in: D.K. Simonton, *Scientific genius: a psychology of science* (Cambridge University Press, Cambridge; 1988) pp. 50–51.

38. A.H. Halsey and M. Trow, *The British academics* (Faber and Faber, London; 1971) p. 304.

39. M. Charlesworth, L. Farrall, T. Stokes, and D. Turbull, *Life among the scientists: an anthropological study of an Australian scientific community* (Oxford University Press, Melbourne; 1989) p. 119.

40. H.W. Menard, *Science: growth and change* (Harvard University Press, Cambridge, Massachusetts; 1971) pp. 103–108.

41. V. Trimble, "Death comes as an end-effect of cessation of personal influence upon rates of citation of astronomical papers," *Czechoslovak Journal of Physics, 36*, pp. 175–179 (1986).

42. B.E. Noltingk, *The art of research* (Elsevier, Amsterdam; 1965) p. 94.

43. H.C. Lehman, *Age and achievement* (Princeton University Press, Princeton, New Jersey; 1953).

44. W. Dennis, "Productivity among American psychologists," *American Psychologist, 9*, pp. 191–194 (1954).

45. R.J. Simon, "The work habits of eminent scientists," *Sociology of Work and Occupations, 1*, pp. 327–335 (1974).

46. A. van Heeringen and P.A. Dijkwel, "The relationships between age, mobility and scientific productivity. Part 1. Effect of mobility on productivity," *Scientometrics, 11*, pp. 267–280 (1987).

47. A. van Heeringen and P.A. Dijkwel, "The relationship between age, mobility and scientific productivity. Part II. Effect of age on productivity," *Scientometrics, 11*, pp. 281–293 (1987).

48. J. Ziman, *The force of knowledge* (Cambridge University Press, Cambridge; 1976) p. 122.

49. H. Small, "Recapturing physics in the 1920s through citation analysis," *Czechoslovak Journal of Physics, 36*, pp. 142–147 (1986).

50. R.K. Merton, *The sociology of science: theoretical and empirical investigations* (University of Chicago Press, Chicago; 1973) pp. 439–459.

51. H.L. Hoerman and C.E. Nowicke, "Secondary and tertiary citing: a study of referencing behavior in the literature of citation analysis deriving from the Ortega hypothesis of Cole and Cole," *Library Quarterly, 65*, pp. 415–434 (1995).

52. J.R. Cole and S. Cole, *Social stratification in science* (University of Chicago Press, Chicago; 1973) p. 228.

53. H. Zuckerman, "The careers of men and women scientists: a review of current research." *In:* H. Zuckerman, J.R. Cole, and J.T. Bruer (eds.) *The outer circle: women in the scientific community* (Yale University Press, New Haven, Connecticut; 1991) pp. 27–56.

54. M.W. Rossiter, *Women scientists in America: struggles and strategies to 1940* (Johns Hopkins University Press, Baltimore; 1982) pp. 172–173.

55. M.F. Fox, "Gender, environmental milieu, and productivity in science." *In:* H. Zuckerman,

J.R. Cole, and J.T. Bruer (eds.) *The outer circle: women in the scientific community* (Yale University Press, New Haven, Connecticut; 1991) pp. 188-204.

56. M.J. Moravcsik, *Science development: the building of science in less developed countries* (International Development Research Center, Indiana University, Bloomington; 1974).

57. Kapil Raj, "Images of knowledge, social organization, and attitudes to research in an Indian physics department," *Science in Context, 2*, pp. 317–339 (1988).

58. M. Bonitz, E. Bruckner, and A. Scharnhorst, "The structure of world science in the eighties," (Fifth International Conference on Scientometrics and Informetrics, River Forest, Illinois; 1995).

59. A.J. Meadows, "Amateur science and communication," *Science and Public Policy, 13*, pp. 285–289 (1986).

60. R.A. Stebbins, "Avocational science: the amateur routine in archaeology and astronomy," *International Journal of Comparative Sociology, 22*, pp. 34–48 (1980).

61. A.J. Meadows, *Communication in science* (Butterworths, London; 1974) p. 196.

62. S.P. Gupta and P.S. Nagpaul, "Organizational structure as related to performance: a study of research groups in India." *In:* P.S. Nagpaul (ed.) *Organization and efficiency of research groups* (National Institute of Science, Technology and Development Studies, New Delhi; 1988) pp. 139–152.

63. D. de B. Beaver, "Collaboration and teamwork in physics," *Czechoslovak Journal of Physics, 36*, pp. 14–18 (1986).

64. A.J. Meadows, *Communication in science* (Butterworths, London; 1974) p. 197.

65. D. de B. Beaver, "Collaboration and teamwork in physics," *Czechoslovak Journal of Physics, 36*, pp. 14–18 (1986).

66. D. Lindsey, *The scientific publication system in social science* (Jossey-Bass, San Francisco; 1978) p. 83.

67. M. Gibbons, C. Limoges, H. Nowotny, S. Schwartzman, P. Scott, and M. Trow, *The new production of knowledge* (Sage Publications, London; 1994) p. 166.

68. P. Wright, "Homework: an international comparison of behavioural researchers' use of computers for work at home." *In:* M. Feeney and K. Merry (eds.) *Information technology and the research process* (Bowker-Saur, London; 1990) pp. 130–145.

69. H.C. Morton and A.J. Price, *The ACLS survey of scholars* (American Council of Learned Societies, Washington, D.C.; 1989) p. 36.

70. The Royal Society, the British Library, and the Association of Learned and Professional Society Publishers, *The scientific, technical and medical information system in the UK* (British Library R and D Report No. 6123, London; 1993).

71. E. Coiera, "Medical informatics," *British Medical Journal, 310*, pp. 1381–1387 (1995).

Chapter 4

1. R.G. Crowder, *The psychology of reading: an introduction* (Oxford University Press, New York; 1992).

2. M.A. Tinker, *Legibility of print* (Iowa State University Press, Ames; 1963).

3. G. Henry, *Comment mesurer la lisibilité* (Nathan, Paris; 1975).

4. A.J. Meadows, "The readability of physics papers," *Czechoslovak Journal of Physics, 36*, pp. 89–91 (1986).

5. M.A.K. Halliday and J.R. Martin, *Writing science: literacy and discursive power* (Falmer Press, London; 1993) p. 71.

6. G.K. Zipf, *The psycho-biology of language* (Houghton Mifflin, Boston; 1935) pp. 20–48.

7. A.L. de Lavoisier, *Elements of chemistry* (Dover, New York; 1965) p. xiv.

8. D.W. King, D.D. McDonald, and N.K. Roderer, *Scientific journals in the United States: their production, use and economics* (Hutchinson Ross, Stroudsburg, Pennsylvania; 1981) p. 164.

9. J. Rolinson, H. Al-Shanbari, and A.J. Meadows, "Information usage by biological researchers," *Journal of Information Science, 22*, pp. 47–53 (1996).

10. D.W. King, D.D. McDonald, and N.K. Roderer, *Scientific journals in the United States: their production, use and economics* (Hutchison Ross, Stroudsburg, Pennsylvania; 1981) p. 175.

11. A.J. Meadows, *Communication in science* (Butterworths, London; 1974) pp. 102–103.

12. B. Shackel and D.J. Pullinger, *BLEND-1: background and developments* (Library and Information Research Report No. 29, British Library, London; 1984) pp. 72–73.

13. I.L. Horowitz and M.E. Curtis, "Scholarly book publishing in the 1990s." *In:* P.G. Altbach and E.S. Hoshino (eds.) *International book publishing: an encyclopedia* (Garland Publishing, New York; 1995) pp. 303–313.

14. B. Biber, *Variation across speech and writing* (Cambridge University Press, Cambridge, UK; 1988) p. 15.

15. M. Charlesworth, L. Farrall, T. Stokes, and D. Turnbull, *Life among the scientists: an anthropological study of an Australian scientific community* (Oxford University Press, Melbourne; 1989) p. 83.

16. D.B. Hertz and A.H. Robenstein, *Team research* (Eastern Technical Publications, New York; 1953).

17. J. Rolinson, H. Al-Shanbari, and A.J. Meadows, "Information usage by biological researchers," *Journal of Information Science, 22*, pp. 47–53 (1996).

18. C.W. Shilling, J. Bernard, and J.W. Tyson, *Informal communication among bioscientists* (Biological Sciences Communication Project, George Washington University, Washington, D.C.; 1964).

19. A.J. Meadows, *Communication in science* (Butterworths, London; 1974) pp. 121–122.

20. The Royal Society, the British Library, and the Association of Learned and Professional Society Publishers, *The scientific, technical and medical information system in the UK* (British Library R and D Report No. 6123, British Library, London; 1993).

21. T.J. Allen, "Roles in technical communication networks." *In:* C. Nelson and D.K. Pollock (eds.) *Communication among scientists and engineers* (Heath, Lexington, Massachusetts; 1970) pp. 191–208.

22. D.J. de S. Price and D. de B. Beaver, "Collaboration in an invisible college," *American Psychologist, 21*, pp. 1011–1017 (1966).

23. S. Crawford, "Informal communication among scientists in sleep research," *Journal of the American Society for Information Science, 22*, pp. 301–310 (1971).

24. G. Taubes, *Nobel dreams: power, deceit and the ultimate experiment* (Random House, New York; 1986).

25. S. Pangasa and G. Mehta, "Pattern of internal and external communication in R & D groups." *In:* P.S. Nagpaul (ed.) *Organization and efficiency of research groups* (National Institute of Science Technology and Development Studies, New Delhi; 1988) pp. 199–211.

26. B. Cronin, "Invisible colleges and information transfer," *Journal of Documentation, 38*, pp. 212–236 (1982).

27. R.L. Dahling, *Shannon's information theory: the spread of an idea* (Institute for Communication Research, Stanford University, California; 1962).

28. W. Goffman, "Mathematical approach to the spread of scientific ideas—the history of mast cell research," *Nature, 212*, pp. 449–452 (1966).

29. P.J. Shoemaker, *Gatekeeping* (Sage Publications, Newbury Park, California; 1991).

30. H. Zuckerman, *Scientific elite* (The Free Press, New York; 1977) p. 108.

31. J. Rolinson, H. Al-Shanbari, and A.J. Meadows, "Information usage by biological researchers," *Journal of Information Science, 22*, pp. 47–53 (1996).

32. M.F. Fox, "Gender, environmental millieu, and productivity in science." *In:* H. Zuckerman,

     J.R. Cole, and J.T. Bruer (eds) *The outer circle: women in the scientific community* (Yale University Press, New Haven, Connecticut; 1991) pp. 188–204.

33.   A.M. Anderson, "The fragmenting world of science communication." *In:* K. Ackrill (ed.) *The role of the media in science communication* (Ciba Foundation, London; 1994) pp. 97–111.

34.   G. Stix, "The speed of write," *Scientific American, 272*, pp. 72–77 (1994).

35.   J. Rolinson, A.J. Meadows, and H. Smith, "Use of information technology by biological researchers," *Journal of Information Science, 21*, pp. 133–139 (1995).

36.   L. Stewart, "User acceptance of electronic journals: interviews with chemists at Cornell University," *College and Research Libraries, 57*, pp. 339–349 (1996).

37.   A. Dillon, *Designing usable electronic text* (Taylor and Francis, London; 1994) p. 42.

Chapter 5

1.   W.D. Garvey, *Communication: the essence of science* (Pergamon Press, Oxford; 1979) p. 282.

2.   S. Hodges, B. Hodges, A.J. Meadows, M. Beaulieu, and D. Law, "The use of an algorithmic approach for the assessment of research quality," *Scientometrics, 35*, pp. 3–13 (1996).

3.   H.C. Morton and A.J. Price, *The ACLS survey of scholars* (American Council of Learned Societies, Washington, D.C.; 1989) p. 26.

4.   B.C. Vickery and A. Vickery, *Information science in theory and practice* (Butterworths, London; 1987) p. 86.

5.   The Royal Society, the British Library, and the Association of Learned and Professional Society Publishers, *The scientific, technical and medical information system in the UK* (British Library R and D Report No. 6123; 1993) pp. 93–94.

6.   D.W. King, D.D. McDonald, and N.K. Roderer, *Scientific journals in the United States* (Hutchinson Ross, Stroudsburg; Pennsylvania; 1981) pp. 66–67.

7.   W.D. Garvey, *Communication: the essence of science* (Pergamon Press, Oxford; 1979) p. 60.

8.   E. Rudd and S. Hatch, *Graduate study and after* (Weidenfeld and Nicholson, London; 1968).

9.   D. Schauder, "Electronic publishing of professional articles: attitudes of academics and implications for the scholarly communication industry," *Journal of the American Society for Information Science, 45*, pp. 73–100 (1994).

10.   M.D. Gordon, "Citation ranking versus subjective evaluation in the determination of journal hierarchies in the social sciences," *Journal of the American Society for Information Science, 33*, pp. 55–57 (1982).

11.   D. Schauder, "Electronic publishing of professional articles: attitudes of academics and implications for the scholarly communication industry," *Journal of the American Society for Information Science, 45*, pp. 73–100 (1994).

12.   J. Rymer, "Scientific composing processes." *In:* D.A. Jolliffe (ed.) *Advances in writing research* [Vol. 2] (Ablex Publishing, Norwood, New Jersey; 1988) p. 223.

13.   J. Hartley, *Technology and writing* (Jessica Kingsley, London; 1992) pp. 23–24.

14.   A.B. Buxton and A.J. Meadows, "The variation in the information content of titles of research papers with time and discipline," *Journal of Documentation, 33*, pp. 46–52 (1977).

15.   T.N. Huckin, "Surprise value in scientific discourse." *In: Ninth European Symposium on Language for Special Purposes* (Bergen, Norway; 1993).

16.   S. Eastwood, P. Derish, E. Leash, and S. Ordway, "Ethical issues in biomedicine: perceptions and practices of postdoctoral research fellows responding to a survey," *Science and Engineering Ethics, 2*, pp. 89–114 (1996).

17. N. Wade, *The Nobel Prize duel*. (Anchor Press/Doubleday, Garden City, New York; 1981) *In:* W. Gratzer (ed.) *A literary companion to science* (W.W. Norton, New York; 1990) p. 390.

18. B. Cronin, *The scholar's courtesy* (Taylor Graham, London; 1995).

19. J.P. Kassirer and M.A. Angell, "On authorship and acknowledgements," *New England Journal of Medicine, 325*, pp. 1510–1512 (1991).

20. L.A. Coser, C. Kadushin, and W.W. Powell, *Books: the culture and commerce of publishing* (University of Chicago Press, Chicago; 1985) p. 229.

21. S. Lock, *A difficult balance: editorial peer review in medicine* (Nuffield Provincial Hospitals Trust, London; 1985) p. 60.

22. M.D. Gordon, "The role of referees in scientific communication." *In:* J. Hartley (ed.) *Technology and writing: readings in the psychology of written communication* (Jessica Kingsley, London; 1992) pp. 263–275.

23. D. Lindsey, *The scientific publication system in social science* (Jossey-Bass, San Francisco; 1978) p. 19.

24. M.C. La Follette, *Stealing into print* (University of California Press, Berkeley; 1992) p. 122.

25. R.L. Daft, "Why I recommended that your manuscript be rejected and what you can do about it." *In:* L.L. Cummings and P.J. Frost (eds.) *Publishing in the organizational sciences* (Sage Publications, Thousand Oaks, California; 1995) pp. 164–182.

26. M. Ryan, "Evaluating scholarly manuscripts in journalism and communications," *Journalism Quarterly, 59*, pp. 273–285 (1982).

27. S.S. Siegelman, "Assassins and zealots: variations in peer review," *Radiology, 178*, pp. 637–642 (1991).

28. V. Bakanic, C. McPhail, and R.S. Simon, "Mixed messages: referees' comments on the manuscripts they review," *Sociological Quarterly, 30*, pp. 639–654 (1989).

29. S. Lock, *A difficult balance: editorial peer review in medicine* (Nuffield Provincial Hospitals Trust, London; 1985) p. 63.

30. A.J. Meadows, *The scientific journal* (Aslib, London; 1979) p. 107.

31. H. Zuckerman and R.K. Merton, "Patterns of evaluation in science: institutionalisation, structure and functions of the referee system," *Minerva, 9*, pp. 66–100 (1971).

32. D.W. King, D.D. McDonald, and N.K. Roderer, *Scientific journals in the United States* (Hutchinson Ross, Stroudsburg, Pennsylvania; 1981) p. 77.

33. H.H. Kornhuber, quoted in: H.-D. Daniel, *Guardians of science: fairness and reliability of peer review* (VCH, Weinheim; 1993) p. 3.

34. R.L. Jacobson, quoted in: H.-D. Daniel, *Guardians of science: fairness and reliability of peer review* (VCH, Weinheim; 1993) p. 63.

35. J. Rolinson, H. Al-Shanbari, and A.J. Meadows, "Information usage by biological researchers," *Journal of Information Science, 22*, pp. 47–53 (1996).

36. H.W. Marsh and S. Ball, "The peer review process used to evaluate manuscripts submitted to academic journals: interjudgmental reliability," *Journal of Experimental Education, 57*, pp. 151–169 (1989).

37. H. Zuckerman and R.K. Merton, "Patterns of evaluation in science: institutionalisation, structure and functions of the referee system," *Minerva, 9*, pp. 66–100 (1971).

38. M.J. Mahoney, *The scientist as subject: the psychological imperative* (Ballinger, Cambridge, Massachusetts; 1976) Chapter 5.

39. H. Zuckerman and R.K. Merton, "Patterns of evaluation in science: institutionalisation, structure and functions of the referee system," *Minerva, 9*, pp. 66–100, (1971).

40. M.D. Gordon, "A critical reassessment of inferred relations between multiple authorship, scientific collaboration, the production of papers and their acceptance for publication," *Scientometrics, 2*, pp. 193–201 (1980).

41. S. Presser, "Collaboration and the quality of research," *Social Studies of Science, 10,* pp. 95–101 (1980).

42. R. Rosenthal, "Reliability and bias in peer-review practices," *Behavioral and Brain Sciences, 5,* pp. 235–236 (1982).

43. M.D. Gordon, "The role of referees in scientific communication." *In:* J. Hartley (ed.) *Technology and writing: readings in the psychology of written communication* (Jessica Kingsley, London; 1992) pp. 263–275.

44. D.P. Peters and S.J. Ceci, "Peer review practices of psychological journals: the fate of published articles, submitted again," *Behavioral and Brain Sciences, 5,* pp. 187–192 (1982).

45. S.J. Ceci and D.P. Peters, "How blind is blind review?" *American Psychologist, 39,* pp. 1491–1494 (1984).

46. R.A. McNutt, A.T. Evans, R.H. Fletcher, and S.W. Fletcher, "The effects of blinding on the quality of peer review," *Journal of the American Medical Association, 263,* pp. 1371–1376 (1990).

47. J.M. Campanario, "Have referees rejected some of the most-cited articles of all times?" *Journal of the American Society for Information Science, 47,* pp. 302–310 (1996).

48. H.C. Morton and A.J. Price, *The ACLS survey of scholars* (American Council of Learned Societies, Washington, D.C.; 1989) p. 28.

49. C.M. Yentsch and C.J. Sindermann, *The woman scientist* (Plenum Press, New York; 1992) p. 136.

50. S. Lock, *A difficult balance: editorial peer review in medicine* (Nuffield Provincial Hospitals Trust, London; 1985) p. 29.

51. M.D. Gordon, "The role of referees in scientific communication." *In:* J. Hartley (ed.) *Technology and writing: readings in the psychology of written communication* (Jessica Kingsley, London; 1992) pp. 263–275.

52. S. Lock, *A difficult balance: editorial peer review in medicine* (Nuffield Provincial Hospitals Trust, London; 1985) p. 59.

53. W.D. Garvey, *Communication: the essence of science* (Pergamon Press, Oxford; 1979) p. 190.

54. S. Lock, *A difficult balance: editorial peer review in medicine* (Nuffield Provincial Hospitals Trust, London; 1985) pp. 67–68.

55. W.J. Broad and N. Wade, *Betrayers of the truth: fraud and deceit in the halls of science* (Simon and Schuster, New York; 1982).

56. A.J. Meadows, *Communication in science* (Butterworths, London; 1974) p. 64.

57. S. Lock, *A difficult balance: editorial peer review in medicine* (Nuffield Provincial Hospitals Trust, London; 1985) p. 48.

58. M.C. La Follette, *Stealing into print* (University of California Press, Berkeley; 1992) p. 130.

59. R. Smith, "Time to face up to research misconduct," *British Medical Journal, 312,* pp. 789–790 (1996).

60. M.C. La Follette, *Stealing into print* (University of California Press, Berkeley; 1992) p. 179.

61. W.W. Powell, *Getting into print* (University of Chicago Press, Chicago; 1985) p. 169.

62. American Council of Learned Societies *Scholarly communication* (Johns Hopkins University Press, Baltimore; 1979) p. 93.

63. L.A. Coser, C. Kadushin, and W.W. Powell, *Books: the culture and commerce of publishing* (University of Chicago Press, Chicago; 1985) p. 236.

64. Y. Lindholm-Romantschuk, *The flow of ideas within and among academic disciplines: scholarly book reviewing in the social sciences and humanities* (Ph.D. thesis, University of California, Berkeley; 1994) p. 53.

65. Y. Lindhohm-Romantschuk, *The flow of ideas within and among academic disciplines: scholarly book reviewing in the social sciences and humanities* (Ph.D. thesis, University of California, Berkeley; 1994) p. 80 *et seq.*

66. J. Bernstein, *Cranks, quarks and the cosmos* (Basic Book, New York; 1993) p. 27.

67. K. Johnson, "Dimensions of judgement of science news stories," *Journalism Quarterly*, *40*, pp. 315–322 (1963).

68. M. Tuman, *Word Perfect: literacy in the computer age* (Falmer Press, London; 1992) pp. 109–110.

69. D. Schauder, "Electronic publishing of professional articles: attitudes of academics and implications for the scholarly communication industry," *Journal of the American Society for Information Science*, *45*, pp. 73–100 (1994).

70. H. Lustig, "Electronic publishing: the role of a large scientific society." *In:* D. Shaw and H. Moore (eds.) *Electronic publishing in science* (ICSU Press/UNESCO; 1996) pp. 127–130.

Chapter 6

1. M.L. Radford, "Communication theory applied to the reference encounter: an analysis of critical incidents," *Library Quarterly*, *66*, pp. 123–137 (1996).

2. D. Ellis, D. Cox, and K. Hall, "A comparison of the information seeking patterns of researchers in the physical and social sciences," *Journal of Documentation*, *49*, pp. 356–369 (1993).

3. A.J. Meadows, *Communication in science* (Butterworths, London; 1974) p. 95.

4. C.C. Gould, *Information needs in the humanities: an assessment* (Research Libraries Group, Stanford, California; 1988).

5. C.C. Gould and M. Handler, *Information needs in the social sciences: an assessment* (Research Libraries Group, Mountain View, California; 1989).

6. C.C. Gould and M. Handler, *Information needs in the social sciences: an assessment* (Research Libraries Group, Mountain View, California; 1989) p. 17.

7. A.J. Meadows, *Innovation in information* (Bowker-Saur, London; 1994) p. 70.

8. D.W. King, J. Casto, and H. Jones, *Communication by engineers: a literature review of engineers' information needs, seeking processes, and use* (Council on Library Resources, Washington, D.C.; 1994).

9. J. Martyn, *Literature searching habits and attitudes of research scientists* (British Library Research Paper No. 14, British Library, London; 1986).

10. E. Almquist, *An examination of work-related information acquisition usage among scientific, technical and medical fields* (Faxon Institute Annual Conference, Reston, Virginia; 1991).

11. E. Almquist, *An examination of work-related information acquisition usage among scientific, technical and medical fields* (Faxon Institute Annual Conference, Reston, Virginia; 1991).

12. J.-M. Griffiths and D.W. King, *Special libraries: increasing the information edge* (Special Libraries Association, Washington, D.C.; 1993) p. 13.

13. J. Rolinson, H. Al-Shanbari, and A.J. Meadows, "Information usage by biological researchers," *Journal of Information Science*, *22*, pp. 47–53 (1996).

14. E. Almquist, *An examination of work-related information acquisition usage among scientific, technical and medical fields* (Faxon Institute Annual Conference, Reston, Virginia; 1991).

15. J. Olsen, *Electronic journal literature: implications for scholars* (Mecklermedia, Westport, Connecticut; 1994) p. 18.

16. J. Palmer, "Scientists and information. Part I. Using cluster analysis to identify information style," *Journal of Documentation*, *47*, pp. 105–129 (1991).

17. T.W. Malone, "How do people organise their desks? Implications for the design of office information systems," *ACM Transactions on Office Information Systems*, *1*, pp. 99–112 (1983).

18. The Royal Society, the British Library, and the Association of Learned and Professional Society Publishers, *The scientific, technical and medical information system in the UK* (British Library R and D Report No. 6123, British Library, London; 1993) p. 115.

19.   J.-M. Griffiths and D.W. King, *Special libraries: increasing the information edge* (Special Libraries Association, Washington, D.C.; 1993) p. 103.

20.   J. Chapman, "Views of a history information officer." *In:* S. Stone (ed.) *Humanities information research: proceedings of a seminar; Sheffield 1980* (Centre for Research on User Studies, University of Sheffield, Sheffield, Yorks; 1980) pp. 31–32.

21.   E. Almquist, *An examination of work-related information acquisition usage among scientific, technical and medical fields* (Faxon Institute Annual Conference, Reston, Virginia; 1991).

22.   C.V. Wedgwood, quoted in: Ved Mehta, *Fly and the fly-bottle* (Penguin Books, London; 1965) pp. 166–167.

23.   D. Ellis, "Modeling the information-seeking patterns of academic researchers: a grounded theory approach," *Library Quarterly, 63*, pp. 469–486 (1993).

24.   R.S. Cahn, *Survey of chemical publications* (Chemical Society, London; 1965).

25.   D.W. King, D.D. McDonald, and N.K. Roderer, *Scientific journals in the United States* (Hutchinson Ross, Stroudsburg, Pennsylvania; 1981) p. 201.

26.   S.J. Cunningham and D. Bocock, "Obsolescence of computing literature," *Scientometrics, 34*, pp. 255–262 (1995).

27.   D.J. de S. Price, "Networks of scientific papers," *Science, 149*, pp. 510–515 (1965).

28.   Y.-F. le Coadic, *La science de l'information* (Presses Universitaires de France, Paris; 1994) p. 70.

29.   H.W. Menard, *Science: growth and change* (Harvard University Press, Cambridge, Massachusetts; 1971) pp. 53–57.

30.   D.F. Shaw, "Input, subfields and ageing of recently cited physics monographs," *Czechoslovak Journal of Physics, 36*, pp. 130–132 (1986).

31.   The Royal Society, the British Library, and the Association of Learned and Professional Society Publishers, *The scientific, technical and medical information system in the UK* (British Library R and D Report No. 6123, London; 1993) p. 105.

32.   F. Narin, "Patent bibliometrics," *Scientometrics, 30*, pp. 147–155 (1994).

33.   A.M. Cummings, M.L. Witte, W.G. Bowen, L.O. Lazarus, and R.H. Ekman, *University libraries and scholarly communication* (Andrew W. Mellon Foundation, Pittsburgh, Pennsylvania; 1992) p. 16.

34.   A.M. Cummings, M.L. Witte, W.G. Bowen, L.O. Lazarus, and R.H. Ekman, *University libraries and scholarly communication* (Andrew W. Mellon Foundation, Pittsburgh, Pennsylvania; 1992) pp. 88–90.

35.   H.C. Morton and A.J. Price, *The ACLS survey of scholars* (American Council of Learned Societies, Washington, D.C.; 1989) p. 46.

36.   C.R.H. Inman, "Scientific publications in English and developing countries: a report of a survey of scientists' experiences," *Journal of Information Science, 6*, pp. 159–164 (1983).

37.   P.B. Kantor, "Information retrieval techniques," *Annual Review of Information Science and Technology, 29*, pp. 53–90 (1994).

38.   J. Rowley, "The controlled versus natural indexing languages debate revisited: a perspective on information retrieval practice and research," *Journal of Information Science, 20*, pp. 108–119 (1994).

39.   T.K. Park, "The nature of relevance in information retrieval: an empirical study," *Library Quarterly, 63*, pp. 318–351 (1993).

40.   T.K. Park, "The nature of relevance in information retrieval: an empirical study,: *Library Quarterly, 63*, pp. 318–351 (1993).

41.   B. Vickery and A. Vickery, "Online search interface design," *Journal of Documentation, 49*, pp. 103–187 (1993).

42.   W.J. Wilbur, "Human subjectivity and performance limits in document retrieval," *Information Processing and Management, 32*, pp. 515–527 (1996).

43. G. Philip, "Use of 'leading edge' information systems by academic chemists in the UK. Part 1. The results of a preliminary investigation," *Journal of Information Science, 21*, pp. 187–199 (1995).

44. J. Rolinson, A.J. Meadows, and H. Smith, "Use of information technology by biological researchers," *Journal of Information Science, 21*, pp. 133–139 (1995).

45. J. Olsen, *Electronic journal literature: implications for scholars* (Mecklermedia, Westport, Connecticut; 1994) p. 43.

46. A.M. Cummings, M.L. Witte, W.G. Bowen, L.O. Lazarus, and R.H. Ekman, *University libraries and scholarly communication* (Andrew W. Mellon Foundation, Pittsburgh, Pennsylvania; 1992) p. 121.

47. L. Stewart, "User acceptance of electronic journals: interviews with chemists at Cornell University," *College and Research Libraries, 57*, pp. 339–349 (1996).

48. K. Willis, K. Alexander, W.A. Gosling, G.R. Peters Jr., R. Schwarzwalder, and B.F. Warner. "TULIP—The University Licensing Program: experiences at the University of Michigan," *Serials Review, 20*, pp. 39–47 (1994).

49. The Royal Society, the British Library, and the Association of Learned and Professional Society Publishers, *The scientific, technical and medical information system in the UK* (British Library R and D Report No. 6123, London; 1993) p. 159.

50. L. Stewart, "User acceptance of electronic journals: interviews with chemists at Cornell University," *College and Research Libraries, 57*, pp. 339–349 (1996).

51. A.J. Meadows, "Preserving the digital imprint," *Learned Publishing, 9*, pp. 215–218 (1996).

52. V.A. Markusova, R.S. Gilyarevskii, A.I. Chernyi, and B.C. Griffith, "Information behavior of Russian scientists in the 'Perestroika' period," *Scientometrics, 37*, pp. 361–380 (1996).

53. L. Stewart, "User acceptance of electronic journals: interviews with chemists at Cornell University," *College and Research Libraries, 57*, pp. 339–349 (1996).

54. J.P. Walsh and T. Bayma, "Computer networks and scientific work," *Social Studies of Science, 26*, pp. 661–703 (1996).

55. J.P. Walsh and T. Bayman, "Computer networks and scientific work," *Social Studies of Science, 26*, pp. 661-703 (1996).

56. B.C. Vickery and A. Vickery, *Information science in theory and practice* (Butterworths, London; 1987) p. 106.

57. H.C. Morton and A.J. Price, *The ACLS survey of scholars* (American Council of Learned Societies, Washington, D.C.; 1989) p. 24.

58. D.P. Phillips, E.J. Kanter, B. Bednarczyk, and P.L. Tastad, "Importance of the lay press in the transmission of medical knowledge in the scientific community," *New England Journal of Medicine, 325*, pp. 1180–1183 (1991).

59. S. Klaidman, *Health in the headlines: the stories behind the stories* (Oxford University Press, New York; 1991) pp. 48–49.

60. S. Klaidman, *Health in the headlines: the stories behind the stories* (Oxford University Press, New York; 1991) p. 5.

61. T.S. Eliot, *The complete poems and plays* (Faber and Faber, London; 1969) p. 147.

Index

Library and Information Science

(Continued from page ii)

Lois Swan Jones and Sarah Scott Gibson
Art Libraries and Information Services

Nancy Jones Pruett
Scientific and Technical Libraries: Functions and Management
Volume 1 and Volume 2

Peter Judge and Brenda Gerrie
Small Bibliographic Databases

Dorothy B. Lilley and Ronald W. Trice
A History of Information Sciences 1945–1985

Elaine Svenonius
The Conceptual Foundations of Descriptive Cataloging

Robert M. Losee, Jr.
The Science of Information: Measurement and Applications

Irene P. Godden
Library Technical Services: Operations and Management,
Second Edition

Donald H. Kraft and Bert R. Boyce
Operations Research for Libraries and Information Agencies:
Techniques for the Evaluation of Management Decision Alternatives

James Cabeceiras
The Multimedia Library: Materials Selection and Use, Second
Edition

Charles T. Meadow
Text Information Retrieval Systems

Robert M. Losee, Jr. and Karen A. Worley
Research and Evaluation for Information Professionals

Carmel Maguire, Edward J. Kazlauskas, and Anthony D. Weir
Information Services for Innovative Organizations

Karen Markey Drabenstott and Diane Vizine-Goetz
Using Subject Headings for Online Retrieval